The
PANAGE PAPERS

From Cyprus to the Ozarks
1942-1955

Edited by
Lisa Brandom

MOON▲LAKE
PUBLISHING COMPANY
Siloam Springs, Arkansas

MOON⧫LAKE
PUBLISHING COMPANY

14213 Lake Forrest Heights

Siloam Springs, AR 72761

The Panage Papers. Copyright © 2005 Edited by Lisa Brandom. All rights reserved. No part of this book may be reproduced in any form or by any electronic or mechanical means, including information storage and retrieval systems, without permission in writing from the publisher, except by a reviewer, who may quote brief passages in a review. Any members of educational institutions wishing to photocopy part or all of the work for classroom use, or publishers who would like to obtain permission to include the work in an anthology, should send their inquiries to Moon Lake Publishing Co., 14213 Lake Forrest Heights, Siloam Springs, AR 72761.

Printed in the United States of America
Design by Joel Armstrong

Library of Congress Cataloging-in-Publication Data
Brandom, Lisa
      The Panage Papers / Lisa Brandom
      p. cm.
      ISBN 0-9755950-3-2

1. Panage, John H.—Diaries
2. Immigrants—Arkansas—Siloam Springs
3. John Brown University—History

LD2601.J8P36 2005
378.12 P191   2005107684

10 9 8 7 6 5 4 3 2
First Edition

INTRODUCTION

According to *The Merriam-Webster Dictionary's* New Edition of 2004, the word *enigmatic* means *mystifying*. John H. Panage, the author and subject of these journals, would certainly fall into that description. He served as a professor of English for thirty-five years at John Brown University located in northwest Arkansas. A native of the island of Cyprus, John arrived on the campus of this small Bible-based college in 1939 determined to become renowned as a scholar in his discipline.

That goal, however, was never to be realized fully perhaps due to the workload he experienced at the college, teaching year round with responsibilities not only for college teaching but also for teaching high school while all the time serving on college committees and chaperoning student events. He also vowed to master the spoken and written English language, yet throughout his life he always had a distinctive accent, revealing that he was not a native-born American. He wanted to achieve fame by writing a great masterpiece, and he promised himself to read one hundred pages of literature a day to become the scholar he hoped to be. Yet he often found himself falling short of that lofty goal and falling instead into campus gossip about the state of the college and its faculty. His friendships were tenuous and often petty in nature. He could be incredibly stingy at times, not buying his closest friends a

Christmas gift and refusing requests from his family in Cyprus for money, for example, yet sending money back home freely at other times and ultimately leaving the bulk of his estate to his family and the college.

As a professor, John Panage was always one of the most popular, if not the most popular, teacher on the campus. His students to this day, though middle-aged and beyond, share stories about his frequent repetition in class of the phrase, "Get the point!" and his incessant use of the blackboard, combined with a familiar tapping sound to make sure the students indeed "got it."

Since he was from the tradition of western learning from the Greeks and Romans, but the base of our own civilization, John often struggled with what he perceived as the college's narrow view of its mission in the world. For John, growing up in poverty in Cyprus, the world's problems must be solved by love and meeting the physical needs of the people. For the founder of John Brown University, the world's problems should be solved by taking the message of Christ to all in light of the Great Commission from the Bible. These two seemingly opposing philosophies were troublesome to John during the years, but he vowed essentially to keep his political opinions to himself because he feared losing his job if he spoke too openly.

In his personal life, John remained a bachelor all of his life. While he had a long standing relationship with a fellow professor whom he calls Sh—an abbreviation for Miss Sherbourne who taught English at John Brown for several years and then moved to nearby University of Arkansas—he was conflicted in his view of women. He spoke in his journals of the boredom with Sh but still longed passionately for other women whom he met and worked with in the small town in which he lived. He often spoke pejoratively about the role of women to bear children and their detracting influences upon his students and friends.

After his death in the late 1970's from complications from a fall, his journals from the year 1942-1955 sat in the English offices of the college. While making an office change in 1996, a couple of English faculty discovered them locked away in an old cabinet. They immediately became interested in publishing them. This project is the culmination of a nine year effort on that behalf. I thank my colleagues Edward Nichols, Gary Guinn, Patty Kirk, Mark Fulk, Angela Fulk, and Carol Nichols for their assistance in editing the first part of the manuscript. In addition, numerous student editors and typists assisted in getting the journals into print form such as Zula Graham, Emily Brown, Billy Nye, Megan McCarty, Joy Ernst, Lee Ella Olgesbee, Carrie Jensen, Joy Weinheimer, and Jessica Highfill. Proofreaders were Mary Habermas, Joy Ernst, and Elizabeth Granderson.

The journals provide insight into the life of a Greek professor in the Ozarks through the war torn years of World War II, through the reign in Russia of Stalin, through the Cold War period, and through the life of the average citizens in a small college town.

His colleague, Edward Nichols, called Dr. Panage "a sage for all seasons."

Our fear, hopes, doubts, and aspirations

seem so trivial and transitory

when we look at the starry skies.

January 7, 1942, Wednesday

Today being my name-day, I decided to start a diary in which to record my thoughts, feelings, hopes, fears, and observations. This is the first diary I have started since 1925 or 1926. Two or three other diaries I've started are lost in suitcase and trunk, left behind in Boston, Massachusetts, and Atlanta, Georgia. I've made up my mind to cling to this diary as long as I can. It might prove my salvation. For years I've been planning to become a writer, and as a matter of fact, I've composed two or three novels, one of which is at present in complete form, but out of sheer laziness and indifference, I've neglected to write at least a line a day.

Today I got up as usual at 5:10 a.m. I lighted up the gas stove, shaved, and washed my hair with the moon still shining bright. I walked from 203/1005 South Wright Street (the Cline's apartments as they are called) to Youree Café for my regular cup of coffee and doughnuts. It was windy and cold—the temperature being in the bleak twenties. I was glad to get a ride the moment I passed the bridge over the creek. Mr. Whaley, the red-haired young man who manages the KUOA radio station, picked me up.

1

I spent the first hour from 7-8 reviewing the vowels and consonants, the accents and the nouns of the second declension in my Beginner's Greek class, which is composed of five boys and two girls. I spent the second hour from 8-9 lecturing on Francis Bacon and listening to reports of my students on *As You Like It* and *The Two Noble Kinsmen.*

At 9 o'clock, my friend Bitzer drove me in Mr. Thompson's car to town for a second breakfast at the Youree. I ate a fried egg and toast and drank my second cup of coffee. While eating breakfast, we read the morning papers, *The Tulsa World* and *The Southwest America,* and discussed the advance of the Japanese in Malaya and the retreat of the Germans on the Russian front. B. was not particularly cheerful because he received a card from the Local Draft Board requesting him to appear on January 9 for medical examination. He had already registered last October, being not yet 35 years old. I have to register on February16, according to the new proclamation ordering all men between the ages of 20 and 44 to register for compulsory military service. After the breakfast, we drove to the "Cottage" and listened to the 10 o'clock news broadcast. Nothing unusual except that business and labor have promised to produce 125,000 planes, and I don't know how many tanks and guns U.S. President Roosevelt asked for in his message yesterday to the Congress.

I taught three hours in the afternoon—one hour of N.T. Greek, one hour of Shakespeare, and one hour of American Literature. I spent time on the Fourth Act of *Julius Caesar* and Bret Harte's "The Luck of Roaring Camp." Because it was chilly in Room 208, I moved into Room 210. My friend Mr. Batchelor, dean of the Vocational School, very graciously invited me to occupy this room, which is warmer than mine. After finishing my work, I drove to town with Mr. Whaley. I reached home about 5:10 and started reading Ovid's *Metamorphoses* in an English blank verse translation by Brooke Nore. At ten minutes to six, I wrote my usual card to Frances (I bought this card at the Robinson's ten-cent store), ate a supper (pork chops, potato, spinach, milk, and ice cream—all for 31 cents), and returned to my room to start writing this first entry in my diary. It is now 7:30 p.m., and I'll undress, take a bath, lie in bed and read for awhile, and then go to sleep.

January 8, 1942, Thursday

Today I walked all the way to the campus at 6:30 a.m. in a temperature that hovered around zero. The worst sufferers were my delicate ears; otherwise, I enjoyed the walk immensely, and I think it did good to my sluggish liver. At one o'clock, I walked to the "Cottage," where my friend Sh. lives. I waited for her to finish the dishes, and then we drove in her blue Ford to Flint Creek. During the ride we talked of war and our mutual friends; she then deposited me in front of the Home Economics building. I spent most of the day reading Ovid. I received two letters from Frances. I'm glad I'm not at present living in Minneapolis because the clipping enclosed in the letter was shouting in headlines that the temperature was as low as 30 below zero. I know what it means. Although I've never experienced such low temperatures yet, I lived through ten and twelve and eighteen below zero. Sometimes I'm inclined to feel sorry for the German soldiers now in Russia who have to fight in temperatures as low as 40 below zero. But they brought it upon themselves. No sane man should leave his own comfortable home and invade somebody else's country for the sake of conquest or fame. The war news is both pleasant and unpleasant. In the

Pacific, the Japs are still advancing in Malaya toward Singapore. But in Russia and Libya, the Axis forces are in full retreat. Everybody who faces the grim prospect of military service earnestly and devoutly prays that the Russians may wipe out the Germans and thus shorten the war. It is the greater irony in history that the life of the two democracies, England and America, depends upon the valor and resourcefulness of the once-despised and ridiculed Reds or Bolsheviks. But for the valiant resistance of the Russians, the Germans would have already won the war. But Hitler made a great mistake when, on June 22, 1941, he attacked Russia, expecting to win as quick and decisive a victory as he won over France in the spring of 1940. In the madness of war and race of armaments, I pray to God that I might be left alone in order to pursue my goal in life, which is and always has been the accumulation and communication of knowledge. Scholars feel out of place in a war-torn world. And yet the scholars in their dark days must keep the love of learning burning bright and transmit it to the coming generation. Otherwise, the world will plunge again into another long, dark age.

January 9, 1942, Friday

It is still cold, clear, and windy. We sat before the blazing fire and discussed the war situation. We bewailed and discussed the stupidity of a politician for not sending abundant supplies of war materials to the British, Russians, and Chinese during the last year so that they would exterminate the Japs and the Germans and save the American boys. Now, of course, we have to ship American armies abroad and keep them supplied, as well as our allies, with communications.

January 11, 1942, Sunday

I went to Chapel for the 9:30 service. D. Bennet preached on the man who is blessed of God and grows like a tree, bringing fruit and always having green leaves. After that, we drove to Tahlequah. At Harry's Hut we ate a nice dinner, a new dish called Fried Chicken in the Bucket. Then we went to the Sequoyah Theater, where we saw Cagney and Bette Davis in *The Bride Came C.O.D.* I saw that show in Minneapolis last summer. After the show, we drove to the grounds of the Teachers College and then returned to Siloam Springs through Westville. I listened to Charlie McCarthy's broadcast and Walter Winchell's news broadcast. Miss Sh. drove me home about 9 o'clock. I washed my hands, and I'm writing now in bed. Thank God the cold wave is over, and I've not yet even lighted the stove.

January 12, 1942, Monday

The weather has changed definitely for the best. It is a joy to walk up and down the Hill. As usual, I lectured for three hours: one hour on Francis Bacon, another on Shakespeare's sonnets and *Othello,* and the last hour on Edith Wharton, Willa Cather, and Theodore Dreiser. Rev. Bennet drove me to town and bragged about his driving from California to Siloam Springs in 30 hours. I hinted that it would be better for both his life and the life of the car if he would stick to 40 miles an hour, the speed recommended by the authorities. Today I got another point straight. I asked Snider why he had to go to Little Rock for his physical examination. He explained to me that, at the Local Draft Board, they examine you only to make sure that you are not rejectable material, so they save the government the expense of a trip to Little Rock. But if you are not rejectable material, Little Rock is the place where the final physical checking takes place. It usually takes a month between the two examinations. They wait until they get a busload for shipment from Siloam Springs to Little Rock. In times of war, an individual is of no more worth than an animal; he is weighed, checked, shipped, trained, and then sent to some unknown destination to kill men he never set eyes on before and to whom, as far as he is concerned, he bears no grudge or ill will. Yet, what can an attacked nation do? We certainly can't allow the brutal forces of the world to gain control of everything and make a hell of earth. The brutal four have already caused untold misery and sent hundreds of thousands of human beings to an untimely grave. They have overrun countries, devastated cities, sunk ships, and made slaves of small nations.

January 13, 1942, Tuesday

I spent the greater part of the day reading Ovid's *Metamorphoses*. In the afternoon, Miss Sh. and I drove to Flint Creek in the warm, bright sunshine. On the way, we discussed the way Flower tries to get hold of B. Miss Sh. also told me that B., in an effort to escape military service, had not only resuscitated dependents in the persons of his widowed sister and mother (who, by the way, live in California), but he has also composed a document setting forth his conscientious objections to war. It seems that, in the United States, everybody expects somebody else to do the fighting while he remains behind, enjoying the comforts and conveniences of modern civilization. The married men expect the young men and the bachelors to do the fighting, while the bachelors and the young men do not see why they will fight for someone else's children and families. I hope the despised Russians and the Chinese, armed with American-made weapons, will defeat the Germans and the

Japs and save our boys' lives—although I doubt it greatly, owing to the stupidity of senators who, for three years, in spite of unmistakable signs of efforts on the part of the Axis powers, have hindered the administration from sending vast quantities of weapons to the British, the Russians, and the Chinese.

January 14, 1942, Wednesday

Today B. underwent what he called a physical inspection preliminary to his physical examination that will take place in a month in Little Rock. I attended the usual Wednesday 11-12 chapel. D. Bennet preached a sermon, "I Thought of My Ways." The point was that most of us do not think before we act and that we never think of our ways but always of somebody else's ways. After the chapel, there was a brief meeting of the scholastic committee (of which I am a member) in order to decide what to do with the classes of Mr. Stewart. Mr. Black presided in the absence of Dr. Willis. We decided to post a note in the bulletin that his classes will not meet till further notice. Although the meeting was only five minutes, it deprived me of the opportunity to get to town for lunch. So I had lunch on the Hill. The meal consisted of beans, chili, crackers, coffee, and gingerbread. I paid the usual price of twenty cents for it. I sat at a table with Max Condor, the teacher of singing, Mr. and Mrs. Weaver, the old couple that run the store, and Mr. and Mrs. Brown, the brother of the President, whose job it is to sweep and dust the classrooms. I missed my "old pals" Mr. Vanderkan, who is at present in Stillwater, and Mr. Bitzer, who at present eats at the "Cottage," Mr. Lord, and Mr. Wright, who have all departed. I felt like a stranger among these people. I also missed old Mr. Pitman, the teacher of carpentry, who has been taken ill and left to God knows where. Mr. Snider and Withers sat at the table with the three young ladies, Miss Buffun, Wright, and Pool. Youth is always happy in any environment, as I could see from the looks of the students, who laughed, joked, made love, and looked as happy as fish in the water.

January 15, 1942, Thursday

I spent the greater part of the day reading Longfellow's prose romance *Hyperion*. Miss Sh. had to buy a license plate for her car, but she could not do it simply because the U. did not pay its teachers as scheduled. This being the last day the car could operate under the 1941 license, I drew money from the bank and lent her ten dollars to buy the license plate, which is commonly called the auto tag. After settling this business, we drove beyond Flint Creek. It was a very beautiful day, with high temperatures and blue skies and balmy breezes. We joked about the finances of the U., which have just gone through a re-organization—bankruptcy. B. and Flower were the most excited of all of us. They almost saw in their mind's eye the U. closed and every one of us condemned to iner-tia, unemployment, and looking for another job. I simply refuse to worry over hypothetical emergencies. No use crossing a bridge before coming to it. I had a haircut and supped at the Youree on eggs, cheese, and vegetables. I read the *Joplin News*. It's not very cheering or encouraging. The Japs are still advancing toward Sin-gapore and the Dutch Indies. The Americans are, however, still valiantly resisting in the Luzon, and the Russians are advancing. The British have had trouble in the Mediterranean with the Ger-mans attacking Malta in an effort to relieve their hard-pressed Army in Libya. The more the war rages, the more I think of Goethe, who said, "The end is everywhere; art has still truth; take refuge there." I'll devote my efforts to the complete mastery of the

English language, both written and spoken. I'll become a master of expression and, thus, be able to express my thoughts, fears, and hopes in memorable prose. My command of English is still far from perfect; I'm still ashamed of my pronunciation, my grammar, my syntax, and my delivery. Unless I overcome these defects, I'm in danger of remaining poor, ignorant, and unknown.

January 16, 1942, Friday

I supped at the "Cottage" with Miss Sh. and B., Flower being busy with a banquet at the Home Economics Building. I had a long discussion with B. about whether merit or influence will get you a position. I supported the thesis that merit is always rewarded and that what one needs is patience—to bide one's time.

Today I met two of our boys walking to town in their Sunday clothes. I asked them where they were going. They answered, "To visit our Uncle." They meant they were on their way to Little Rock for physical examinations and to join the Army. Another boy, who has just finished taking American Prose, told me he was not coming back next semester because he was going to join the Navy or some other branch of service. When I asked him why he was in such a hurry, he answered that, by joining now, he would select the branch of service he wanted, but if he waited to be drafted, he would be consigned to the duties of a private soldier in the Army. With our students literally streaming out of the classrooms, I wondered whether we shall have enough students to carry on next semester or next summer.

January 17, 1942, Saturday

Today I worked with Mr. Batchelor and Dr. Smith. I prepared the library for next Monday's registration. We had fun moving the tables and chairs and setting out the name cards. We drove beyond Flint Creek. The weather was fine, and I enjoyed the ride immensely in spite of the fact that I had to pay 53 cents for three gallons of gasoline. On my return home, I finished Longfellow's romance called *Hyperion,* and then I went out to supper. I'll start re-reading Eugene O'Neill's plays. I'll shampoo my hair with Fitch in an effort to get rid of my dandruff, and then I'll go to bed. Since this is the last day of the first semester, I feel bound to thank God for preserving me in health and happiness during this semester. When I started this semester back on September 18, I was suffering from such a headache and general weakness that I could not walk up the Hill. Many a time I taught in misery. But thank God, I feel much better at present, and I can walk, talk, and eat without headache or dizziness. D. Williams, whom I consulted, gave me some green pills to rouse my sluggish liver and recommended exercise. I think these are unmistakable signs of age, and a wise man will take care of himself to the best of his ability to pass the remainder of his life in freedom from pain and care. From now on, I'll concentrate on my work, which contributes to my mastery of the English language. I'll talk less and do more. Of late, I have acquired the bad habit of spending too much time in gossip and nonsensical arguments. I'll study more, walk more, teach better, and be kinder to my students and my colleagues. The dreams I dreamt in my youth must be realized. It is not too late to leave behind something to conquer time.

January 19, 1942, Monday

Everyone was in high spirits since the paychecks were out. I must have money, since there is little hope of my ever recovering the 1,000 dollars the U. owes me in bonds, savings, and back-salary. At least I must have money enough to keep body and soul together next summer. I'm not as strong as I used to be twenty years ago when I used to spend my summer working and at the same time reading voraciously. My legs are not strong, my eyes are weak, and my head swims when I overexert myself. For a while at the beginning of the year, it seemed as if I were doomed to perform only my duties and have no strength to do any outside reading or study. Thank God, I have improved greatly, but I'm far from being as peppy and strong as I used to be. By exercise, diet, peace of mind, cleanliness, and adequate sleep, I hope to keep on studying and teaching without feeling pains and inconvenience.

January 20, 1942, Tuesday

Today the scholastic committee, of which I am a member, held a meeting at 1 o'clock to decide about giving degrees and transcripts to students who are called to service. I saw one student, suitcase in one hand and overcoat in another, leaving the campus. One of my students who took the final examination in American Prose asked me to correct his paper and turn his grade in before Friday because he was leaving on that day to join the Navy. It breaks one's heart to see young men taken away from the pursuit of knowledge for the manual training to kill. But what can one do? As a senator said today, "Damn Hitler and all his people." Because I had to give an examination today, I spent almost the whole day reading O'Neill's *Lazarus Laughed* and *Strange Interlude*.

He is certainly depressive with his insistence that human beings speak and act according to the rule of the Freudian psychology.

In order to keep myself fit, I walked three times up and down the Hill; it is a very fine day, reminding me of the glorious winter sunshine of distant Cyprus. I wonder whether the poor inhabitants have anything to eat. According to the dispatcher from Europe, Finland, Croatia, and Greece are suffering for lack of food. Today I've seen neither B. nor Flower nor Sh. I think it is good for all of us not to see much of each other. Sometimes we get on each other's nerves.

January 21, 1942, Wednesday

So God help us! Third day without seeing any of the inmates of the "Cottage."

January 22, 1942, Thursday

I gave two exams, and I spent the day reading the February edition of *The Reader's Digest*. The most interesting item is "Education for Death," an account of the German boys and girls under the Nazi regime. All they are taught is that their lives belong to Adolph Hitler and that dying for him is the duty of every German. Another interesting anecdote was "The Last Days of the Bismark," which recounts the sinking of the German ship by that name in the Atlantic by the British fleet and air force. The scenes of the sinking ship are horrific. Once the Germans lost their faith in their invincibility, they behaved like a panicky mob. Because the day was fine and warm, I walked up and down the Hill four times, the last time carrying my overcoat over my arm. It is such a relief to have the warm sunshine streaming on my face and the blue sky smiling at me.

January 15, 1942, Sunday

Sh. drove me to the "Cottage," since B. and F. went to the Presbyterian Church. We were left by ourselves. For reasons which

I could not understand and which she would not divulge, she was on the verge of tears. Sometimes I wish I could understand women, but who ever did? We dined at the Youree with F. and B. and then went out for a ride. I spent the whole afternoon reading O'Neill.

Tomorrow we start the second semester, and everybody is wondering how a university with such a small number of students can function. As I understand it, the university has enrolled about 137 student—a very small number. Most of the boys were either drafted or volunteered, and most of the girls are rushing to jobs made available to them by the defense program and war demand. Only a quick victory can save the teachers from lecturing to empty benches, and the end of the war is not even in sight. The Russians are advancing toward the Germans, but in Asia and Africa, the Allies are still on the defensive.

January 26, 1942, Monday

I saw B. for a moment. His face was wrinkled, and he seemed to have not slept at all last night. He has been expecting an answer from the Local Draft Board concerning his clarification. Any way one looks at things, they don't look bright. If one is called for Army service, it is bad, especially for some of us who are no longer young and have little relish in marching up and down in uniforms and learning how to kill our fellow men. On the other side, most of us professors will probably be left without students, hence without jobs, and would either starve or go back to the work we used to do so many years ago that, naturally, we hated. But I'll press valiantly forward. One more goal—the hardest and the most glorious—the art of writing, and thus becoming independent of employers and work hours and at the same time serving more men and women than I do at present in the ill-ventilated classrooms.

Unless I achieve that goal, my life has been wasted. I'll have nothing to show when I cross the bar. It is about time to offer to God and my fellow men a gift in appreciation of the joy and happiness they have given me.

January 28, 1942, Wednesday

Since I'm chaperoning this week, I saw the couples to the California Hall, and then I separated them. I don't blame the things for wanting to cling to each other; the night was bathed in a white, warm moonlight, and the stars twinkled bright and remote in the depth of the sky. I walked home in the moonlight, looking at the stars and wondering how many generations of men they have seen appear and disappear on the face of the earth and how many generations they will see yet. Our fears, hopes, doubts and aspirations seem so trivial and transitory when we look at the starry skies.

January 29, 1942, Thursday

Dr. Brown made some announcements, the most important of which was that, on account of the present war crisis, some members of the faculty will be asked to teach some subjects not strictly belonging to their fields.

January 30, 1942, Friday

What is my goal in life? Until 1939, I had only one goal—"to get a Ph.D. degree." But what is my goal now? I thought of setting a new goal in my life and bending all my energies toward achieving it, but the phantom of being called to the Army interfered. It seems fantastic that I should ever become a soldier—a man who has never handled a weapon—but stranger things have happened in this mystical world of ours. Boys of my acquaintance are now in the AEF in Ireland; others are serving as Marines in the Pacific, while others are in the Air Corps. B. has been classed as 1A, and he will probably be inducted very soon. Millions and millions of men and women have undergone radical changes in their professions, fortunes, and lives. But, as always, one can only say, "Let His will be done in everything."

I set my goal: I want to be president of a university. To achieve that, I need absolute mastery of the English tongue, both written and spoken. It can be done, provided I stop discovering difficulties in order to excuse myself for not achieving what I ought to. God helps those who dare, and I'll dare once more to hitch my wagon to a star.

February 3, 1942, Tuesday

Last night I came home late on account of my supping at the "Cottage," going out for a ride with Sh., and then visiting with my landlord and landlady. I spent most of the day reading Booth Tarkington's new novel, *The Heritage of Hatcher Ide*. In the afternoon, I went out for a ride with Sh. toward Gentry. Especially memorable were my last year's night rides with Gussie, who at present works as a librarian at Washington College in Tennessee. We used to ride far and fast beyond Decatur and Gravette in all kinds of weather. Sh. is not so good a driver as Gussie. She is easily tired, and she lacks vitality. But one must be satisfied with what one can get, especially a man of my age, poverty, and clumsiness.

Today, I sent a card to the U.S. Civil Service Commission, requesting forms for an application for examination for the position of translator. Colleges are heading for closing on account of the draft, volunteering, and defense work. The U.S. government seems to be in need of translators, and at least one can try.

February 4, 1942, Wednesday

I taught four hours instead of five, having decided to meet my Shakespeare class, consisting of two not very industrious students, only twice a week. I spent most of the day reading Tarkington's *The Heritage of Hatcher Ide*, which I finished about noon. I walked to the "Cottage" with B., and then we drove to town. I ate a supper consisting of a tiny pork chop, mashed potatoes, and peas, washed down with a glass of milk. It cost 30 cents. The prices are going up steadily and slowly, but still, in Arkansas, we are far from feeling the effects of war—yet. Only the boys who were drafted complained of the Local Draft Board as being too tough. They put everyone in a 1A class. Some of the boys think that, in their hometown, they should have received more consideration and won deferment. The nation demands men, and everyone is trying to gain a deferment. In the meantime, who will man our ships, planes, and batteries? It seems that the whole world depends on America not only for munitions but also for men. In the beginning, everyone said, "Give us weapons, and we will defeat the enemy." We gave them their weapons, and now they are clamoring for men. Americans are now in Iceland, Ireland, Australia, Singapore, Persia, and Libya. Already over one million men have been sent abroad, and more are to follow.

February 6, 1942, Friday

I had a rather good time because two of my classes failed to meet on account of the Missionary Conference. I attended one meeting at 11, where the guest speaker, James Stuart, spoke on the text about how Christ sent His disciples to teach all nations, saying that He would be with them always. Last year we had McGinlay, upon whom the University bestowed an honorary doctorate. This man is for evangelizing Europe. Other missionaries who preached for former conferences were for evangelizing the Mohammedans. In my humble opinion, we need to teach our own people.

February 9, 1942, Monday

First day of the so-called "war-time." Seven o'clock classes meet at a most unholy hour, and the 8 o'clock classes met at seven. I guess very soon we will get used to the new time. Yesterday, B., Flower, Sh., and I drove to Fayetteville, where we ate a nice steak dinner at the Blue Mill and saw a funny show called *Hellzapoppin'*. It was an unusual production, employing all the conventional devices of the motion picture technique. I supped with them at the "Cottage," and for reasons, which I could not easily understand, they attacked me rather violently on account of my choosing English literature as the special field of my endearment. They were of the opinion that I was unsuited for teaching English on account of my inability to speak correct, clear English. If it were not for the fact that I've already taught English for five semesters, I would have been almost persuaded to resign and go fishing. But, of course, they are wrong. A man can't live by accent alone. It is much to be regretted that I have not yet gotten rid of my foreign accent and that I don't speak English like a native, yet my knowledge of the classics, French, and modern Greek gives me formidable equipment for a professor of English. Well, they were probably activated by a slightly secret jealousy—a real interest in my welfare. Anyhow, I shall keep on working, and I shall never give up the struggle for the mastery of both English literature and the English language. To the brave, there is nothing impossible, and our defects are the very weapons with which one conquers both fame and fortune.

February 11, 1942, Wednesday

Yesterday I gave a brief talk to the Fortnight Club about Cyprus. I gave the same address months ago to the Rotarians. It proved a great success. This time, however, it proved a dismal failure as far as I'm concerned. My pronunciation of certain words was exorable, my sentences were anything but grammatically correct and clear, and they were certainly unworthy of a man who heads the English department of a university.

After the talk, I went out for a ride with Sh. as far as Gentry; it was a rather silent and gloomy ride. I supped at the "Cottage," and then I attended a general meeting of the staff and faculty in the Chapel. Dr. Willis stressed the subject of "civil pride."

Today, with the help of my friend Snider, I filed and dispatched my income tax. I was surprised to discover that my net income during the last year did not amount to more than 800 dollars. JBU went bankrupt and then went through a state of reorganization and owes me over 1,000 dollars. Last year I paid $16.28 in income tax; this year I did not pay any, and I really wanted to pour some dollars into the U.S. Treasury since the need is great. I hope that not many others are in the same predicament. Today I could not get a cup of coffee at any of the three restaurants in town, owing to the fact that they open at 6:30, and I can't afford to wait till they get their coffeepots boiling. I decided to do without my cup of coffee. I bought some chocolate bars. I'll eat one every morning and wash it down with a glass of pure water. I'll not ever be a slave to such a mild intoxicant as coffee. As it is, I drink too many cups of coffee.

February 14, 1942, Saturday

I spent a few hours preparing for my Shakespeare and English Literature classes for Monday. I went out for a ride with Sh. The weather is spring-like. I'm at present reading *The Little Minister* by J.M. Barrie. I enjoy it very much. Everyone is worried over the war. The Germans' battleships escaped from Brest through the English Channel to Bremen. I simply don't see why German boats can go from one port to another when they are protected by shore batteries, airplanes, and mosquito torpedo boats. Singapore is still holding out, and if it holds three days more, it will probably hold out as long as Leningrad and Moscow. The thing that wins wars is courage. It seems some people lack courage, and they easily swing from elation to despair. If I really were over 45, I would have continued my peaceful activities unworried, in the assurance that Russia, the United States, China, and the British Empire will win the war. But, unfortunately, I'm under 45, and I have to register next Monday and will probably be called to some kind of military service if I pass the physical examination. But just the same, I must continue to study and teach and write as usual. My chief worry is that I have not yet completely mastered the English language, and, without the absolute command of the English language, my future will be neither bright nor brilliant. Hence my goal is still this: Get rid of your foreign accent. This is of more vital interest to me than anything else.

February 15, 1942, Sunday

At 3 o'clock, we listened to Winston Churchill's speech. He told the English, who seem to be restive after the loss of Singapore, the retreat of Libya, and the escape of the German battleship under the very noses of the British coast defenses, that they are much better off than in June 1940, when France collapsed, and in August 1941, when the Russian armies were in retreat. Now they have powerful allies in the United States, Soviet Russia, and China, and although the road is hard, the victory is certain. He also pointed out to them that the Russians were saved from disaster by uniting behind their rulers. The radio of the lady who occupies the ground floor is filling the house with the laughter from the unseen audience on the celebrated Charlie McCarthy show.

February 20, 1942, Friday

Last night I was excited over the receipt of the application forms for a translator position. Today I visited D. Sampson to inquire whether my eyes meet the specification prescribed of the applicant's vision, and I was told that one eye does not meet the requirements. I guess it is not so great a loss since translation has never been my favorite activity. Another loss sustained this week was the sale of Sh.'s car. She sold it for 150 dollars. It was an impulsive act. I'll miss the rides to Flint Creek and Gentry, but one can live comfortably and sanely without driving aimlessly from place to place with a lady by his side. It was good as long as it lasted. Sh. is my third driver since I came to Siloam Springs—the first being "Old Stevie" and the second, "Gussie." Well, God will provide another driver.

February 21, 1942, Saturday

This morning I found a drawing of myself in chalk on the blackboard with the inscription, "The Honorable Dr. John H. Panage." I dined at the "Cottage" with Sh. and B., Flower being away at a Home Economics meeting in Fayetteville. After the dinner, Sh. asked me to help her dry the dishes. I don't know why—unless it's because I hate to be bossed by anyone—I refused. B., to my surprise, sprang up to help her, and then both of them proceeded to take me to task for failing to help, to play ball, etc. It is certainly not fair of them to invite me to dinner (for which I always pay) and then expect me to dry dishes. But somehow Sh., and especially B., think they do me a valuable service by inviting me to the "Cottage" for meals. If it were not for the fact that both were under nervous strain on account of the war, the fear of losing their jobs, and the lack of exercise, I would have bidden them good-bye and never set my foot inside the threshold of the "Cottage" again. Sh. walked to town with me and tried to apologize. I told her that it was such an insignificant incident that one must forget it right away. This is the second time within a week that F. or B. or Sh. has been unduly hard in their remarks to me. Sometimes I wonder why I put up with them. It is simply because in this small village, I'm as lonely as I used to be at the time I was teaching and studying in Boston, Atlanta, and Minneapolis. Tonight at the U. is the annual George Washington Banquet. During the three years I've been in Siloam Springs, I have attended only one banquet. Last year, to the great disappointment of Gussie, who wanted to be seen with me, I persuaded her to go to Fayetteville and see a show. This year Sh. served notice that it would be proper that she and I be seen together at the banquet. If there is anything that vexes me, it is to be seen escorting—like an obedient valet—a lady who thinks that she must display to the envious eyes of her sisters the man she has captured! This year I put off Sh. by pleading the inadequacy of my wardrobe. I told her frankly that I couldn't attend a banquet in my present work-day suit of clothes, already slightly shabby from two years' wear (my other suit being too light for this season). She agreed, or she pretended to agree, and so I stayed at home to read and write.

This day reminds me of the day in 1927 when I got my naturalization papers in New York. At that time I was teaching in Boston and staying with Lucas, who at this moment is in Cyprus.

I remember it was a cold, sleety day, and Costa accompanied me to the court. I also remember the trip back to the shoreline. It was sleeting all the way, but, in my youthful expectation, I smelled spring in the air. How the years fly! I often wonder what Lucille, Costa, Lucas, Nike, and the other friends of those days are doing now. I don't even write to them now, except at Christmas. I've lost track of Lucille and Costa, but wherever they are, I wish them health and happiness. They were of great help to me—Lucille by teaching me all the torments, fears, hopes, and doubts that an unrequited love is heir to, and Costa by teaching me that a bank account and a full stomach might make a man forget to pursue knowledge and wisdom. Love and hunger have made me eat humble pie. Someday, I'll tell the world in memorable words the sufferings of the timid, inefficient, dreamy youth on the streets of New York, on the uneven sidewalks of Boston, and under the blazing sun of Atlanta. I forgot to mention Mary, who studied Greek under me and was experimenting with weaving in colors and materials reminiscent of the ancient Greeks. She was beautiful and loved me, but I could think only of Lucille, and there hangs another tragedy of my life. But all is well since it ended well.

February 23, 1942, Monday

Nobody wants war; nobody wants to be killed; no one wants to be taken from his peaceful routine of life and thrown into camps, trenches, mud, etc. But what the average man wants to know is what one must do when attacked. Nobody in the country wanted war, but we are attacked, and if we fail to fight, our fate shall be like the fate of France. We will become slaves to brutal masters who will not respect anything and who will make us work for them and keep us starving so our ideals, hopes, and dreams will turn to dust and ashes. In times like these, everyone must put his shoulder to the wheel and help produce tanks, planes, and guns by thousands to overwhelm the enemy by sheer metal superiority. Machines are cheaper than human bodies, and this is the war of machines. The fastest and sturdiest machines always win.

Tonight President Roosevelt will talk over the radio at 9 o'clock. His speech has been greatly advertised in advance, but since I don't have a radio, and since I must get up at 5 o'clock, I'll miss it. I'll read it in tomorrow's papers.

Today I've only gotten glimpses of Sh. and B., and I certainly feel much better for it. The girl with her petty fears and worries and the man with his pessimistic philosophy sometimes upset me and make me unable to concentrate on my work. The thing that matters is doing one's work and increasing one's knowledge by reading, observation, and thinking. There will be a draft-lottery, the third since March 17, 1940. I'm keenly interested since, if my number comes out, I'll have to join the Army, and God only knows what that will lead to. They are to draw between 8,000 and 9,000 numbers, and today I told Helen, the waitress at the Youree, that my number is sure to come up. I'm so luckless. I repented later on. I'm still a little superstitious. I still carry a stone, a ring, and a counterfeited silver dollar. One can only say God's will be done in this as in everything. One, however, can't but rebel against such a nonsensical procedure as having his happiness, health, and life decided by blind luck. But that is still much better than being pressed into service by force.

February 25, 1942, Wednesday

All day long I felt tired and worn out, owing to the fact that, last night, I went to bed late on account of a faculty meeting and was awakened in the middle of the night by a fire that broke out in a garage and automobile showroom just two blocks away from the place I'm staying. At the meeting I was asked to say a few words about my way of teaching English. I explained to the faculty the cooperation system and my objective essay exams, and I ended with the remark that we seem to cultivate the memory of the students and not their thinking. The aim of college is not to pump knowledge into the heads of the students but to teach them how to think. This last remark stirred a great deal of discussion.

February 26, 1942, Thursday

B. and I breakfasted at the Youree. He told me that Dean Willis visited him last Tuesday evening and somehow hinted to him that he must marry Flower. B. was exceedingly mad. He thinks that Dr. Bennet is again displaying undue interest in the welfare of Flower. I told him that the best thing for him is to try to get away from the U. He did a rather silly thing. He has bought the "Cottage," and he is so attached to it that his attitude toward life may change. I personally think that marrying Flower is not going to hurt him. Flower's besetting sins are boundless energy and a disposition to domineer. Energy is a virtue rather than a vice, and where can one find a woman who is not directly or indirectly trying to domineer someone?

On account of the meeting that lasted till 12:10, I took my lunch at the California Dining Room. I sat beside the plump, buxom nurse, and I ate a piece of steak with more bone than flesh, mashed potatoes, corn, beets, and coffee. It is the first meal I have eaten at the Cafeteria since Christmas. It reminded me of the first and second year of my sojourn in the U., when I used to eat there every day and sit beside and joke with a person who left the

U., as it seems, ages ago. I felt lonely, and although I tried to be bright and smart with the nurse, the presence of Mr. and Mrs. Weaver and Mr. and Mrs. Brown—all past 50, overworked and weary—dampened my spirits. There is certainly nothing certain in this world but change.

March 1, 1942, Sunday

It has been raining and snowing all day long. I spent the entire day in my room, except at noon I met the inmates of the "Cottage" at the Youree for lunch. We talked as usual about the U. and the war. After lunch I saw about 30 boys taking the bus for Little Rock, where they will be inducted into the Army. Among them was Charles Wilson, one of our seniors. I shook hands with him and wished him good luck. There was a small crowd to see them off, but as far as I could see, there were neither cheers nor tears.

March 2, 1942, Monday

I attended a faculty meeting at 12:45 in the Chapel. Dr. Brown announced that he has some difficulties with the lawyers and that he is going away for two months and has turned the U. over to a board of three, consisting of Mr. Cox, Dr. Willis, and Mr. Springfield. He also announced that the checks for the last half-month are out, but God knows how the payments for the next month will be provided. I supped at the "Cottage." Everyone was very gloomy and discussed the meeting. Even I suggested to B. that we start raising chickens—if we can get the money to buy chickens, wire chicken houses, and other necessary equipment. I drove to town with Dr. Durham and kidded his daughter. I told her that I was sorely in need of a girl with a car. She offered herself.

I turned her down for being yet an undergraduate. I wrote a card to Frances, who seems to be excited over her son's spending his leave of absence with her. I spent almost the entire day reading the March edition of *The Reader's Digest*.

March 4, 1942, Wednesday

Today being an intramural day, I rode to Tulsa with Mr. Cook, his wife, and Sh. We visited nearly all of the stores in Tulsa, including Dunkin, Sears, and Five and Ten. We dined at Schoeffields', and Mr. and Mrs. Cook visited some friends. At about 2 o'clock, we started home with our purchases. On the way we picked up one of our high school students, who had thumbed his way to Tulsa and was trying to thumb his way back to Siloam Springs. How on earth a boy of fifteen or sixteen can escape the supervision of the responsible ones and make his way to a distant town unnoticed is beyond my comprehension. I hope some of our girls do not travel unnoticed so far. I almost always feel gloomy after my return from a big city, and yet I like small towns, where one can breathe and live sanely. City life is artificial life. I envy big cities for their libraries, shows, restaurants, and communication.

March 5, 1942, Thursday

I went to the City Library and got Mark Twain's *A Connecticut Yankee in King Arthur's Court*. I remember two screen versions of this story: a silent one about eighteen years ago and another "talkie" version in Atlanta about ten years ago. During that time, Will Rogers was in his glory, and he was playing the Yankee's part. How fast the years fly! Just now everyone is worrying about Java, which, according to the newspapers, seems doomed. The Japs are advancing everywhere after occupying five or six of the principle towns.

March 8, 1942, Sunday

Very windy day. I spent the entire day reading Stuart Chase's *The Tyranny of Words*. It is a study in the science of semantics. He keeps repeating with tiresome reiteration the four cardinal ideals of the writers of semantics. Words are not things. Don't misuse abstraction. Find the referent. Turn false meanings into no meanings. But just the same, he is very interesting and stimulating. He suffers from verbosity. It seems to me that one can say certain things in fewer words. But still, who am I to criticize men who write books read by millions? It would be better for me to study their technique and profit by their example.

March 10, 1942, Tuesday

I wasted the day in committee meetings and chapels.

I finished Stuart Chase's *The Tyranny of Words*. Is it possible that men do not know what they are talking about? Is it possible that we have peopled the world with objectified abstractions that do not exist anywhere except in our heads? From now on, I'll not use a single word whose referent I do not know. I'll give abstract words a wide berth, and I'll always ask what, where, and when! Such rigid discipline will free my mind of verbal cobwebs and enable me to see life as it is. Today, while I was drinking a cup of tea at the Youree, the nine-year-old son of the waitress came in. She kissed him on the lips and patted his cheeks while her eyes swam with such a desire as one feels before embracing his beloved. The son is, of course, spoiled to the very marrow of his bone, and once he had wheedled her out of a dime, he ran away to buy something.

March 12, 1942, Thursday

I'm waiting to get my serial number. A drawing of lots will

take place next Tuesday starting at 5 p.m. wartime. If one's number falls among the first, he has an excellent opportunity of being inducted into the Army by next June. I hope—I devoutly hope—my number comes last. It would be the grimmest joke of my life to find myself in uniform at such an advanced age simply because I devoted my time and effort to self-development and neglected to marry and raise a family. I'm 42 years and five months old, but I wish I were 45. Yet in this, as in everything, one can humbly say, "Let His will be done!" One may be a philosopher to many current beliefs, but when one has to face a situation over which one has no control—like the lottery—one can only say, "Let His will be done!" Today, Sh., being ill, could not attend to her freshman class. Dr. Willis got hold of me and made me take care of it. For one hour, I listened to reports on aliens, Japs, etc. I contributed little to the discussion because I was as hungry as a bear and tormented by a slight headache. However, I smiled and tried to be witty. I dismissed class five minutes ahead of time, and B. and I walked through the rain to Flower's car and drove to the Youree for break-fast and a cup of coffee.

March 14, 1942, Saturday

A very quiet day. I spent most of the time reading Virgil's *Aeneid* in an English translation. I read it in the original—at least Books I and IV—25 years ago as a student of the sixth class in the Cyprus Gymnasium. The professor who taught it has been dead for a long time, and I've not seen some of my fellow sufferers these 22 years. God knows whether any of them are still alive. I relived once more the terrible night when Troy fell, Priam was killed and Aeneas escaped. I also, once more, felt sorry for poor Dido, who fell in love with Aeneas, who was reminded by the gods that he had to build his city and, therefore, could not afford to waste his time with a widow.

I visited the "Cottage" in the afternoon about 3:30, and I had a long conversation with B. and Sh. Flower, as usual, spent her time more profitably washing and pin rolling her hair. Flower is a practical girl. She prefers dating to thinking, she does things, and she is always immaculately dolled up, but she is not happy. She rarely smiles, and she often looks sour. She can't relax. Mere activity will not bring happiness to anyone.

The news is not so good, but the Japanese stopped advancing, I guess, out of sheer exhaustion, and the Germans are on the defensive in Russia. The war in Russia has degenerated into a war of attrition, and, unless Germany resumes her advance, she will lose the war from mere loss of men and ammunitions. Meantime, the British are bombing western Germany and making life uncomfortable for the Germans.

March 19, 1942, Thursday

I spent most of my time reading *The Big Money* by John Dos Passos. I looked up my serial number: it is 733. Then I looked in the papers for my order: it is 1,578. I guess it could be worse, but 1,578 is not as good as 5 or 6,000. Today I walked up the Hill with Sh. It seems that Flower is upset because I visit the "Cottage" often and since B. made some remark about my conduct toward Sh. I've made up my mind not to call again at the "Cottage," and that will save time for me and improve Flower's temper and disposition. Few friends wear longer than a year, especially when women are involved. I'll concentrate on my work and especially on improving my English—both written and spoken.

March 25, 1942, Wednesday

I spent most of the day browsing among the April issues of different magazines. *National Geographic* magazine contained a very interesting article on Egypt and the Mediterranean Sea. It included some notes on Cyprus and a picture of the Port of Cyrenia, the very place where I first set eyes on the sea, where, about 30 years ago, I was the guest of Mr. Fiero at Easter. Today, by the way, is the 25th of March, the Greek Independence Day. When I was a schoolboy, I used to take part in the parade of the high school students and get up early and go to the stadium to witness the firing of the so-called "mascula." During my stay in the United States as a principal of various schools in the Greek community, I had to coach my students for dramatic performances and recitations of poems, and I had to deliver highly patriotic speeches in honor of the revolutionary heroes. I still see the audiences in Boston, Atlanta, New Brunswick, and Minneapolis staring at me as I read my prepared speeches. I always used to prepare my speeches. How glad I was when the whole affair was over and I was at liberty to return to my English studies.

March 29, 1942, Sunday

I spent the whole day reading Hitler's *Mein Kampf.* It is as interesting as a novel. His attitude toward nationality and race is not different from mine. Born in Austria of German parents, he could not accept the Austrian government, but he longed for union with Germany. I was born in Cyprus, under English government, of Greek parents. When I was young, I was agitating for union with Greece. It was lucky for me that I migrated to the United States. If Hitler knew anything of the United States, which I doubt greatly, he would have striven for a United States of

Europe ruled by Germany as Germany was once ruled by Prussia.
He studied history and boasts of it, but he seems to have never
studied the history of the United States or the history of the British Empire. He knows only German history. Frederick the Great
and Bismark are his heroes. He is nationalistic; he never thinks in
terms of a small country. He hates the Jews; he thinks that they
control everything from business to white slavery. He abominates
Marxism and Parliamentarianism. His idea of a nation is a nation
armed to the teeth, ready to kill Jews and invade countries in order
to acquire colonies of Germany in Europe. He has succeeded in
plunging the world into a great world war. A little education—the
very thing he scorns—would have made a human being of him
instead of a fanatic fool.

March 31, 1942, Tuesday

I spent most of the day reading Hitler's *Mein Kampf.* I finished the first volume. His ideas about the Jews, race, purity, and
nationalization sound like a fanatic's. By this time, he has attained
his goal: He has driven the Jews from Germany, the masses are
over-nationalized, and the purity of race has been attained, but
where is the German nation? It is in the throng of a terrible war
against the three mightiest empires of the globe: Soviet Russia,
the British Empire, and the United States. Hitler's chance of
subduing all three is nil. Last year he could not subdue England
alone, and this year he faces an England who has gone on the
offensive, an expanding American force, and a determined Russia.
He is in a mess. I don't feel sorry for him, but I feel deeply sorry
for the German people and the poor French, Greeks, and other
Europeans who at this moment experience hunger and unheard-
of deprivations.

Today Sh. made a second appeal to me to accept an invitation to dinner at the "Cottage." The whole affair has become ridiculous, but she seems to suffer. This is definitely the last time I'll involve myself in any way with any woman. There are so many things to be done and learned, but women must have a man under their complete dominion. They must wreck his life by driving him into all kinds of illogical actions.

April 2, 1942, Thursday

I did not attend the Founder's Banquet because my suit of clothes is too shabby for such an affair. On my way home from supper, I met Sh. going to the post office. She seems to think that I didn't attend the banquet because I did not want to be seen with her. She looked pitiful. I guess for her sake I'll have to swallow my pride and begin going to the "Cottage." How I hate women! They always find means—tears, entreaties, sweetness, etc.—to bend a man to their will. Above all, they want a man to dance attendance on them, to be seen with them. Somehow, on account of my early education, I hate to be seen escorting ladies to banquets, restaurants, shows, or other public places. But how can one make women understand anything? When they want a thing, they want it unreasonably, illogically, impulsively, and fiercely.

April 3, 1942, Friday

Today is Good Friday, but we worked as usual. I spent the day reading Shakespeare's *Antony and Cleopatra*. It was warm. I supped at the "Cottage" for the first time in a month, and I did it in order to please Sh. The meal was good: steak, boiled potatoes, cauliflower, salad, tapioca pudding, and milk. One can't get such supper in town either for love or money. B. was trying to dig some row of fence posts. They got a chicken house, and before they install chickens, they must fence the place. Not a few of the professors spend their spare time milking cows and feeding chickens. It is certainly a waste to use their trained minds in feeding animals. But I guess every one of us is a farmer under the skin.

April 6, 1942, Monday

Sh. told me that she had been told by a person whose identity she refused to divulge that B. is fired. That would be a terrible blow to the poor fellow since he bought the "Cottage" and spent all his salary paying for it in monthly installments. But one can't rely on rumors, and especially at this time, rumors are flying faster than the bullets from the guns' muzzles.

April 7, 1942, Tuesday

It is cloudy and rainy. I attended a meeting of the Scholastic Committee, in which we decided what kind of credit shall be given to two students who are leaving for military service.

I've not received a letter from Frances these last four days— an unusually long silence for her. She must be busy shipping her boy back to camp.

I've finished *Mein Kampf.* It is quite a remarkable book. The writer may be mistaken in his views about labor, race, nation, etc., but he has a shrewd and dynamic personality. The events of today, however, prove him mistaken. He thought that no Marxist would defend his country. The Russians disappointed him. They have not yet collapsed after ten months of bloody struggle. His friends, the Italians, are not giving him the military assistance he expected, and instead of preserving the best blood of the race, he is certainly spilling it at the battlefields of Russia and Libya. In addition, the

British are bombing Germany savagely, and very soon the Americans with their heavy bombers will join them in the raids. Until now he has not yet felt the might of America. He will probably begin to feel it the moment his offensive against Russia starts.

April 9, 1942, Thursday

The news of the fall of Bataan has just been broadcast. General Wainwright has opened negotiations for surrendering to the Japs. We pay for years of unpreparedness, bickering, and mere talking. The men did their job, but our own politicians failed them. While Marshall and the President are sending men abroad, the politicians blocked the way until we were attacked and there were no sufficient powers to repulse the enemy. Our fleet, instead of attacking the enemy, was employed in escorting convoys, and the Japs had time to lord it over the Pacific. Let us hope that the worst is over and that from now on, putting our shoulder to the wheel, we shall give stunning blows to the enemy.

April 10, 1942, Friday

It is strange how tired and blue one feels by Friday afternoon. Life to him seems flat and unprofitable. Then one recovers over the weekend and begins the week with cheerfulness and courage.

Dr. Davis and I discussed the question of whether it would not be more profitable for the United States to send ammunition and men to only one front in abundant quantities instead of sending men and weapons to twenty different fronts. Of course, we are what one may call parlor strategists, but we are often right while staff and the so-called war experts have proven to be wrong.

April 12, 1942, Sunday

After dinner we paid a visit to Dr. Cook's home to see his chickens, his garden, and his alfalfa field. B. and Flower have already established a chicken house some distance from the "Cottage." They have fenced ground and wanted to get some information concerning the purchase of chickens, the kind of feed, etc. We stayed until 3 o'clock. They drove to the "Cottage," and I walked home. The snowy white hens looked pretty among the green, luxuriant alfalfa.

April 13, 1942, Monday

Dr. Brown called a special chapel and a special faculty meeting today. He had received a letter from a girl student who accused professors and students of smoking, drinking, and motion-picture going. Even Mr. Black, the registrar, was accused of smoking. Dr. Brown said he knew that my friend B. and Mr. Condon were in the habit of smoking. He said that he would tolerate smoking and picture going, but liquor is liquor, and any student caught with liquor either in the bottle or in his car is to be shipped home without ceremony. I drove to town in Mr. Stout's car with Mr. Durnham's daughter. She told me that my friend B. filled the classroom with tobacco smell. The day was consumed in discussing "smoking" and "motion-pictures."

April 15, 1942, Thursday

I deposited fifty dollars into my account, thus bringing my bank account to 1,470 dollars, not including the 150 dollars I have in my Minneapolis bank account. Besides my life insurance, that's all I have in the world. The U. owes me approximately 1,100 dollars in bonds and back salary, but I'm not quite sure of ever collecting it.

At 10 o'clock B. and I drove to the "Cottage" to see the new pump he is installing. It will cost him about 120 dollars. The pump is a nice-looking fixture in blue and red, it is electrically propelled, and it is guaranteed for five years. This morning on my way to the Hill, I met Sh. She immediately corrected my pronouncing "shoes" with "s" instead of "z" (Shuz) and my wrongly using "either." It seems that I can scarcely open my mouth without making a mistake either in syntax or pronunciation.

The return of Laval, head of the French government, has stirred great fear and speculation. What will France do? I guess Laval will play Hitler against Roosevelt and try to get something for France; after all, why should a Frenchman care for Germany or America? The Germans have enslaved them, and the Americans had deserted them at their hour of need. Of course, with a disarmed nation at the mercy of a brutal conqueror, there is little that even the altruist politician can do. But Laval is not a baby, and he is probably a match for Hitler. One thing is becoming clearer day by day—the Anglo-Americans are getting stronger in the air, and it is the aeroplane that will decide the fate of humanity. The huge American bombers are produced by men. They will spread havoc in Germany and paralyze its communication and production system.

April 20, 1942, Monday

Of all my old friends—the four original ones—only I was left on the Hill, and God only knows for how long.

Everybody is discussing the raid on Tokyo. The Japs say that they were bombed by American bombers, but our government is still silent. The Japs do not know how and when the planes appeared over their capitol, and Washington is not in a hurry to tell them. Hitler is stepping up his offensive in Russia, and Marshall has returned with Hopkins from England. Last night I supped at the "Cottage," and we had fun trying to get the thirteen pullets Flower bought last Friday to roost in the neat chicken house. They began counting the eggs—they had only one on Sunday—out of five laying hens. They think the hens are too well fed and, therefore, have grown lazy and don't care to lay eggs.

April 21, 1942, Tuesday

It was clear about noon, and tonight is a very lovely evening with the leaves and the grass at their greenest, the sky at its bluest, and the birds at their merriest. How I long for Gussie, who used to pick me up about 7 o'clock for a long ride in the cool evening! I saw Mr. William Winter on the campus, who last year was student instructor at the University and was drafted for the Army last fall. He wore a neat, well-fitting uniform, and he looked brown and tough. He has just returned from Fort Benning, Georgia. I asked him whether he ever took a trip to Atlanta. He said, "No, I've been always broke." His month's pay amounts to about 36 dollars.

I spent most of the day correcting papers, filling cards with grades, and reading Robert Burns' biography by Neilson. No great news from the war fronts except that the Japs are still wondering whence the raiding American planes came! The news on the front page announced that American bombers will soon join the British in bombing Germany. Well, last year seemed to be Hitler's year, but this year he is hemmed by the Russians on the east and by the British and the Americans on the west and can't make up his mind whether to attack or not to attack. Hitler has done so many things deemed impossible that people can't believe that he is weak and that there is a limit to his planes, gasoline, tanks, and men. This summer will tell whether he is still strong or at the end of his tether.

April 23, 1942, Thursday

Mr. Springfield offered to sell his car to B. and me for 600 dollars to be covered by four of my bonds and two of B.'s bonds. That shows that the bonds are good. But B. thinks that the coming of gas rationing and the scarcity of tires, as well as the uncertainty of whether we will soon be in the Army, make such a purchase unwise.

April 24, 1942, Friday

I received a card from Christ Pappan, whom I knew in Minneapolis. He is now a private for Basic Training at Roberts Camp, California. He writes that so far he likes the Army life and that California's climate is like that of Greece. It is thundering and raining. If it were not for Mr. Schrag, who drove me home from the Hill, I would have been soaked to the very marrow of my bones, and my suit of clothes would have been completely ruined.

May 1, 1942, Friday

After two or three days of tornado weather, we have sunshine and cool breezes. I talked about Browning's *Winter's Tale,* along with Greek infinitives and participles. I walked to town with Sh., who has just returned from Delaware, Ohio, where she went to bury her father. She complains constantly of B., as he complains of her. I listen to both, and I say nothing. It is about 6 o'clock wartime.

May 5, 1942, Tuesday

Today I received two questionnaires from the Local Draft Board. The one called "Occupational Questionnaire" I studied carefully, but I could not find any occupation for which I can fit.

It seems that literature is a forgotten goddess in this world of machines, hatred, and war. The nearest I can come to is a "Personal Manager" or an "Interpreter," although I have no experience in either of these professions. I also received 540 dollars worth of debentures payable on December 1, 1961. Well, I guess I must forget the war and the back pay and the bonds and live as merrily and happily as I can. Fear of what might come and worry over loss of money (especially since I don't need it very urgently) must not interfere with my work or my enjoyment of life. My work at the U. must also not interfere with the main aim of my life, which is not so much service as self-improvement and self-development. As long as I hold to this aim—to improve myself in every way—I'll be happy and hopeful of reaching a great haven, and this haven is nothing but the power of expression in faultless English, both written and spoken. I might become immortal, or I might die poor, ignorant, and unknown. It depends upon me. God has always called me to attain my goal. He shall not fail me now. Even in the darkest hours of despair in my earlier life, when even to hope seemed insane, I trusted in God. He saw me through. When I was wallowing in the misery of teaching Greek in the afternoon schools, with insufficient salary and under excessively trying circumstances, the belief in self-knowledge, self-control, and self-improvement saved me from a stagnating life. I have raised my head above the waves of the sea of life, but I have not yet reached the solid rock of success. I'll never reach it unless I completely master the English tongue. Sometimes I despair of even doing it, but courage and cheerfulness will enable me to win the fight. It is a hard fight, but the reward is great. It is fame, fortune, and immortality.

May 8, 1942, Friday

I walked with B., discussing one of our most indolent students who tries to get by with minimum effort.

Yesterday being intramural day, I stayed in town and supped at the "Cottage." I developed a good appetite mowing the grass for one hour. Sh. cooked an excellent meal, and she looked pretty and happy when I praised her cooking. We call it "practicing Carnegie," who recommends "lavish praise and hearty appreciation" for encouragement of people. Then we walked to town, and, as the students met us on their return from Lake Wedington, they yoo-hooed us. It was great, and we laughed heartily.

May 12, 1942, Tuesday

I turned in my two questionnaires, and thus I've given hostages for my future to unknown men and incalculable forces. In two weeks, I'll know my classification. I earnestly hope it will not be 1A since, at my age, I would hate to put on a uniform, take a gun, and be trained to kill people I've never seen. To me, as I sit on this beautiful May evening by my window, it seems that I've done enough for the United States to justify my exemption from any further annoyance. For 22 years, I taught generations of Americans how to be honest, have industry and be good. Owing to my absorption in study, I neglected marrying, and now my chief appeal to the Draft Board is that I have no dependents. I have also, by diet, exercise, and sober living, overcome some diseases that threatened to send me to a premature grave. What I most resent is the fact that I, who have spent my best years in educating the children of others, must also put on the uniform to protect the prosperity and the families of others. But, of course, crazier things than these have happened in this mysterious world of ours and are constantly happening. In situations like these, a poor, defenseless individual among people not his own can only say, "Let His will be done!"

May 14, 1942, Thursday

I got up as usual at 5 o'clock, bathed, shaved, and rushed to the Youree Café for the annual Senior Breakfast, given by the faculty to the graduating class. Mr. Whaley was master of ceremonies, and he introduced Ch. Willis, the president of the senior class, who gave a brief address. Then Dr. Brown gave a short speech interspersed with his usual anecdotes, and then every graduating student was asked to say what he was planning to do after graduation. Most of the graduates declared their intention of entering theological seminaries, the Army, or the Navy, and one of becoming a soldier in the King's Army and serving as a missionary. Then some of the professors were asked to give fatherly advice to the graduating class. Mr. Davis suggested that, since we have so many graduates from the Bible school, it would be a good idea to start raising chickens. Since it has been rainy and I did not have my raincoat, I bribed Flower with seven cents to let B. drive me home.

May 16, 1942, Saturday

Sh. tried to get me to go to Dr. Brown's farm, where a buffet supper was to be given to the staff, students, and alumni. I had already made up my mind not to go, although it is hard to say why. She phoned twice to persuade me to go with Mrs. Buffum, and she would follow in F.'s car. If there is anything I most cordially dislike, it is a woman who tries to work me up with breaking voice. I get immediately antagonistic, and the more she insists, the more antagonistic I become. I guess it must be something wrong with me, but, just the same, I resent any kind of interference with my plans by a third party. Sometimes I wonder whether it is a blessing or a misfortune to be loved by a woman! If you happen to love a woman, she probably does not care for you, and if she loves you, you probably don't care for her. There is neither rhyme nor reason in this mystical world of ours.

May 26, 1942, Tuesday

It is really hot today. I doffed my waistcoat. About 7 o'clock I walked up to the "Cottage" and lingered there for about one hour. Flower, her mother, and B. were sitting on the back porch. I told them how I was annoyed with Sh.'s interfering with my last night's slumber when I rode with her in Dr. Willis' car to Springdale to see her off. It was a mistake talking to them about it. They may repeat it either to Sh. or to Dr. Willis, and they will think me an ungrateful dog. Anyhow, I must not talk too much even to my closest friends. Silence is golden. Last year about this time, B., Mr. Vanderkamp, his wife, and I took a trip to Oklahoma City. I also used to go riding with Gussie almost every night.

May 27, 1942, Wednesday

The second time B. picked me up. He told me that he rented the "Cottage" to some friends of his and that, in a few days, he is leaving for Texas. He is furious with Sh. He gets mad at several people several times. He is then very bitter and abusive, and by the end of the week, he selects another person on whom he pours the vials of his wrath. I have a sneaking suspicion that he is going to marry Flower very soon, and that counts for his nervousness during the last few months.

May 28, 1942, Thursday

On my way to town, I met a tiny snake. It looked like a bright, gold twig. I touched it with a stick, and it immediately vanished into the hedge. I also saw Flower and B. sitting on the swing. I waved to them, but I did not walk up the drive to them. I guess they have seen enough of me these last two weeks.

May 29, 1942, Friday

Robert Johannes, one of my students, picked me up and drove me to Dr. Smith's farm. I found him milking a cow in a miserable shed. There were chickens, sheep, goats, cats, dogs, and even a horse. I played with a cute, white pup. The farm is large but not well kept. Dirt is everywhere. I carried a stick, with which I hit stones for exercise.

May 30, 1942, Saturday

It is Memorial Day. I spent it reading on the porch. Of all the Memorial Days, I remember the one I celebrated in New York in the year 1934. I was living then on 112 or 113 Street, and I happened to be on vacation, so I witnessed the parade up Riverside Drive. There were planks of sailors and Marines in the parade. I've not yet heard from the Local Draft Board. It is really a pain in the neck. It is not enough that one has one's own personal worries, but one must also worry about the nation and the whole world. There are indications that the Americans will join the British in the aerial offensive against Germany. It seems that the Germans have been stopped in Russia, although they are making claims of annihilation. Russian armies are capturing immense amounts of guns, tanks, and men. Also in Libya and in China, the Allies are holding steadfast. If they just hold long enough, the Axis powers will exhaust their resources of men and ammunition, and the war will be brought to a speedy conclusion.

May 31, 1942, Sunday

The setting sun shed its rays across the green boughs and leaves of the oak trees. The boys and girls sitting on benches, their feet on the green grass, made a very beautiful and peaceful picture.

June 1, 1942, Monday

I spent the whole day in JBU's library registering students for the first part of summer school. There were not many students to register, and we professors had a good time discussing the war and especially last night's blasting of Cologne by 1,000 RAF planes.

June 2, 1942, Tuesday

One of the strangest things happened to me tonight. About 8 o'clock I dropped into the "Cottage" to say good-bye to B. and Flower. I was received with coldness. I was not invited to sit down. "How are you young fellows?" I said. "You didn't come to see me!" B. snarled. Then he got up from the chair and walked out of the "Cottage." Soon F. followed, and I was left with F.'s mother who, out of politeness, tried to keep up a conversation. At last I rose to go and walked onto the lawn, where F. was watering the flowers and B. was smoking.

"Are you going away tomorrow?" I said.

"That's none of your business," was the cold answer. "The people in this house do not want to see you!"

"That's O.K. with me," I answered. "I don't want to inflict myself upon anybody."

"You sneak to see what is going on!" he said.

"What has come over you?" I said.

"You know!" he said. "Shirley will be back in three months. You can't get anything out of me anymore."

"Will you tell me what is going on?"

"You know," he said.

"Well," I said, "Good-bye and good luck to you," and I walked away, entirely baffled and mystified. To say the least, I'm deeply hurt. Here are two of my best friends, leaving—perhaps forever tomorrow morning—and treating me like an outcast dog without ever explaining. This is a lesson to me. I've been too familiar with them. I treated them as brother and sister and talked to them freely about things nearest my bosom and business, and overnight they turn upon me like dogs to tear me. From now on, I'll give everyone my ear but few my heart. Well, I'll forget it and get down to work. There are still good books, green fields, and leafy trees, God's wide sky, the stars, and the birds.

June 6, 1942, Saturday

Exactly one year ago today I arrived in Minneapolis for my summer vacation, and about this time I was waiting at the Corner Drugstore for the rain to abate in order to walk to F.'s house. How fast the time flies! Last year I was worried by financial difficulties. This year I'm vexed by the fear of being drafted into the Army. I guess there is no rest for the weak and the wicked. It is best, therefore, to enjoy the present without fear for the future and regret for the past. After all, what can a man do, being caught in unusual times brought about by forces he cannot control?

June 10, 1942, Wednesday

I met B. twice today, once on the Hill—he was carrying his

laundry—and once on the road to town. In both cases we spoke as mere acquaintances. He looks thin and worried. He asked about Sh. There must be more between him and her than I'm aware of. She must have stung him badly as only a woman can sting.

I'm glad to read in the papers that Air Marshall Harris of England agrees with Seversky on the question of eliminating Germany by continuous air raids. Rule the Air and Rule the World. It is so simple and so self-evident, and yet we spend billions of dollars building obsolete battleships and training old-fashioned armies. I hope this self-evident truth will dawn on the minds of our conservative leaders who think in terms of the past instead of the present and the future.

June 12, 1942, Friday

Today about 12:30 a violent rainstorm struck Siloam Springs. The houses withstood the rush of the wind and the rain, but many trees were blown down. The electric wires were also down. Five trees were uprooted on the campus, and two or three around the "Cottage." The little creek that runs through town has swollen to a mighty, surging river. During the storm, I stayed in my room watching the trees struggle with the wind and the rain. Everything is covered by semi-darkness, and, for a moment, I thought that the end was close at hand. The storm lasted about 35 minutes. At 1:30 I went out to lunch. People were out on the streets and in the park thoughtfully watching the fallen trees. Relieved from great fear and anxiety, they were unusually friendly and talkative. About 2 o'clock I walked up the Hill; it was cool and clear. At the store, the books I ordered for my freshman class had arrived at last. I bought one copy, and I began to study it because I'm as innocent of teaching English Composition as a newborn baby. I had a haircut, and since the barber could not use his electrically propelled clipping machine, he used the old-fashioned one. That reminded me of the haircuts I used to get on the blessed island of Cyprus. After a light supper, I took a short walk and returned home to study and go to bed. Owing to the wartime, daylight extends to 9:10 or 9:30. It is the earliest one can go to bed. The papers today carried the headlines that the United States, England, and Russia have agreed to open a new front in the year 1942. This indicates that the United Nations have made up their minds to finish the war before the year is over. It all, however, depends upon the ability of the Russians to repulse the new Nazi drive that has just been launched. The results of the Coral Naval Engagement have just been announced. The Japs lost heavily, owing to our air superiority. All the Japanese ships had been sunk or damaged by aircraft. That proves Dr. Seversky is right. He insists that battleships are obsolete. Bombers escorted that pursuit because planes are the modern weapons.

June 19, 1942, Friday

A week ago we were bashed by the storm that uprooted many trees. How timid and apologetic we are when compared with the bold, adventurous, and lusty heroes of history. We simply vegetate, tied down to a job in order to keep body and soul together. We love comfort. We are unwilling to take pain and face danger for fame and fortune. Nothing ventured, nothing had. For a cup of coffee and a shower bath, we have sold our birthrights.

June 21, 1942, Sunday

Mr. Gilbert Galen picked me up and drove me to the Hill. While sitting in the car, we listened to a transcribed speech by Bevin on the first anniversary of Russia's entrance into the war. It was a very fine speech—just as good as if it were one by Churchill. Walking down the Hill, I met the lady who runs a millinery shop, and we walked to town together. She is short, soft, and plump. She shows unmistakable signs of maturity. She is pretty in a Jewish manner. We talked about war, the U., and her business. At our parting, I told her that I enjoyed walking with her immensely and invited her to repeat the experiment. Sometimes it is refreshing to talk with persons who do not belong to the profession. Their views are different. The lady seemed perfectly sensible and well informed. She had directed plays before opening her shop. I don't even know her name.

June 30, 1942, Tuesday

Snider is leaving on Thursday for Little Rock for his physical examination and induction into the Army. He married Miss Buffun about a month ago. B. has visited me more than once during the last eight days. Our relation is formal and friendly. Since his rude and inexcusable behavior, I'm trying to treat him better than any of my acquaintances.

July 2, 1942, Thursday

Everybody is excited over the situation in Egypt. The Germans have advanced perilously near Alexandria. Churchill won a vote of confidence, and reinforcements have been rushed to the Allies. B. dropped in to see me at about six, and then we listened to the news. After a supper at the Youree, we walked up the Hill. He told me that Mr. Jackson had returned from Little Rock to work for JBU again. I've not heard from Frances these last four days, an unusually long silence. She usually writes every day. Sh. sent a letter special delivery about Mr. Snider's car. Sh. wants to buy it and borrow 80 dollars from me. Mr. Snider left this morning for Little Rock to be inducted into the Army. When he comes tomorrow, I'll speak to him about it.

July 14, 1942, Tuesday

I've not seen B. today. Three more days of work, and then I'm on vacation. I've not yet made up my mind whether or not to go to Minneapolis some other time. I've spent so many summers in Minnesota that I've gotten tired of it; besides, I don't want to go back to Frances. She is not a very cheerful companion with the eternal talk of her operations, illnesses, and hard luck. I'll make up my mind.

July 21, 1942, Tuesday

B. left last Sunday evening with Fred Moulton for California, where he will be inducted into the Army on the fifth of August. Sh. has returned and is at present staying at the Jones's. I'm still at a loss where to spend my summer vacation. I spend most of my time on the porch reading, resting, and dreaming. With the war raging fiercely on three continents, with the Germans in the suburbs of Voronehz and Rostov, with Rommel within sight of Alexandria and the Japanese in the Aleutian Islands, I thank God that I'm allowed to spend my leisure hours reading books and resting. It is selfish, but my stake in the struggle is very small. If I'm called to serve, I'll willingly serve, but otherwise I'll lie low and let the storm blow over me. With B. gone, I'm the only bachelor left on the JBU staff. I never accepted the principle of "dependency" as a criterion for serving one's country. Some of us have given our best years in acquiring knowledge and in teaching the youth of the nation. We were too poor to even think of getting married. After teaching one's children, it is too much to be asked to shoulder a gun and defend them also. The parents ought to be more solicitous about the future of their children than the bachelor.

July 23, 1942, Thursday

Just sleeping, reading, walking, and eating. If I were a millionaire, I would keep this kind of life to my dying hour. I could probably have added love, although even at present I'm not erotically starved. The Germans are still advancing on Rostov and Stalingrad. Our candidates are campaigning; our boys are trained in flying and fighting, and the ladies, as usual, are cooking, sewing, gossiping, shopping, and painting. The future historian will probably fail to note that even during the greatest upheaval the world has ever seen, men, women, boys, and girls are walking in the streets in slacks and eating ice cream.

July 25, 1942, Saturday

I met our students in line with Mr. Jackson and Mr. Whaley, taking a moonlight hike. On my return, I was picked up by Joe Smith, who deposited me in front of Dr. Williams' office. The city was crowded with cars and people Saturday evening. War seems so far away in the heart of the beautiful Ozarks.

July 31, 1942, Friday

I supped at Sh.'s, who, in preparing supper, unfortunately burnt her left hand. She must have suffered severe pain, but she repeated that she could take it. I sent her to the hospital to have her hand dressed. After supper and listening to the 8:30 KUOA news broadcast, I took my regular walk up the Hill. I stopped at Sisco's for a drink. I asked for a cone of ice cream, and the careless high-school girl that waits on customers brought me a half pint of ice cream. It is rather warm, and I'm glad that tomorrow I'm getting away for my annual vacation. I'll go first to Kansas City and then probably to Minneapolis, where I have so many friends and acquaintances. Today I had my first dealing with the Local Draft Board. I sent them a card notifying them of my absence from Siloam Springs. I earnestly hope that this will be the only dealing I'll have with it.

September 14, 1942, Monday

I returned from Minneapolis yesterday afternoon. During all of August and the first half of September, I vacationed in Minnesota. I stayed at 1613 West 31st with a family called Bigelows. I spent as much time as I could by Calhoun Lake.

Usually three or four times a week, I visited F. at her apartment on 125 Oak Grove Street. There I got acquainted with Ann, the woman who is manager of the apartment house. She is in her early forties, a shapely brunette with sparkling eyes and a pouting mouth. She is married to a wealthy man 27 years her senior. She spends most of her time in arguments with renters of the various apartments, smoking Kool cigarettes, and gossiping. I went more than once to the movies. Among the memorable films I saw were the *Gay Sisters, Mrs. Minniver, Gold Rush, Tortilla Flats, Fantasia,* and *This Above All.* I breakfasted at the Rainbow mostly on hot wheat cakes, whole-wheat toast, and coffee. When there were no customers, I talked with Esther, the young waitress, whose husband had just been drafted and sent to Missouri. She liked to talk about him and to hear me talk about the mysterious South. Every Tuesday at one I would lunch at the Luxe Café or Hennepin and at twelve with Spell and company. After lunch, Spell usually drove me any place I particularly desired to see. Once he drove me to the vast naval airfield and Fort Snelling and Minnelake Falls and Saint Paul. Another time he drove me to New Brighton, where I saw the vast plants, and last Tuesday he drove me to Saint Paul to see the Capitol. In the last trip, we visited different apartment houses in our effort to find a nice apartment for him. That gave me first-hand information about the scarcity of apartments, high rents, and the unwillingness of the owners to accept families with children.

Evenings I either supped at the Dean's Coffee Shop, Lake, and Hennepin or at F.'s. My friend Ari was not in Minneapolis. He had been drafted last April, and he had been stationed at Fort Riley, Kansas. When I wrote a card to him, I received—through a chaplain—the message that, by accident, a nurse put acid in his right eye and that he was in danger of losing his eyesight. I wrote him another card, promising to visit him on my way south. Last Friday morning I received a telegraph instructing me not to go to Fort Riley since he had been removed to Fitzsimmon's General Hospital, Denver, Colorado.

This summer I did not miss the fabulous old man Bousalis, who is in his late seventies and still vigorous and ruddy. He is the richest Greek in Minnesota. He had spent his winter in Phoenix, Arizona, where he met a monk from Jerusalem—a famous theologian who had fallen in love with and married an American woman, fled the monastery, come to the United States, and turned farmer. His American wife deserted him, and he is now leading the old, cheerless bachelor life. The story of this man lends itself easily to fiction, and someday I'll write the story of the monk and the woman.

On Monday at the Rainbow I met Rev. Spyropoulos and

Mr. Xanthes, who were going to northern Minnesota to solicit advertisements for the Picnic Book of the Greek community. I joined them and got a delightful ride to Saint Cloud, Princeton, and Brainerd. I also got a glimpse of the vast Mille Lacs, by the shores of which I spent one delightful week with Lucy. The most memorable character I met on that trip was a 46-year-old, wealthy bachelor who owned a luncheonette and many slot machines. Everybody was urging him to get married. I pointed out to him how lucky he was to be free from the clutches of war, women, and sickness. On the beach, I met, as usual, Walter, Jay, Jack, and company. All these are wealthy bachelors, Walter and Jack being Jews owning shops, theaters, and vital industries. Jay is an insurance man who drove me once to Saint Paul, where I called on George Phanaris and his wife, both from the island of Cyprus. They were so busy in their little restaurant that we did not have time to visit. They served a lunch of fried pike that upset my stomach. At the Richman store I also bought a suit of oxford gray clothes. The pants are without cuffs, and I look very funny in them. On the train I met three remarkable women. The one who sat beside me all the way from St. Paul to Kansas City was a high school teacher from Missouri who was teaching English to the Indians on a government reservation in North Dakota. She was rushing home to see her dying mother. The other lady who sat beside me from Kansas City to Siloam Springs was the wife of a defense worker who was rushing to her home in Stillwater to celebrate her 29th birthday. She was a rather attractive woman with powerful appeal; her father was a Frenchman and her mother an Irish woman. She had already had three husbands; she thought that the one she now had was too good for words. While with the teacher, I discussed literature and politics; with this married woman I discussed food, family, and crops. I met the third woman in the dining room of the Southern Belle. She was a woman of majestic proportions with large black eyes, black hair, and pale skin. She was going to Freeport, Louisiana, and she had lived a long time in Long Island. With her, we talked of New York.

When I reached Siloam Springs yesterday, I was exhausted but suffering neither from headache nor dizziness. Since it was awfully warm—about 95 in the shade—I perspired freely and abundantly while unpacking my cardboard suitcase. Just now, my prayer is "God, deliver me from the clutches of war, women, and sickness that I may devote my energy and time to study, and thus become a thinker and a scholar and give Thy people a new message of the joy of life and the joy of beauty. Give the world peace with justice for everyone. Amen."

September 16, 1942, Wednesday

Last night Sh. told me that Dr. Willis wanted to see me, so this morning after a good breakfast, I started walking up the Hill in my shirt sleeves. Charlie, who has taken over the taxi business relinquished by Glynn, who was drafted, picked me up and drove me to the Hill. I saw Dr. Willis, who was busy trying to arrange the program for this semester's classes. He wanted to give me a high school Algebra class. I hope he will not because I hate to teach subjects in which I am not interested. Mr. Snyder drove me to town. I dropped in to see Sh. about going to Dr. Willis's party given in honor of the Cooks, who are leaving the U. to teach at the Japs Concentration Camp in South Arkansas. The weather has been pleasantly cool, and I spent the whole day reading on the porch.

September 18, 1942, Friday

I supped at Sh.'s with F. After the supper, the girls washed the dishes, and then they joined me and we talked about our colleagues, school affairs, sugar, prices of things, etc. Just eight days ago at about this hour, I bade good-bye to B. Last night I went to Dr. Willis's party given in honor of the Cooks. There were only the Schrags, Sh., F., and myself. We ate in the open air in spite of the flies that swarmed over the food. After the meal, Dr. Willis showed us his garden and vegetable patches. Then we went indoors, and Mrs. Willis played the piano while we sang some hymns. About 9 o'clock we departed; I felt sleepier than ever.

September 19, 1942, Saturday

A cold, cloudy, rainy day. About noon I took a short walk to town and returned dripping water. About 5:30 I availed myself of a brief dry spell and took a walk to stretch my legs and rest my eyes. As I sat in my room reading, I recalled the past especially cold, dreary, rainy days in Boston and Minneapolis spent indoors. I also dreamt of a glorious future—the future of a thinker and a scholar. It seems idle to dream of the future in my age, at a time when the Army is after me and diseases are threatening me. But in the past, I pulled through poverty, bodily weakness and adverse, hostile environments; so now, with God's will and my efforts, I might get out of the draft, diseases, and Siloam Springs and amount to something. It is never too late. One thing stands in the way—my inability to speak English fluently, correctly, and without accent.

September 20, 1942, Sunday

About noon, F. and Sh. and I dined at the Kay-June's on fried chicken. B. was missing, being in the Army. We talked of chickens, professors, and restaurants. After the dinner, we drove to Lake Frances. The sun shone bright and chilly on the green grass and the clear leaves of the oaks and elms. We drove the same road I drove with Wright, Lord, Vanderkamp, B., Gussie, Stevenson, and Sh. Well, time flies, individuals come and go, but the hills and the lake remain forever. After the ride I walked home from the post office and read for three hours on the porch. About 5 o'clock, I took a walk up the Hill; on my return I was picked up by Mr. and Mrs. Biddle. I stopped at the Youree for supper. I ate a Heinz vegetable soup, a cheese sandwich, and a glass of milk. It cost me 35 cents. And now I'm lying in bed, at 8:10 p.m., but before I turn off the lights and go to sleep, I'll also do some reading. No man goes to bed early, and yet one has to think of his eyes and his feeble body.

September 21, 1942, Monday

I attended the first general staff and faculty meetings at 10 a.m. There was not much said nor done that needs recording. I returned home about noon. I supped at the "Cottage" on baked ham, fruit salad, tomatoes, ice cream, and milk. There were only three of us: F., Sh., and I. We talked about the new voice teacher, who was supposed to stay at the "Cottage," but she will stay at Campus. She comes from New York City, and, according to F., she has just married a lawyer who is trying to get into the Intelligence Department. I returned home about 9 o'clock, suffering from a slight headache I must have contracted from eyestrain caused by reading in the sun. I ought to know better than that. I received two letters from Frances. They sound queer and distant with her eternal love and devotion. And yet it is only ten days since I left Minneapolis.

September 22, 1942, Tuesday

This is officially the last day of my summer vacation. Tomorrow at eight registration starts. As the new school year opens, I thank God for the health, happiness, and pleasure I've enjoyed during the summer, and I pray that I may be allowed to spend the coming year in health, happiness, success, and usefulness. The clouds of war are ominously hovering over me, but God's will be done in this as in everything. I spent the day reading the *Lives of Millions* by different men. The best I read was by an anonymous writer, and the second best by Edward Phillips' cousin. Reading *Lives of Millions* made me wonder whether I could write a short life of myself, presenting in a concise and clear way the most important events in my insignificant and unimportant life. My grandfather John David, as he was called in the Cyprus dialect Laviois, was a substantial farmer in the small village of Voni, about nine miles east of Nicosia, the capital of the Island of Cyprus. He was married to a stout, short woman called Photine or Photou, who bore to him four sons and two daughters. Of the sons, George had migrated to Greece before I was born, and I know him only by his photograph, shown wearing the uniform of a Greek soldier of the Balkan Wars. I've never seen him. Basil was living in Joppa, where he married an Arabian lady and had two or three sons. He paid us some visits before World War I. During the war, he returned to Cyprus and made his home in a village near Lemessos. He was a shoemaker by trade, and he was known for being hen-pecked by a nagging wife. Nichola was a priest and had a numerous family. His daughter got married before I left Cyprus to a young man who migrated with me to the United States, but since we left Famagusta, we parted ways, and since then I've not seen him. His Christodoulos a Toolis, about my age, was an apprentice to my father for years and used to stay at our home. Of the daughters, one was married to a wealthy man from Voni, who was famous for his stinginess, and the other to a man from Angastina, a small village on the railroad line from Famagusta to Nicosia. None of the sons and daughters could measure up to my grandfather, who, besides being a good farmer, was also distinguished for his thirst for knowledge. He learned to read and write at a very advanced age, and reading the papers and the selections from the Apostles at Church and singing in church were some of the ways he expressed his intellectual hunger. He used to visit us often and always brought us sweetmeats and candy. The last time I walked with him, it was when I was recovering from typhoid fever in the summer of 1917, when he took me to the station and accompanied me to Agastina to my aunt's. How well I remember his stopping the train by raising his cane! It was many years later that I met a man who bore a striking resemblance to him. It was Professor Kittredge of Harvard University. Both men greatly influenced my life, and both are remembered for raising their canes: one to stop a train, the other to cross Harvard Square. My grandfather was influential in my being sent to the Gymnasium. He paid my tuition fee and gave me a nice Swiss watch as a present, which I unfortunately lost when I came to the United States. I don't know whether my father was the youngest son in the family, neither do I know how he met and married my mother, who was an adopted child of two poor workers, George and Helen Savas. My mother and her adopted parents came to the capitol from a small village called Acaci, near Morphou, in the center of the island. I remember my father dressed in his zimbouke, naka, and fez and being usher at the chapel of St. Elefterion, which belonged to the Monastery of Mahaira. My grandfather George was the janitor. They called him Yewuopn, "temple keeper," of the chapel. My mother and my grandmother Helen were very pious people. They kept the fast days, attended all the services, masses and vespers, and from my early childhood, they were accustomed to attend service and go to church. My favorite retreat was the part of the church called "holy" (iepor), where I used to help my grandfather George in the performance of his duties. Through my grandfather and my father, I was acquainted with the Monks who were in charge of the chapel. They were beaded, dark-haired fellows who were sent from the monastery to study at the Gymnasium. I even tried my voice as assistant cantor, but I soon gave it up from bashfulness. One of my favorite hobbies was to ring the bell, especially during funerals and the Holy Week.

I was sent to school rather late in the seventh year of my life, owing to the system then employed in teaching, which was nothing but whipping. It took me a long time to master my letters. My first teacher was the legendary old Michael, a man in his late seventies, wearing a fez and Turkish trousers and armed with Knotted cane. My mother—being more practical—sent me to a private teacher called Black Zoe during the summer. She was the wife of the well-known George the policeman. Black Zoe managed to teach me how to read and write the letters of the alphabet.

After that I was sent to the elementary school run by the so-called Kyreniae party, which was supporting the Bishop of Kyrenia in his efforts to become Archbishop of Cyprus. The school was crowded, and the teachers were brutal. My mother, who seemed to always know what was good for me, took me away from that school and enrolled me in the famous school of the Citians, the party that was backing the Bishop of Citium in his efforts to become Archbishop of Cyprus. From the third grade to the sixth grade, I stuck to the Citiac School. The school's program suited me admirably. I became a star scholar; I took history, literature, and mathematics in stride. I graduated at the head of my class in the year 1911. In the following year, I entered the Pan-Cyprus Gymnasium; it was the first year of the unification of the two parties after the elevation of the Bishop of Citium to the Archbishopric. I stayed in the Gymnasium at the Normal School for seven years, graduating in the summer of 1918 at the head of the graduates of that class, composed of 22 students. For my fine scholarship, I was appointed as a teacher to the elementary school of St. Anthony in Nicosia with a yearly salary of 50 English pounds. I was given the second graders. I taught reading, writing, and arithmetic. The work was pleasant and easy for a boy of eighteen who liked to learn and to teach. I was reappointed for the following year, 1919-1920, but I quarreled with the principal, borrowed 46 pounds, and on May 1, 1920, took my suitcase made by my father and an overcoat, bade farewell to my two sisters, and took the train for Famagusta. My brother had already been dead for six years, and I was sure that I would never see my father again because he was in very poor health. At Famagusta I boarded the fast steamer Tanta, which took me to Port-Sand and Alexandria. At Alexandria I boarded the Indian liner Politania, which took me through the Cyclad Islands to Piraeu, the port of Athens, Greece. I stayed at Peraeus and Athens for 10 or 12 days, visiting some of my old Gymnasium schoolmates who were there in Athens studying law and medicine. Gerge, my best friend, died shortly afterward. I left Athens on May 26 on the good ship Themistoles. I was traveling third class and suffered greatly for lack of proper food, cleanliness, and good companions. Of the boys who took that trip with me, I have not yet seen any except Anthony, who died later in London. He lent me the money that I showed at Ellis Island previous to my being allowed to disembark. I'm ashamed to record that I've never repaid him that money. I reached New York on June 19, 1920, and a taxi driver deposited me at the door of the confectionery at 192 Court Street, Brooklyn, just off Borough Hall. The confectionery was owned by Marcus Thalassinus, a former schoolmate of mine. He and his wife welcomed me warmly, helped me to secure a room on Berger Street, and took me to Manhattan to be introduced to George, for whom I had a letter. George took hold of me with vengeance. He urged me to stay in a room rented by a Greek lady who occupied an apartment at 900 6th Avenue, the place now occupied by Rockefeller Center. The beds were infested with bed bugs, and there was no hot water to waste for a bath. Then he took me to work with him as a busboy at an American Chinese restaurant in Brooklyn off DeKalb Avenue. I worked from 11-2 in the morning. The salary was 60 dollars a month, besides tips, which were not very big. Lucky enough for me, the Chinese restaurant closed for repairs, and I was left to shift for myself. I never loved work. It was just for the mere sake of making a living. For me, there was neither rhyme nor reason to carry dishes, glasses, bread, and butter to idle customers just for two or three dollars a day. I began to scan the want columns of the Greek-American newspapers for open teacher positions. I easily obtained one as a teacher at Lynn, Mass., with a salary of 125 dollars a month. On September 1, I left New York for Boston. It was my misfortune, green and crude as I was, to fall in love with Lucille, my colleague. She was a short, rather plump, dark-haired, black-eyed girl. When I fell in love with Eudosie, a girl slightly older that I, I spent delicious hours kissing and fondling her in the sesame fields of Cytherea where I used to spend my moments at my God-mother's. But this love for Lucille made me dreamy and unable to concentrate on my work. With Lucille, I went to Salem Normal School for six months, the fall term of 1920. Of the teachers who most influenced me was Miss Harris, the teacher of English Literature. In the second semester, I enrolled in Boston University College of Liberal Arts on Boylston Street, Boston. I got fired from my teacher's job on January 1, and I had to work my way through college by washing dishes at a Waldorf restaurant from 4-6 and giving private lessons. Lucille had left for Washington, DC, and my father died. Being torn between love and financial worries, I had a hard time that spring of 1921. Even during the summer vacation, when I returned to New York for work, for the first time I faced the specter of unemployment and depression. I pulled through by washing dishes at a Thompson Cafeteria on Broadway near Madison Square. In that summer I met my friend Costa, who was working in Vander-bilt Hotel as a dummy-man or assistant waiter. Labor Day came, and I had neither job nor money; and yet I was burning with desire to go back to Boston University and get my M.A. degree. I bor-rowed 50 dollars from Costa, took the train, and returned to Boston. I enrolled at the U. on money extorted from George and started classes, not knowing whence my next meal would come. Luckily enough, the Boston Greek School needed a teacher. I was employed to teach at 50 dollars a month. I was rooming in a small room on Washington Street. I did my own washing and bought cheese, bread, and ham from the grocery store and borrowed shamelessly. I read voraciously and, generally speaking, except for my longing and love—melancholy for Lucille and my worries for my sisters and brother, I was very happy. What sources of delight and power were opened to me that year! Chaucer, Spenser, Shake-speare, the Elizabethan dramatists, the Romantic poets, and the modern novelists began to speak to me. I must have been a sight to linger in the mind with my unpressed clothes and only one suit, which I wore every day, my home-washed collars, my monthly haircuts, and my shabby overcoats. Years later a Bostonian passing through Atlanta learned that I was teaching there and inquired whether I was still wearing old clothes and old hats. During that year, 1921-1922, I literally lived alone. I had neither friends nor acquaintances. Some of the professors, like Professor Black, liked me and smiled on me encouragingly, but others, like Professor Rice, would sneer on the pretensions and aspirations of a scantily fed and poorly clad foreigner who could scarcely speak understandable English. I got an M.A. degree in June of 1923, but owing to my inability to speak English fluently and correctly, I did not even try to get a teaching position in an American college or high school. That timidity and hesitation cost me dearly. I could have easily gotten a job as an instructor of French or Latin. I continued, therefore, teaching in the Greek School of Cambridge, Massachusetts. And I went to Harvard just for the sake of learning. I never dreamt that it was possible for a poor man like me to get a Ph.D. from that august institution. I took a course in Shakespeare under the fabulous Kittredge and another in Romantic Poetry under Lowes. At the end of the school year of 1924, I gave up hope of ever securing a job as a teacher. I worked for two years as dummy-man at Vanderbilt Hotel with my friend Costa. I used to work from 4 p.m. to midnight. I attended classes at Columbia, taking Shakespeare under Thorndike, Chaucer under Ayres, and Contemporary Literature under Stephens. During these two years, I was rooming with my friend Sifas, a boy from the island of Crete, at an apartment at 521 122nd West, one block from Broadway and two from Riverside Drive. One reason that kept me in New York was the fact that Lucille was living just two blocks away in Morn-ingside Drive. At that time, she was employed by the *National Herald,* and one of my chief delectations was to take her on my days off to Broadway Theater and walk in Central Park and River-side Drive. As I look back on those walks and visits with her, one thing struck me as rather remarkable, astonishing, and unusual. I never kissed her. This fact, when compared with my behavior with other women, seems stupid to me—the sign of an underdeveloped personality. Another remarkable woman came into my life during those two years. She was May, a charming young widow who almost tried to seduce me, but even to her I denied my caresses. After staying two years in New York, I moved back to Boston and took charge of the Boston Greek School, which by that time had moved into the new building on Boylston Street. I had the hardest time of my life. The students, my colleagues, the preachers, and the school committee were dull and unimaginative. I went back to Harvard and took two other courses: one in Elizabethan non-dra-matic literature and another in short story with Professor May-nard. I stayed with my friend Lucas in an apartment opposite the YMCA. I gave up my job in February of 1928 and went back to New York and worked at the Vanderbilt. This time I was so tired of going to the universities that I didn't enroll in any institution. I kept on, however, reading in the New York Public Library on 42nd Street and Fifth Avenue. In September of 1928 I was appointed teacher of the Greek School of New Brunswick, New Jersey. I didn't go to any school, but traveled up and down to New York in aimless efforts to secure an extra job. In the following year, Sep-tember 1929, I left for Atlanta, Georgia, where I was destined to spend four delightful and profitable years as principal of the Greek School of Atlanta. For the first time here, my salary was over 100

dollars a month. I went to Emory University, from which I graduated in 1931 with an M.A. in English. Again I missed an opportunity to secure a job as professor of English in the College and
kept on teaching Greek for two more years. In November 1934, I
moved to Gatonia, North Carolina, where I worked as assistant to
the Dean in the now-defunct Greek-American College. I worked
harder than ever, and in the end I failed to collect four months'
salary. I returned again to New York and went back to my old job
in the Vanderbilt Hotel, where the faithful Costa was still working. In the fall of 1934, I returned to New Brunswick, and for two
years I taught Greek under the most distressing of circumstances.
During those two years, 1934-1936, I went to Princeton in a vain
effort to get a Ph.D. degree. They would not even consider me as a
graduate student. They believed me to be queer and stupid. But I
did satisfactory work in 17th century prose, criticism, and Elizabethan prose. During those two years, my life was brightened and
enriched by my acquaintance with Ruby, a married woman of
exceeding beauty and vitality. She undertook to correct my accent
in exchange for my teaching her French. Because her husband,
whom she later divorced, was away and because she had a car and
leisure, we went out riding. For the first time I knew the joys of
being loved. After being fired from the Greek School of New
Brunswick, I spent a wretched summer trying to get a new teaching position. For a moment it seemed that I had to start a new
career. But on September 11, 1936, I received an appointment as a
teacher to the Greek School of Minneapolis, Minnesota. I reached
that city by Saturday evening, September 12, by way of Chicago. I
decided to get that Ph.D. degree by hook and crook. I went to the
University of Minnesota, and in three years of not very arduous
work, I got a Ph.D. degree on June 18, 1939. It seemed almost

impossible to get a job, but my good fortune held. I got the job I'm now holding as head of the English department at John Brown University in Siloam Springs, Arkansas. After living in some of the greatest metropolises of the world, I've been living in a small village of 3,000 in the heart of the Ozark Hills since 1939.

September 26, 1942, Saturday

It rained all morning. The afternoon was cold—the thermometer fell to 41 degrees. I began to hunt for my winter underwear. On account of the rain and the cold wave, I have attended neither the 11 o'clock special chapel called by Dr. Brown nor the 7:30 faculty reception for the students. I started today writing my novel *The Monk and the Woman*. Briefly, the plot is this: "I meet a farmer in the Ozarks. By accident, I immediately recognize him. He is a monk. He tells me the story of how he fell in love with an American missionary, eloped with her, married her, and came over to the United States. She left him, and he has lived a monk's life in the United States. He tells me how he has prospered greatly and wishes to return home." I'll create the monk out of the many monks I got acquainted with in my childhood, and the woman shall be modeled after Ruby. Some of the incidents of my life shall be woven into the story. I hope to write a very good novelette of about 150-200 pages. It is about time that I give the world something.

September 27, 1942, Sunday

I went to chapel twice, at 11 and at 7. Dr. Brown preached in both services. At the morning service, his message was "You were sold." Everybody is sold to bad habits like smoking, drinking, and dancing, but bought by the blood of Christ. At the evening service, the subject was repentance, regeneration, conversion, and consecration. He made a distinction between conversion and consecration. Conversion means turning away from your bad habits and sins; consecration means dedicating your gifts and abilities to the service of God. I dined at the U. and supped at the Youree. After the evening service, F. drove me to town. We had our ice cream at the drugstore and talked of B. Then she drove me home. It is exactly 9 o'clock. Thank God! It is much warmer, but I have already put on my winter underwear.

September 29, 1942, Tuesday

I taught two hours: one hour of American prose and the other, Beginner Greek. I attended chapel at 11 o'clock. Dr. Brown preached again on repentance and being born again. I supped at the "Cottage" with F. and Sh. I heard that two of my students in Greek have won the highest honor in Dallas, Texas, where they entered a seminary. Well, it is only 9 o'clock, but since I have to get up early at 6 o'clock, it is time to sleep.

September 30, 1942, Wednesday

I attended chapel twice, once at 11 o'clock and again at 7 o'clock. I taught four hours—two in the morning and two in the afternoon. I walked up the Hill this morning, and the walk has contributed to the elevation of my spirits. Today Dr. Brown amplified the term *repentance* by stating what it is not. He said it is not conviction, it is not fear, it is not feeling, it is not sorrow. It is the human side of redemption. He also elaborated the excuses for not accepting Christ. Churchmen are hypocrites, saying, "I don't feel like it." Five or six boys and girls came forward. Mr. Hodge drove me to town and deposited me in front of the Post Office. We talked about Dr. Bennet's illness. He scratched his hand, and blood poisoning has developed. He is at present in the hospital.

October 4, 1942, Sunday

During the past week we had "Revival Services."

The past week was the first week of the fall semester. I teach 17 hours a week. My hours of teaching are scattered from 8 a.m. to 6 p.m. All my life it seems I'm doomed to work from 4-6.

During the week, I ate lunch at the U. I supped once at the "Cottage" and twice at Sh.'s. Considering the war, food is plentiful in Arkansas and not too expensive. This is in sharp contrast with some localities where defense industries or military camps are located. Today I even had bacon and eggs—bacon is regarded as a commodity hard to get. I'm glad, however, that President Roosevelt has frozen both the prices and the wages, thus saving the nation from possible inflation.

The war news is heartening. The Russians still hold Stalingrad, the Japs are retreating in New Guinea, and the Americans have established bases on the Aleutians very close to the Japanese base of Kiska. Big bombers are going to smoke the Japs out of the Aleutians. I don't share the opinion of those who think that the war will last long. Once we build sufficient numbers of bombers, the end of the war will be in sight.

October 6, 1942, Tuesday

Dr. Brown had the chapel moved to Tuesday in order to speak once before he went to California. He preached a sermon on the open door and the adversaries that guard it. Selfishness, laziness, and the lack of purpose or plan in life all prevent men from entering the open door that leads to success and the good life. I spent most of the time reading *War and Peace*. I supped at Kay-June's with F. and Sh. as my guests. Both looked tired and worn out, and I was not in much better spirits, so our conversation never rose above the level of gossip. F. was glad to hear that Mr. Durham leased Dr. Lewis's place for a year, which is adjoined to the "Cottage."

October 8, 1942, Thursday

I received a letter from B. He is in Nashville, Tennessee, working in an Army Air Corps Classification Center. He can't write details about his work; it is a military secret, but he says that he enjoys it. I'm glad he enjoys his work since he was so averse to enlisting in any branch of the service. I also received a letter from F., telling me that she had received a check from the U.S. government as a dependent. I'm still reading *War and Peace*. The weather is ideal, neither too cold nor too warm.

October 11, 1942, Sunday

I spent the week, as usual, reading, teaching and walking. During the week, I read the first and second volumes of Tolstoy's *War and Peace*. I dined out twice, one time with Sh. and the other time with Sh. and the Cooks, who are still with us. I received a letter from B. He has not been away even for three months, and everybody, except F., has forgotten him. Occasionally, people, from idle curiosity or for form's sake, inquire about him, but all are so intensely absorbed in their own affairs that they do not care what has become of their brother. Yesterday I received the first paycheck of the year. It was 70 dollars for September 15 to the first of October. That means that my salary was raised by five dollars a month.

October 13, 1942, Tuesday

Today I drove with the Stewarts to Fayetteville. We attended a session of the teachers meeting. It was a panel discussion on the vital question: the place of school in wartime. They stressed the fact that mathematics and science must be taught as never before and that the students must help in harvests and in raising chickens and cattle. The vexing problem of whether labor is educative was touched on but was soon dropped like a hot potato. There is confusion between the terms *training* and *education*. *Education* has to do with the development of the intellect, esthetic sense, moral sense, and religious sense. Do milking cows and feeding chickens really educate persons? It is good to have a trained hand, but let us not confuse the training with education. We returned to campus about 2:30, and I went to the library, where I read in the *Tulsa World* two speeches: one by Roosevelt and the other by Churchill. Both speeches had this in common. The strength of the United Nations is increasing while the powers of Germany, Italy, and Japan are waning. They also noticed the increase of air power, which in my mind will end the war. There was a lot of cheer in the speech of President Roosevelt. The United States will send abroad armies consisting of the youth, age 21-24, and the young men between ages 18 and 20 are to be drafted soon. I wish that this fear of being drafted be removed from me. I'm too old to serve in the Army, and I'm too unskilled to work in the factory or on the farm. I guess education is my proper field, and I'm where I belong.

October 18, 1942, Sunday

It is a rainy Sunday, and I think I'll spend it in my room reading Tolstoy's *War and Peace*. I spent a very delightful week. On Monday I supped at the "Cottage" and on Wednesday and Friday with Sh. On Tuesday I took a trip to Fayetteville, and besides attending a teachers meeting, I looked at the Ozark hills and the buildings of Arkansas University. There is no comparison between JBU buildings and Arkansas University buildings. We struggle to get hundreds of students, and they struggle for thousands. I don't know anything about the AU faculty, but it cannot be as ill assorted as ours is. Yesterday I met Mrs. Frisco, the former Frances Counsel, in front of the University Store. She and her husband were on the campus for a weekend visit. Mr. Frisco is at present a teacher in A&M College in Stillwater, Oklahoma. She told me that Mr. Vanderkamp is a full-time instructor at the A&M and that he had plenty of doctors' bills on account of Alma's ill health. I requested to be remembered to them.

The bill for drafting the youth of 18 and 19 has passed. God only knows its effect on me. It might save me from being drafted, but at the same time, it might close JBU and set me hunting for employment. But God's will be done in this as in everything. By this time I've learned one lesson. Everything that happens to me is for my good.

The war news both in Russia and in the Pacific tells of renewed attacks on Stalingrad and the Solomons. It is easy to repel an enemy if you have the weapons, and I devoutly hope that we and our allies have the necessary weapons.

Today is St. Luke's day. When I was young, I used to go to St. Luke's church and spend the day on the fairgrounds. The church lies beyond the Turkish quarter, and even in the twentieth year of my age, I could never find my way through the narrow and involved streets of that old quarter of the city. I remember two events connected with that day. The first event occurred when I was a student of the third or fourth class in the Gymnasium. Our new textbook had just arrived from Athens, and I spent the day reading the history textbook. Another event was when my godfather and friends from Cythrea quartered a visitor on us for the fair. It rained heavily on St. Luke's Eve, and I remember my godfather said that he had to stop a spouting water pipe with his palm in order to allow his party to cross the street. There is something reassuring in tradition and habits that come down through centuries. Probably my brother, my cousin, and their children are attending the fair today with the same zest and gusto that my father and I used to have. Wars come and go, and empires fall, but the common people—the masses—keep on performing the rites and the observances handed down to them by their forefathers.

October 20, 1942, Tuesday

Today I underwent my preliminary physical examination for classification in the military service. I was given papers and a paper receptacle containing a glass tube for blood. I went to Dr. Williams' office at 2 o'clock. There was another fellow sufferer, a toothless bachelor of 40. Besides us, there was a young mother, rosy, plump and pretty with her two-month-old baby. She was interested in us and talked about her husband's classification being 3B. There was also the nurse, black haired and clad in white with a sallow, tired face. The examination proved very different from what I expected. I undressed in the office. The doctor told me to open my mouth. He looked me over, and that's all. Then he filled the papers and took blood for the test. It happened that Dr. Martin dropped in to have his throat examined. He drove me to the Hill in time for my 4 o'clock Greek class. Sh. looked sad. She thinks that the world will come to an end if one is called to the service.

October 24, 1942, Saturday

Today, the 24th day of October, is my birthday, although

it is not exactly my birthday since I was born on the old-style October 24. I'm now 43 years old. I've been teaching now for 25 years, having started my career on September 14, 1918. It is a pity that I have nothing to show for the 43 years of my life. I've read much, I've traveled much, I've suffered much, and I've loved much. I saved no money, I established no family, I wrote no book, and I have dozed my life away. And the worst part of it is that just now the armed forces of the United States are stretching their powerful hands to snatch me from my books, walks, lectures, and loves. It seems that God has gotten tired of my eternally being a consumer and not a producer, a sponge and not a giver, and He is now by force going to teach me a lesson of self-sacrifice, service, and production. The cup is bitter. I cry, "Take this cup away from me," but God's will be done in this as in everything.

I have only two friends—both ladies—who are my friends because they hope or expect to marry me. One of them is anxiously waiting for me to secure a more lucrative position in order to fasten her feelings on me. The other seems more unselfish, but at the bottom of her heart lingers the hope and the belief that someday my steadfastness shall crack, and she shall win a meal ticket.

As I complete my 43rd year of life, I thank God for the health, the help, the books, and the friends I have enjoyed, and I pray that this mighty scourge of war might pass away from me and from the whole world and that new opportunities be opened to me. If life begins at 40, I'm only three years old, and yet something may be done not unbecoming men who come from a race famed in arts and literature. At least after years of doubt and fear, I have gained a clear view of my object in life, which is nothing else but "the power of expression." I must be able to express myself or perish. There is no compromise.

October 25, 1942, Sunday

At about 5 o'clock I took a walk in the cold, crisp weather. I met Mary, who runs the only millinery shop in town, in her smart sweater, her graying hair, and cheeks colored by the exercise and the wind. She looked pretty. She is over 40, but she is plump, pretty, and rosy.

October 27, 1942, Tuesday

I cashed my check and deposited 30 dollars in the bank. I sent 15 to F., and with the rest, I'll live comfortably. I talked with no one except old Pitman, who was repairing the wooden stairs that lead up the Mechanical Building I. He is old, almost deaf, and rheumatic; but he is a glad man and bears the evils of old age with fortitude and cheerfulness.

October 29, 1942, Thursday

Today I received my classification. It was as I expected: 1A. This creates a huge problem for me. I don't know whether I ought to appeal for reclassification or ask the university authorities to apply for my deferment. It is a nasty situation for me. Here I am, over 43 years of age, and the state demands that I leave my work and shoulder a gun. I would not mind if all men my age were called to service, but to be called only because I've no dependents is simply idiotic. The land is chock full of young men—married and unmarried, childless or with means enough to be indepen-dent, men born and bred in this country, men who received a free education at the expense of the state, men who possess property and children to defend—and they will stay snug and comfortable, fattening themselves, going to the shows, drinking and fornicating, while men who simply couldn't marry because they were too poor must do the fighting for them. I don't expect to do any fighting, but, just the same, to be taken away from one's job—a job that cost me 19 years of struggle and privation to prepare for—is maddening to say the least. Anyhow, stranger things than these have happened. I'm still not in the Army. I might be deferred, or I might be rejected for some kind of disease. As for appealing for reclassification, it would be a further waste of time and energy. The members of the Draft Board would probably get mad at me and not even grant me a deferment. So tonight, unless I'm deferred or rejected, I must consider myself to be in the Army. And another problem bothers me. Here I am without relatives or next of kin and without friends who will take care of my affairs. And yet why should I care what will happen to my insurance or my small bank account? Money has never done anybody good.

November 1, 1942, Sunday

Dr. Willis is trying to get me deferred for three months. I wish him success, but I doubt it greatly if the Local Draft Board would deign even to consider such an application. I feel like a lamb among the wolves. As I consider the five million boys already drafted—drafted simply because they had no dependents, which is equivalent to having no means—I see them as lambs sent by wolves to fight for interests and causes they don't share in the least. I thought the selective service was a Democratic measure, but not now. I see it is merely another of the ingenious and fraudulent ways through which the powerful exploit the weak and the poor. I don't think it is fair when a poor youngster has to fight to protect the investments and the gains of the businessmen who never produced anything, who were merely sponges and consumers. We, the poor without dependents, don't have the slightest chance of ever reaping the rich reward of political offices or business enterprises, but we are given the chance to suffer and be killed for them. The state can afford to sacrifice us to the grim idol of Moloch; we don't cost much, but a fellow with dependents costs about 500 dollars more a year than we do. This is the most egregious fraud ever practiced by the members of the state against its weak and unprotected charges. And to think that some of us spent sleepless nights and laborious days working hard and late to accumulate knowledge and skill to serve those who are now coolly, deliberately, and cruelly sending us to sacrifice life, limb, health, and time for them. If they were at least generous enough to share our labors and cease profiting by our misery, I would not be so bitter. But while the boys are fighting in the jungles of the Pacific islands, in the Libyan deserts, or in the torrid zone of India, the contented and the useless ride in new cars, hoard food delicacies, accumulate money, get elected to offices, and complain if the sugar is rationed. But they always had their wars, and they will probably always have them because their father is the Devil, and they have sold to him their immortal souls for the luxuries and trifles of this world.

November 2, 1942, Monday

I am thinking of writing a dialogue in imitation of Plato's *Apology,* in which a man of my education, age, and profession refuses to obey the Draft Board and is judged by a hostile jury. He will base his speech on the following arguments: (1) Selective Service is unjust; it drafts those who have no dependents, i.e. the young and the poor. It preserves the old and the rich, for only the rich can marry young and rear a family. Since the law is unjust and one is not bound to obey it, it is better to suffer than to obey an unjust law.

I walked to town with the shapely and vigorous Miss Wright, who teaches typing. I did not eat at the Youree but at another restaurant. Dr. Most, who used to eat at the Youree and whom I met at the Post Office, remarked that she didn't like the looks of the cook at the Youree. He seemed tubercular to her. That scared me away. So here I am! I paid 50 cents for a chicken dinner tonight. It was like throwing good money away.

November 4, 1924, Wednesday

I gave a form for Occupational Deferment to Dr. Willis. I hope he will fill it in and hurry it to the Local Board on time. I might get deferred for six months, but no one can tell.

November 7, 1942, Saturday

Dr. Brown talked optimistically about the war on account of the defeat of the Axis forces in Africa. He was also optimistic about the future of his scholars. They are our cash basis now. Mrs. Stewart gave a report on what the scholars have to face after the war is over. At the store I met F. I bought three pounds of sugar on my ration card, and I gave them to her to prepare cookies for both her boyfriend and me. This is probably one of the last Sundays I'll be in town since I've been called for induction on November 18. All my friends think that I will not be deferred and that I will pass the physical examination easily. They think that the Local Board is tough and does not care for intellectuals and that worse-looking specimens of humanity have passed the none-too-rigid physical examination. Well, it is pitiful when one's fate depends upon the whims, digestions, and dispositions of others. Until now I've endured hardships and undergone a discipline for the sake of a great aim. I imposed them upon myself. But now it is different. The State, by its interests, stupidity, and inertia, has found itself involved in war. A little thinking and planning would have averted the war, but the god of activity, to whom we bow down in worship, blinded us. We rush like fools. We speak for the sake of hearing our own voices. We play politics. We read trash. We get drunk and fornicate, and then we wake up one morning to find ourselves either in war or depression. The fear and want gnaw at our own ears. We spend slumberless nights. We grow neurotic. We shout at the 40-hour week. We decorate our heroes. We draft the young and the poor. We send soldiers to all parts of the world. We pay high taxes. We buy bonds. We listen to the news over the radio. We read the headlines of the morning papers. Some live to see the end; some die hoping that their efforts and sacrifices have not been in vain. Lucky are those whom chance spares. Woe to those who are caught in the throes of fighting, sickness, and poverty.

November 14, 1942, Saturday

This has been a memorable week. It was consumed in efforts to persuade the Local Draft Board to defer me until the end of the semester. First, they rejected my application for not being properly filed; second, when I proved to them that they were in the wrong, they told me that I might request to meet with them. I met with them on Thursday evening, and in order to corroborate my arguments, I took Dr. Willis with me. The Board thought we had a very good case, but they kept on telling us that "the law does not allow any deferment." We wasted our time. On November 18 at 2:30 p.m., I have to put in an appearance for the induction. If I pass the physical examination, a new phase of my life will begin. The very one I hated from my childhood—uniforms, drilling, barracks, nakedness, lack of privacy, empty and meaningless activities, subordination to stupid, conceited officers, unpleasant fellowship and whatnot! It is hard to believe that the change will be for the best. It would mean destructive activities and waste of time and energy that makes nobody better, stronger, nor nobler. It will be worse than loafing. It will mean that I'll relinquish my teaching of literature, my preaching of the gospel of the Good Book, my job scattering ideas—for the training to kill my fellow men. It cannot be for the better, no matter what the whole world says. The war was brought about by monomaniacs like Hitler and Mussolini, by stupid and corrupt politicians, by faulty economics and whatnot! It is fought by the poor against the poor for the benefit of the rich and the unscrupulous. While the poor are working in the factories, the mines, and the fields, or fighting in jungles, in deserts, and on the oceans, the wealthy and the unscrupulous become sleek and fat and talk and agitate for longer work hours. They have already been elected to the senate and the congress. What should a decent man do in a situation like this? Shall he become a tool of the stupid and the unscrupulous, or shall he resist the law and be cast into a dungeon where disease and undernourishment will undermine his health and end his earthly career? Will he say to them, "To Hell with you!" and save his soul but lose his body? Will he blindly crack jokes, look and act stupid, and make the best of a bad business? Shall he try to evade the main issue by saying that service in the Army will enrich his life by new experience and that he will defend non-existent freedoms and Democratic ideals? These questions have been bothering me the last few days, and the more I revolve them in my mind, the more confused and confounded I become. Now I understand why the ordinary person relegates the arduous task of thinking to a priest or a politician. By telling you what to do, they relieve you of all mental effort, but at the same time, they make you their prey. By sheer mental laziness, man has sold himself to what he calls the Church and the State!

November 15, 1942, Sunday

It is windy like March. Around any room on the South Hill of Siloam Springs, the wind howls and sends countless leaves to the ground. My mind dwelt on the writing of a story with the title "The Lord Among the Soldiers." I'll represent a soldier who was formerly an evangelist but is drafted because he is not an ordained minister. He preaches to the soldiers in a camp as follows: "Brothers, last night while I was trying to get a wink of sleep in the guardhouse to which I was relegated for disobeying orders, the Lord Jesus stood beside me and said unto me 'Be of good cheer, My son. Let not your heart be troubled!' I startled and answered, saying, 'Lord, the guardhouse is no place for you!' 'My son!' He answered, 'I am always with the poor and the oppressed of the earth, and you and your fellow soldiers are the poor and the oppressed ones, so I say peace unto you!'

'But Lord,' I cried in agony, 'we are not the poor and the oppressed of the earth. We are the best fed, dressed, and sheltered soldiers in the world, and we are not trained for you, the Lord of Peace, but for (Moloch) the grim god of war!'

'I know it, My son, you are the poor in spirit, and yours is the kingdom of Heaven.'

'We are not the poor of spirit; we are the flower of a mighty nation; we are the smartest, the fastest and the most daring men in existence.'

'Blessed are you, My son, for you are the dullest and the most stupid. The Pharisees, the sleek and fat businessmen, the wily and corrupt politicians and their tools, and My so-called servants and ministers have deceived you with lies and promises. Why, My son, are you here?'

'I was drafted, my Lord. I was hailed before the Local Draft Board and told that since I had no dependents and am not an ordained minister and have preserved my bodily vigor by abstaining from drinking, smoking, and wenching, it would be given unto me a gun to kill my fellow men. If I refused, the dungeon and the concentration camp were ready to receive me. For days I debated within myself whether to obey man or God, and in the end, the fear of man prevailed.'

'I've seen their suffering, My son, and I've bled for you. You are not alone in the world; all your fellow soldiers have gone through the same struggle. It is human to be weak, and your Father, who is in Heaven, sees thy weakness and will use it for His greater glory. The sleek, the fat, the wily, and the corrupt shall perish from the face of the Earth. They think that they are wise. While you, My son, and the soldiers, thy brothers, suffer humiliation and unheard-of hardships on land, in the air and on the sea, the fat and the sleek slumber in soft beds, drink delicious wines, ride in luxurious cars, accumulate wealth, and consolidate their power. They agitate for longer hours of work although they never did an hour's honest work in their lives. They have seduced My so-called servants by bribing them with big salaries and exemption from military service. They draft the young and the poor. They joyfully rub their hands in expectation of great profits and honors. They pay cold and insincere praises to the killed soldiers. Their iniquities offend high Heaven. From now on, I'm through with them. The Kingdom of Heaven shall be taken from the merchants, the politicians, and the priests, and it shall be given to My sons, the soldiers, the workers, the farmers, and the evangelists!'

Thus spoke the Lord, and He vanished. I lay awake wondering how I'll ever be able to deliver the message of the Lord to my brothers, the soldiers! But He found a way! I was released from the guardhouse this morning. I was asked to preach to you because the chaplain was smitten with sickness and is lying in the officers ward of the hospital. Indeed the Lord moves in a mysterious way, His wonders to perform. Let us rise. God bless and guard Thy children everywhere, for Christ's sake and glory, amen."

Then the visitor will wonder whether the preacher is a madman or a genius, whether he is inspired by God or whether he is a crafty fellow who wants to have his radical ideas sanctioned by Christ. But his sincerity is evident, and the soldiers listen to him with undivided attention. His words carry conviction.

November 22, 1942, Sunday

The past week has been one of the most important of my life. Last Sunday I was Dr. John H. Panage; today I'm Private John H. Panage in the United States Army. Last Wednesday at 2:30 p.m., I went to the basement of the Methodist Church, and I was given a cup of coffee, a piece of cake, and a sandwich. Then I walked to the Local Board office. There were about 34 fellow sufferers and many others who came to see us off. Mr. Mitchell, the clerk, put us in line and gave us a short address, the gist of which was to behave and stick together, to take it easy and relax. Then Reverend Brandom, the president of the Siloam Springs Ministerial Alliance, introduced another minister, a pale, small, thin youngster who delivered us another address, giving us the Peace of Christ and telling us how much everybody cares for us and how proud we ought to be for the privilege of serving the country. At last, at 3 o'clock we were crowded into the bus and were off for Little Rock. Some of the boys uncorked their whiskey bottles and began taking liberal doses until they got drunk, tried to sing, and then sank into a heavy sleep. Two or three times, the bus stopped at dingy and dirty cafes on the highway, and ugly looking ladies served us coffee. We reached Little Rock about 10:30 and were unloaded at the backdoor of the Headquarters of the Station, a building that once must have been a large garage but now serves as the place where men are herded in order to be examined by youngsters who are supposed to be doctors and judge whether men are fit or unfit for military service. First, we were given a ticket to go to Frank's Cafeteria and get lunch. The cafeteria was as shabby and repelling as those lunchrooms outside the Great Northern Station in Minneapolis where the people on relief used to get their ill-cooked meals of stale vegetables and rotten meats. There were four counter girls: two who were white, of not-too-healthy appearance, and the others were Negro girls. The upholstered seats showed their dirty insides, and in one booth, a heavily rouged and painted young lady was sitting smoking. She was perhaps one of the waitresses, but she looked and acted like a streetwalker. Over all this mockery, there was the sign: "This establishment is under the supervision of the State Health Department." I asked only for vegetables, which looked better than the meats, a glass of milk, and bread. The spoon was rusted, and the fork and knife must have been manufactured before my birth. The milk was hot, but the bread was good, and I like bread. When we returned from lunch, we were given our papers, and after two youngsters typed our names on a piece of paper, we entered a room where we peeled off our clothes and stood as naked as the day we were born. We were only allowed to put on our shoes, and then we walked first from one doctor to another doctor to have our urine looked at, to have our organs squeezed and pressed, to have our chests X-rayed, and to have our blood pressure measured.

It was a slow and humiliating process, all useless and meaningless. Any doctor would have examined one in half an hour, but here, with 700 waiting in line, it took half a day. As for the examination, it was anything but thorough. It was hurried, careless, and superficial. Organic defects could not be discerned by a doctor who looks at you one minute and then says okay and passes you to the next one. The doctors themselves are tired to death of doing the same thing over and over again. Then, before you are aware of it, you are in the Army. At a desk sits a distinguished-looking gentleman, Jewish in appearance, who looks over your chart with a bored air and signs his name. You are in the Army. Then you are asked to name your beneficiary and whether you want to go to the camp that very night or ask for an eight-day furlough. Then you are fingerprinted and given the oath of allegiance, and you become a private. Those who are rejected try to appear sad, but in their hearts, they are glad to be free again—free from Local Boards, silly Army regulations and the fear that someday they may have to kill a fellowman whom they have never seen before and with whom they never had a quarrel. The accepted ones try to look cheerful and heroic, but in their hearts, there is unutterable grief—grief that their life's work must be discontinued, their harmless habits of life must be abandoned, and they must learn a new trade—the trade of killing men. I noticed that the men on their return were much more quiet than they were on their morning drive. They sat silent and sad, thinking and thinking. I was so tired and crushed that I didn't taste any food. I drank coffee and soft drinks and thought of my miserable condition. People might think that one who objects to military life is a coward. That's not true. I object to it because it means the loss of my freedom from action, thinking, and movement. I object to it because it will turn me from a thinking man to a robot, from a human being to a brute. There still lingers in my heart the hope that, owing to my age, I would probably be spared the trials and tribulations of drilling, handling weapons, and long, arduous trips by land, sea, or air.

Since I came back on Thursday, I've been living on borrowed time. I kept on teaching, reading, and walking. I've been thinking of making my will and disposing my books and clothes, but like all men without relatives and close friends, I'm at a loss how to go about it. There is not even one of my own faith and nationality in this town to whom I can entrust my affairs. The curse of being a stranger in a strange land has hit me in the face. But God has always been and shall be with me. The Eye of Heaven shines everywhere, and to wise men where the sun shines is port of happy Heaven. The stars and winds are always with us, and there will be books, newspapers, magazines, and fellowmen everywhere I go. God has probably given me just what I needed to develop my personality and character. He will province me with means and ways of profiting by this new experience and will lead me with a strong hand through the dangers that will face me.

May 30, 1945, Memorial Day

Thirty whole months have elapsed since I've written in this book. During that time I've been with the Armed Forces of the United States. I left Siloam Springs on November 27, 1942, for the Reception Center, Camp Robinson, Little Rock, Arkansas. I was "processed" there, i.e. I was given a pay book and three or four shots and dressed in OD's and fatigues. I attended lectures by officers and the chaplain, and then I was shipped on December 4, 1942, to the then-unoccupied "New Area" and assigned to Co. C, 766 M P Bn. For a time I had to march in darkness and rain, mud, and misery to a distant mess hall for my meals. Later on, our own mess hall started serving meals. Before I proceed further, let me say something about the Army meals. Every morning they serve either scrambled eggs, cereal, fruit, coffee, and hot cakes or French toast. The noon meal consists of meat (often uneatable), mashed, fried or boiled potatoes, beans, salad (tomatoes and lettuce), with coffee or tea. The evening meal is about the same as the noon meal; the meals are served in the Company Mess Halls with a sitting capacity of 250. There is always noise and rushing and no lack of dirty habits. If you are not fastidious, you are likely to enjoy the food, and even if you are fastidious, in the end you get used to everything, and "chow call" sounds good to your ears. The 766 M. P. Bn. had just been activated and consisted mainly of "limited service" men, i.e. men suffering from some physical defect that renders them incapable of combat duty or over-aged men. But the ambition of the commanding officer Colonel Houston and his officers turned the M.P. battalion into infantry plus unit. Every morning for eight long, interminable months, there was "close order" drill, to be followed by "extended order" drill, and classes on "first aid," "map-reading," "bayonet practice," and "grenade throwing." As a rule, they kept us busy from 7:30 a.m. to 4:30 p.m. We were usually free evenings unless we occasionally caught "guard." I employed my free time in reading. At first, because of my ignorance, I could not get any worthwhile books, but I soon discovered the excellent library housed in Service Club No. 1, and I began to draw books, and in reading I forgot my longings, my loneliness, and my misery. I also acquired the habit of going two or three times a week to the motion picture theaters. Reading, walks, and "shows" have kept me sane and sensible. In order to avoid the excessive fatigue, I occasionally used to put myself on the "sick book" and spend some pleasant mornings reading in the waiting room of the infirmary. The doctor who came to know my ailment invariably gave me "pills" and sent me back to duty. I took two or three "hikes," but as they grew longer and the weather warmer, I acquired the habit of "falling out" and riding comfortably in the ambulance that, by a wise Army regulation, always trails the hiking troops. Except for moving from barracks to barracks and bring transferred from company to company, nothing worthy of note happened till September 1, 1943, when Co. A, to which I was then attached, was ordered to Fort Wardsworth, Staten Island, New York. I enjoyed the trip from Little Rock to New York through St. Louis; Chicago; Pittsburgh, Pennsylvania; Washington, DC; Philadelphia; and Trenton. On Staten Island we lived in tents by the ocean, and except on rainy days, we didn't suffer any hardships. I used my spare time to revisit New York, where I spent my first years of residence on this continent. I revisited Bryant Park, the New York Central Library, 42nd Street, Broadway, Park Avenue, and Fifth Avenue. I walked those sidewalks absorbed in recollections. Out of false shame, I did not contact any of my old friends. I don't know why. I was so much averse to being seen by my friends that I escorted only two trainloads of German and Italian prisoners. One trainload was taken to Ft. Buckner, North Carolina, the other to Ft. McAlester, Oklahoma. During most of the time on the train, I peeled potatoes and furbished spoons because I was, through no fault of mine, placed in the "overhead." Peeling potatoes and shining silver was much more agreeable to me than guarding human beings herded in trains like cattle. On September 26, 1943, we returned safe and sound to Camp Robinson. Between that date and October 18, when I was transferred to the Headquarters M. P. Detachment, nothing important happened. As a member of the Headquarters M.P. Detachment, I had a very good time. At first I was sent to guard the "Magazine Area." I used to walk around the extensive area, a rifle on my shoulder and a pistol on my belt, practicing my phonetics and reciting poetry. About December, when the weather grew cold, I was given the pleasant job of guarding the "Stockade," where misbehaving soldiers are kept in custody. My watch was from 12:30 a.m. to 6:30 a.m. I used to sit in a booth that was sometimes cold like an icebox and either review my notes or recite poetry. At 6:30 I would eat breakfast and go to bed and sleep till noon; then after dinner, I would read and relax.

On February 6, 1944, I was transferred to Camp Crowder, Missouri. I was put into the Language Group on account of my supposed knowledge of foreign languages. After being processed at B-35, I was sent to C-27 for a three-week "refresher," and then I was transferred to D-33 and sent to the Switchboard School. This is neither the time nor the place to discuss or describe the Army Educational System. Those who do not know it at first hand are apt to praise it to the skies. We, however, who went to Army school and sat long, interminable hours listening to instructors who lacked both enthusiasm and knowledge, are apt to sneer at them. I was allowed to finish the school, but I was not allowed to go CPX (Command Post Exchange) and was sent to C-26 as Basic Instructor. I stayed in that capacity for 15 days, and then I was transferred to D-31, where I stayed 48 hours and hence to B-31 May 1, 1944, where I stayed till my discharge from the Army. During the time I stayed with B-31, I was part of the "Cadre," and I was performing the easy and pleasant duties of the company mail clerk. Since the company was at no time in full strength, the mail was negligible, and I had plenty of time to read, relax, visit the PX, gossip, and go to the shows. About December 15, the company moved to the corner of Benton Street and Domphan Drive, opposite the Motor Pool, and only one block away from the Service Club No 1. On January 6, 1945, I was sent to the hospital for discharge from the Army, according to the provision of Section X. I stayed there for 15 days, appeared before the Board, and was recommended for discharge, but before my papers reached Omaha, Section X was frozen, and I was left "to sweat it out" in the Army. On my return to my company, I found two other mail clerks, Mosby and Carolli, and the three of us managed to have a good time at the expense of the taxpayers. Sometime while I was on furlough in March, I was made casual and available for shipping. About this time the B-31, reduced to 10 to 12 men, began moving from Barrack to Barrack till it reached Francis and Coehran. On the last week of April, the long-awaited news came out of Washington that men over age 42 should be discharged from the Army by simply requesting their separation from it. About May 15 the news had officially reached our orderly, and I immediately filed my application. On May 23, I was told that my application had been approved. On Saturday, May 26, I took the K.C. Southern train for Camp Chaffee, Ft. Smith, Arkansas, where I was to be "processed" for discharge. I reached Ft. Smith about 5:15 p.m. and was taken by an Army bus to the camp. After registering and delivering our papers, we were taken by the C9 to Barrack 5 and were given two sheets, a pillow, and a comforter and were told to make ourselves at home. On Sunday we had our physical examination and then rested all afternoon. On Monday morning each one of us met his counselor and helped him make a record of peacetime and wartime activities. My record is ridiculously simple and short. It reads thus teaching: M.P. guard duties, clerk mailing. We rested rather easily till 5:15 p.m., when we were told to take our bags and report first to Last Records Building, where we signed four or five documents and received our eagle button. Then we marched to the Finance Building, where a Major gave us our Discharge papers, and the "mustering out money." I received 50 dollars in cash and 93.97 in check. That's more than I expected. After that, all of us, glowing and seething with excitement, boarded the bus for Ft. Smith. After eating my first civilian meal at the Broadway Café, at last I reached the vast and empty L.C.S. Station. I bought a ticket for Siloam Springs at the reduced rate of 1.44. Since the bus for Spiro, where I was supposed to board the train, was not due till 11:45 p.m. and I could not check my heavy barrack bag, I sat on a bench and reviewed the *Plain English Handbook* by J. Martyn Walsh and Anna Kathleen Walsh. Later on I was joined by an ex-sailor and a soldier on furlough and kept on talking till the bus came. At 1 a.m. I took the train at Spiro, and by 3:30 I reached Siloam Springs. I took a taxi for the Youree. I slept in Room 27, and I woke up on Tuesday at 8:30. I ate breakfast and then, taking my bag, I walked up the Hill to 1005 S. Wright Street, where I used to room before I was drafted. Last night I slept in my own bed, and today I unpacked my books, notes, and clothes and then spent most of my time reading on the porch and walking the streets of the town. I have already visited Mr. Stout, who works for the Brown Hatchers. He used to be a member of the JBU faculty. I also dropped in to see Mary who owns and manages the Shop o' Style. I'm still wearing my soldier's uniform, but I'm glad my Army days are over. I thank God that He helped me to pass thirty months of military life in health, happiness, security, and usefulness.

June 2, 1945, Saturday

A very cool and delightful day. I spent most of my time reading short stories. I was so lazy that I did not even take a walk. I visited the library for the first time since I was discharged from the Army. I'm at present wearing civilian clothes, and I feel almost naked—they are so flimsy and thin in comparison to the Army uniform. The only military things I've retained are my underwear, my eagle buttons, and my brown shoes. I'm fired with desire to start writing a short story and a novel/letter that I had already meditated on while I was in the Army. But somehow my proverbial indolence and laziness still get the upper hand. I must, however, get down to work. There is no other cure for my poverty and obscurity. If I work, I'll thrive; if I loaf and indulge in daydreaming, I'm doomed to die without leaving footprints on the sands of time. And what am I living for? Do I have a family or relatives or even a country? I have only one friend, and that is literature, and one aim, that is to become immortal, that is to say, to live in the memory of coming generations, to be known to posterity. Otherwise, I've lived in vain.

June 4, 1945, Monday

Tomorrow I'll start teaching. I must thank God for delivering me out of the clutches of the Army and depositing me sane, sensible, and sweet back to my room, library, and classroom. I don't like to be heroic. I like to be humbly useful, and I'll try to do my best as a teacher, student, and writer. I'll keep on working. There is no other salvation for me.

June 10, 1945, Sunday

Since both of my classes meet in the afternoon, from 2:15 to

4:45, I'm spending the mornings reading on the porch and in the library. It is exactly the kind of work I like. Like Venerable Bede, my ambition is to learn, teach, and write. I've not yet developed a system of philosophy as a mode of worship. I'm still undecided whether God or Luck rules the world, whether social justice can be achieved by democracy, monarchy, communism, world peace, or whatnot. I'm not yet quite sure whether I'm here to live, make a living, improve myself, serve others, write a book, produce children, or accumulate wealth.

My conscience is bothering me nowadays. I've not written a letter to my brothers, to Eve, nor to others whom I met at Camp Crowder. I'm certainly not a good correspondent. I'll try to at least write to Eve. She proved to be a great friend during the long and interminable months I've spent in the Army.

June 17, 1945, Sunday

Last Friday I attended a party at D. Cook's new—or rather—old place. It was given on account of his birthday. The Schrags, the Wills, the Cooks and Sh. formed a formidable crowd with their children, mothers, and in-laws. As usual, eating formed the principal and most important element of the party. There was plenty of fried, tender chicken, potato salad, tea, ice cream, etc. Everybody—especially the young ones—seemed to enjoy the whole affair. As the only bachelor in the party, I looked with fear and trembling at the children, mothers-in-law, and the wives. Taking care of them absorbs all the time and efforts of the husbands. They must be hard up for time to improve themselves and live the higher life. Sometimes I wonder whether the purpose of life is the reproduction of the species.

June 25, 1945, Monday

I took a long walk in order to explore the town of Siloam Springs. I'm really ashamed of myself. I've been living in this town since 1939, and I've scarcely mastered one third of the town, and it is the smallest town in which I've yet resided.

July 4, 1945, Wednesday

I spent my Fourth of July reading John Galsworthy's *End of the Chapter* on the porch of 1005 S. Wright Street, while the scholars I'm rooming with spent the day at Lake Wedington. I ate three nice meals. In the evening, I took Sh. to Kay June's, where we ate chicken dinners at 65 cents each. We also bought a pint of ice cream at 20 cents, which we carried to Sh.'s apartment and ate at our leisure. I also took a walk at 1 o'clock because the weather was unusually cool, almost verging on chilly. Yesterday I received the second check for 100 dollars of my mustering-out pay from the Army. It is not even 40 days since I bade an affectionate farewell to the Army life, and yet the whole experience seems so unreal and distant to me as if it were a bad dream or a nightmare. Yet very often, while I walk the shady streets of this peaceful village or while I eat my meals or go out for a walk with Sh., I think of the millions of boys in uniform who are pulling guard, going to schools, and C9's. B.O.'s are in the hospitals and AWOL. These are the boys I knew. What is the life of the others who are fighting and dying in the Pacific Theater of war? I don't know first hand. But it must be hell on earth. So I pray to God that this scourge of war might speedily pass away and that men might unlearn war, slaughter, greed, and selfishness.

July 14, 1945, Saturday

I've been very remiss in writing daily in this book in spite of my conviction that my survival depends on my ability to express myself. Laziness, indifference, and indecision keep me from writing every day as much as possible. Life seems dull, drab, and barren to me, and yet while I was in the Army, I dreamt of the time when I, as a free man, would devote my time and efforts to writing.

July 16, 1945, Monday

About 6 o'clock Mr. Cook drove me to Dr. Brown's farm. Everybody was there, including grandmothers and grandchildren. We had fried chicken, potato salad, beans, and watermelon. There was God's plenty. Mr. Cook and I visited the pigs, the cows, and the cornfields. The farm is kept spick and span, but it is rather isolated and cannot be reached except by a seven-mile drive over a dirt road full of ruts and pools of water. We returned to Siloam Springs about 8:30 after dropping Sh. at her house. Farm life appears good, but the pigs smell, the cows have flies, and the grass is full of chickens. I prefer a comfortable apartment in a city with a good restaurant, a rich library, a good movie house, and a park within five minutes' walk or ride. I care more for the nourishment of the mind than the body, and the city contains libraries, schools, theaters, and people who can improve me in every way.

July 18, 1945, Wednesday

At 11 o'clock I attended chapel. Dr. Brown talked about his plans for building the Cathedral of the Ozarks. At 12 o'clock we went to former Athletic and witnessed the bulldozer "pushing dirt" for the excavations of the Cathedral building. It was a solemn moment. It might be the beginning of something or nothing. The future as always lies in the lap of the gods. I also bought two cakes of Lifebuoy soap. I intend to build up a supply of six cakes of soap in case of dearth. I can do without sugar, meat, potatoes, and underwear, but not without soap.

July 21, 1945, Saturday

It is a hot, clear day, and I spent it sitting on the porch, reading G. B. Shaw's *Man and Superman*. The first time I read it was as far back as 1924, twenty-one years ago, when I took a course on Contemporary Literature at Columbia University. At that time I used to work at D. S. of Vanderbilt Hotel from 4 p.m. to midnight and spend my day attending classes, reading, and loafing. I was young and adventurous then, and the world seemed wide. Now I'm a disillusioned, middle-aged man who has been a teacher for twenty-five years, a soldier for two and a half, and lived in the South, the North and the Midwest. I'm a man who has learned that the road to success lies through hard work, disappointments, fears, hopes, and despairs.

July 30, 1945, Monday

Last Monday, July 23, I rode to Tulsa, Oklahoma, with the Cooks and Sh. We started before sunrise. We breakfasted at Choteau, crossed the Grand River by ferry, and reached Tulsa by 9 o'clock in the morning. It was very hot. I kept in the shade as much as I could and drank many glasses of ice water and Pepsi Cola and ate many cones of ice cream. We started on our return trip about 4 o'clock in the afternoon and drove through a desert of heat and sun that caused us to perspire profusely.

I went to the bank and deposited 60 dollars. My savings bank account stands at 800. I must build a strong reserve against unemployment and illness and for vacations and travel. Some summer I'd like very much to take a trip home and see once more the blue mountains and the blue sky of Cyprus.

August 6, 1945, Monday

I bought two cakes of Palmolive soap and a tube of shaving cream. I have an unreasonable fear of being deprived of soap and shaving cream. It is a far cry from the boy who used to get a bath once a semester to the man who bathes every morning, from the young man who used to shave once a week to the middle-aged man who shaves every day.

August 8, 1945, Wednesday

Everyone is talking about the atomic bombs and the entrance of Russia into the war against Japan. If it is true what the papers say about the atomic bomb, then mankind will someday be wiped out by bombs that our scientists have invented. It is like giving sticks of dynamite to little children to play with. They are certain to kill themselves and others.

August 15, 1945, Wednesday

Today the war ended with the unconditional surrender of Japan. The day has been proclaimed a national holiday. I celebrated by reading poems by Fletcher and T.S. Eliot, eating good meals, and taking an afternoon nap. At 10 o'clock I attended a meeting at the Community Building, at which the City Band played two or three marches, and two or three ministers gave addresses on how thankful we ought to be that the war was over and that we must remember the dead and the maimed, and let us win the peace. About 7 o'clock, after half an hour's waiting, I got a "vegetarian" at the Carman's Café. The place was chockfull, and the waitresses and the Carman family looked worn out and ready to collapse. Thank God, the weather is cloudy and cool.

This day reminds me of two other armistice celebrations: the first on November 11, 1918, in Nicosia, Cyprus, at the end of the First World War. At that time I had been teaching for only two months, having obtained my teacher's diploma in June of the same year. The second celebration was in Camp Crowder, when Germany surrendered. I remember the faces of the German prisoners as they were marched to the barracks, excused from work for the day. I also remember the party we had at the mess hall and the boys drinking beer and soft drinks to excess.

Wars come and go. I distinctly remember half a dozen wars. The Italo-Turkish War, the Balkan wars, World War I, The War against Russia, and this war. Thank God, I escaped unscathed, although I served thirty whole months. Wars never settled anything. They will send millions of fine young men to untimely deaths. They destroy towns and cities and unfavorably affect the morals of the people. But to me, war or no war, my problem is to find my rock upon which to build my house.

August 22, 1945, Wednesday

I got my laundry. I'm lucky to get my laundry washed at the University laundry. My old laundry man, Lynn, has gone to war, and he has not yet returned. It is about three months since I left the Army, and my whole Army career looks so unreal and so distant that sometimes I wonder whether it were not a bad dream.

August 30, 1945, Thursday

It is exactly six years ago today that I signed with JBU. Since that time I have taught English and Greek and served with the Armed Forces of the Nation. How much better, wiser, nobler am I now? As far as I'm concerned, I'm not at all satisfied with myself.

September 15, 1945, Saturday

I read stories about battles on land, sea, and in the air in *Men at War.* I really admire the courage, the stamina, and the patience of men at war, but I cannot help pitying men for their stupidity for being engaged in wars. To my mind, war and unemployment represent man's inability to deal with social justice at home and with international justice abroad. Besides, war is wrong in principle, and nothing can make it right in practice. We have emerged victorious out of the war, but we have left on the shores of the four continents and on the plains and islands of the world numberless dead, and we have filled our hospitals with sick, maimed, and deranged men. And yet, after this frightful price paid in blood, work, worry, money, and moral deterioration, the powers of reaction, greed, and selfishness are paving the way for new discords both at home and abroad. It seems that those who have learned the lesson of the futility, unreality, and uselessness of war are either dead or indifferent. The veterans returning home after years of hardships, degradations, and danger are satisfied to sleep with their wives and get back their old jobs. They have no dreams of a new, brave world. They go back to busy idleness and do not care about anything as long as love and hunger are satisfied. I, sitting in my room and reading Beowulf, Chaucer, and Spenser, look, smell, and feel like an anachronism.

September 23, 1945, Sunday

I'm still young and vigorous. I've plenty of time and numberless opportunities. God has freed me from war and women. This year will decide my fate and destiny. Shall I keep on growing, or shall I begin to retrograde? But peace unto my soul! Whining and complaining will not help me in the least. Let me return to the simplicity, sincerity, and silence of my former days when I strove valiantly and hopefully among difficulties in a hostile environment for a haven.

October 1, 1945, Monday

It has been raining since September 24. Even the little creek that flows under the cliff on which the house I'm staying in perches has assumed the dimension of a mighty and swift river. I spent Sunday afternoon visiting Sh., who had just recovered from an attack of flu. She and her mother regaled me with fried pancakes, which I ate with plenty of butter and pure honey.

The present faculty of JBU consists of elderly men. Even I, who used to complain to the Army authority of my age, feel like a youngster, and with the exception of D. Wills and two or three others, I might consider myself to be the baby of the faculty, although I'm over 45 years old.

October 8, 1945, Monday

It is a cool, clear day. I put on my winter underwear, and I lighted the gas stove in my room. I sat down and wrote a brief letter to my brother in Cyprus. He must have grown uneasy on my account, since he wired to JBU, asking about my whereabouts. I'm really to blame for not writing to my relatives, friends, and acquaintances more regularly. I do not know why, but today my mind was full of plans for visiting Cyprus and spending a summer among the hills and on the shores where I passed the first twenty years of my life. Of course, I'll never put into effect any such plan, for there is nothing at home for me to see. I'm likely to catch malaria or some other disease. It will be more profitable for me to stay in Siloam Springs, buy books, read books, and write books. Traveling in the East is not for poor fellows like me. One must be able to pay for first-class accommodations in order to be safe.

October 15, 1945, Monday

I spent a quiet weekend reading Dickens and visiting at Sh.'s. On Saturday evening Dr. Haley, the McCurdies, and Mr. Caywood and I entertained a group of twenty-five students at a party given at the Baptist Assembly Grounds. We served hot dogs roasted over a bright and roaring fire, doughnuts, and cold drinks. We returned to the campus by 8 p.m.

December 21, 1945

I've not written in this book since last October. I have been writing a novel about a soldier who has returned from the Army, gotten his job back, married twice, and can't make up his mind whether or not to desert his wife and daughter! I'm not proud of the performance. My conception is great and glorious, but my performance is poor and ignoble. When it comes to expressing my thoughts and feelings in words, the result is poor. And yet I must not despair.

I bought ten Christmas cards. I did not feel like mailing them. I'll probably muster energy enough to mail them tomorrow. I must also buy some Christmas presents for at least ten persons.

December 22, 1945

I have to buy about ten presents for friends and their children. The Christmas spirit has certainly become the soul of commercialism. The storekeepers and the owners of busses and railroads are gathering money. The people, as usual, are conditioned to part with their money by buying spurious goods while lacking genuine goods. Meantime, in all the buying and selling, the message of Christ, "love God and love thy neighbor as thyself," is forgotten. Of course, we will send a present to those who lie in hospitals, parole a few prisoners, and send a basket of provisions to a poor family. We do those things because our conscience is bothering us. But, anyhow, I'm enjoying this, my first free Christmas since 1942. In 1942 on Christmas I visited Little Rock and drank a cup of coffee at the U.S.O. and got a box of toilet articles at the Baptist Center. In 1943 I guarded the Stockade from 12:30 a.m. to 6:30 a.m., and last year I sorted and delivered mail. One simply can't tell what might happen to a man in this mystical world of ours. In spite of the fact that we possess intellect and will, it seems that chance very often disposes of lives. It also seems that we survive by accident; but just the same I thank God for being back to my job and doing the work for which I'm fit and which I like.

March 12, 1946

I've not written in this diary since December 22, 1945, because I devoted my time and energy to writing a novel; but somehow I reached a blind alley; I lost sight of my characters, and my plot has become too complicated to be unraveled even by a deus ex machina. I'll follow the advice of Mark Twain. I'll leave the book alone until I gather more material and see my way through it. Meantime, I've been reading books as usual, teaching as usual, and walking and visiting as usual. I concentrate more and more on my English. I received a raise of salary. According to Mr. Snider, I now receive 190 dollars a month. I ought to earn more, but it is more than double the amount I was earning ten years ago.

Let me forget the Army life and the long, painful years of preparation through universities, and let me forget my disappointments in love and ambition.

March 15, 1946

I read about a dozen of "Cypress Mail" sent to me by my brother, who is at present manager of the Sorong-Vacuum Oil Co. office at Famagusta, Cypress. I really feel sorry for my poor fellow islanders. They are like sheep without a shepherd. The British do not care about them; they are too poor and too few for the empire to bother about them. The islanders are a mixed population: Turks, Greeks, Americans, Jews, Lavantines, and whatnot. Each group is subdivided into factions, and they waste their time waging quarrels either with the government or among themselves.

March 16, 1946

A rainy day. Sh. phoned through Mrs. Cook that she wanted to see me this evening. I met her on Main Street going to the Telegram office to wire her sisters to rush to their dying mother's bed. I worked all day, suffering with a headache. I read Churchill's speech in answer to Stalin with interest. As long as they don't come to blows, let them discuss things, but I'm afraid that blows will follow words. The most vital idea I acquired today is the idea that to know a nation, one must study not its history but its literature, and the idea that World Peace is threatened not only by Russian aggression but also by colonial unrest. The U.S. government will have a hard time persuading Russia to stop its expansion and convincing England that it is in her interest to set free her colonies.

March 18, 1946

I spent the day reading *Brideshead Revisited*. In the morning I wrote a letter to Bitzer. In the afternoon I read in the English Room while the freshmen worked on their themes. Sh.'s mother died yesterday afternoon, and she is taking a 15-day leave of absence to go carry the body to Ohio for burial. I supped at the Brownie, the Youree being closed. I had to wait about half an hour for a fried-chicken steak. It reminded me of nights last summer when one had to wait about three-quarters of an hour for fried eggs or fried chicken. The place was crowded, the service was very slow, and I read the *Joplin Evening News* slowly and deliberately. The Russians seem to give great concern to the United States on account of their activities in Iran, Manchuria, and elsewhere. One thing I cannot understand is why our government does not ask them what they really want. It is apparent that they want a share in the oilfields that have been appropriated by the Anglo-Americans and that they also want a port in the Indian Ocean. I think they are entitled to this privilege, being land locked on all sides. We are really trying to pull chestnuts for the British Empire, which is an anomaly and an anachronism in our age. For reasons known only to themselves, the British have blocked the Russians' way to the sea for centuries. The Russians want ports like Trieste, Salnika, etc., just to export and import their good products. By prohibiting them from using those ports, we force them to grasp them, and then we will proclaim them aggressive, declare war on them, and proclaim that we are fighting for the UNO charter.

It is a cloudy, cold day. Some trees are in blossom in spite of the cold weather.

March 19, 1946, Tuesday

I've been teaching all day long. I was in rather good shape in spite of the fact that our famous Coffee Shop is closed for remodeling, and I'm deprived of my two regular cups of coffee. Sh.'s uncle came to the U. on purpose to see me. Sh. and Mrs. P. have been trying to get me to dine with him. It irritates me beyond description or narration to have people act as if they own me. Another thing that annoyed me is that some girl who signed herself an honest Coed wrote a poem about SP, who is supposed to be Mr. Pugh, and since she refers to him as Mr. P and some of the general remarks may apply to me, apparently not a few thought that I'm the object of her silly remarks. Whether she refers to me or to Mr. Pugh is immaterial. The point is that the students ought not to be encouraged to write about their teachers. There are so many subjects to write about.

March 20, 1946, Wednesday

I spent the day correcting papers and substituting for Sh., who left last night for Ohio to bury her mother.

Tonight both the Youree and the Brownie were closed. I had to walk all the way to Kay-June's Café to get my evening meal. Now I realize how much my comfort depends on the town's two restaurants. Without them I should have been reduced to either boarding with a family or getting married. Sometimes I wonder if it would have been more profitable and sanitary for me to rent a small apartment and prepare my own frugal meals. The restaurants are by no means over-clean, and the foodstuff they serve is not the best by a long shot. One also pays exorbitant prices and has, sometimes, to wait half an hour for service.

On my way to Kay-June, Mr. Jim Reed picked me up and

gave me a ride. He is a former JBU student who completed 50 bombing missions over Germany and returned home to his young wife and tiny baby. He is at present associated with a garage run by an automobile dealer. He is a hero who performed a disagreeable task and returned to his humble, peaceful occupation. He is not yet 30. He might do some fighting yet. Almost one year since the collapse of Germany, there are rumors of war already. This is certainly a restless, wicked world.

March 21, 1946, Thursday

It is a really spring day with clear skies and balmy breezes. This morning both the Youree and the Brownie were closed, so I went to Nora's Café for two cups of coffee, cookies, and two Baby Ruths. The old janitor who cleans the JBU buildings gave me, as usual, a ride to the Hill. We reached the Hill the moment Dr. Saleski was emerging from the cemetery where she takes her daily morning walk. She is the professor of modern language and successor to Pamblad and Mrs. Guernsey.

March 24, 1946, Sunday

God has wonderfully preserved me and guided me! He has guided me with a strong hand from Cyprus through the misery of Greek-American school, through the long years of the supposed meaningless and purposeless studies to this present position, from which I can see new, wide horizons of usefulness and service. It is so easy to get discouraged, being the only foreigner on the faculty and having students and some members of the faculty making fun of my pronunciation, or telling me that I would be better off teaching Greek than English.

March 26, 1946, Tuesday

Sh. is still away in Ohio, and Wills is leaving for St. Louis, Missouri, to attend one of the educational meetings. Mr. Haley has left for Chicago to attend Central College. The weather is fair and warm, and for the first time in my life my month's salary is 190 dollars. It's not much, considering my degrees and education, but it is in some respects more than I deserve. After all, I'm plagued with a terrible accent; I'm neither eloquent nor intelligent nor well informed as professors of English go. I'll keep quiet, thank God, work hard, and behave. Exactly ten years ago, I was making only 75 dollars a month teaching Greek to the children of the immigrants in New Brunswick, New Jersey.

March 27, 1946, Wednesday

Tonight Soviet Russia walked out of the UNO over the Iran question. In my opinion, the delegates of the other ten nations have been unduly severe. Russia promised to get out of Iran by April 30, and she regarded the problem as closed. But, unfortunately, the British and American delegates wanted explanation and investigation. They apparently don't care very much about peace as much as they care about humiliating a nation that fought on their side against Hitler for three long years. We certainly treat the Russians not as allies but as enemies. We have become a little arrogant and dictatorial since we have developed the atomic bomb. Most of us have scarcely gotten out of our uniforms, and our politicians are starting a new war. Most of us thought that once the totalitarian states were crushed, we should live at peace the rest of our lives. We have already lived through two world wars and half a dozen small wars. But now we discover Russia and communism, and we begin to prepare to crush them. And after that, we will probably discover China and

Yellow Peril and so ad infinitum. It seems that a madness innate and inexplicable drives mankind toward suicide and self-slaughter.

March 30, 1946, Saturday

It is the first really warm day of the year. Most boys appeared on campus in shirtsleeves. The sky was of the loveliest blue, and the grass was of the most soothing green. I bought Stag Shaving Lotion and Stag Perfumed Hand Oil in order to improve my looks. I need a new suit of clothes, and it is almost impossible to get one as things are now. Anyhow, as always, one should take care of one's soul and skin, and the other things will take care of themselves.

Miss Luella Smith gave me a ride to town in the President's car. Three other pretty young ladies who live in the guesthouse were with her. They are really pretty and well dressed, and I guess they must be lonesome because there are no men of their age and station in life to take them out for rides or meals. They are like beautiful flowers, sighing and smelling, unseen and untouched in the wilderness.

April 5, 1946, Friday

The weather is ideal for elegant idleness. I received a letter from B. He hints that he is suffering the effects of his campaign in Leyte Island. He was very cynical and pessimistic before he was drafted, but by now he maintains that he lost his faith in both God and man. There was no hint why he resides in Nashville, Tennessee, nor how he is earning his living.

I'm glad that the Iranian question has been settled so the UNO can go ahead with its work of creating eternal peace on our troubled planet.

April 6, 1946, Saturday

It seems that as one advances in years, one must be more careful about his physical and mental condition. One must do his work and never worry. One must work hard and behave. Still the two roads to salvation must be traveled: the road of self-improvement and the road of service. Life is short and uncertain, but two things are certain: one must love himself, and one must love his neighbor; one must try to improve himself and others. As Johnson phrased it, let us be kind to one another.

April 8, 1946, Monday

While looking for summer underwear, I met Mr. Stout, who runs the Penney's store, and he confidentially informed me that he received five or six suits of clothes. Since all were of the same color, I did not have much choice. One in size 38 fit me perfectly. It is not so good a suit to deserve the 34 dollars I paid for it, but I need a suit of clothes desperately, and I can't be a chooser. Now my problem is whether or not I'll muster courage enough to put on a gray suit in the middle of a semester and appear in front of my students in an entire new color ensemble. Some of my colleagues change suits almost every day, but somehow I'm averse to changing into a whole new suit of clothes myself. I feel ill at ease and embarrassed. It must be the result of my childhood experience when I was so poor that a new suit of clothes was much noticed and commented on. It is strange how our responses are conditioned by early childhood experiences. All of us are far from logical. We are emotional. I wrote a short letter to B., and I enclosed three clippings: one of which, I'm afraid, will revive his flame for F., whose marriage is narrated with the silly description of dresses, flowers, and ceremonies.

April 12, 1946, Friday

It is very difficult to tell whether I'm happy or unhappy at this moment. I'm certainly too busy lecturing, correcting papers, and preparing my lessons to worry about the future or shed tears over the past. One should live wholly in the present. I wish I could get rid of my foreign accent. It seems almost impossible, and yet nothing is impossible to a man who can will. Not only my accent needs improvement but also my grammar and syntax. I'm still guilty of the most atrocious and obvious mistakes. I'm still using the present tense instead of the past tense, and I always get my time sequence mixed up. But all these difficulties will be conquered. Concentration and practice will win me the race.

April 15, 1946, Monday

Yesterday I went to chapel, where I heard a minister talk on the mission to the Lepers. On Saturday evening I went to chapel, where I heard Dr. Woodland, of our own faculty, give a lecture on the Atomic Bomb. It seemed to be easy to construct a bomb if one gets the right kinds of uranium, finds the right kind of moderator, and constructs the right kind of cyclotron. Of course, the expense seems to be prohibitive and the materials very hard to get. But men who will not spend money on education and sanitation will certainly cheerfully vote billions of dollars to develop, perfect, and speed the production of the atomic bomb.

Last night I had a dream that I might use as a starting point for a short story or a novel. I dreamt that I was the survivor of three or four brothers. And on my return home, the wives of my deceased brothers who apparently perished in the war were courting me, especially one with dark hair, dark eyes, and a woebegone face. How on earth I dreamt of sisters-in-law is beyond me. I've two brothers-in-law, but as far as I know, I don't have any sisters-in-law. But, of course, there is neither rhyme nor reason in dreams.

April 18, 1946, Thursday

I received two letters: one from home, from my sister who is now called Mrs. Teggeraki for reasons hard to explain since her husband's name is Christopides. She wants me to advise her son Byron to pay more attention to his lessons since his grades are very poor. Well, I don't know what influence an uncle can have on a nephew he has not seen! I'll probably write a letter to my brother Takis and mention this fact to him. He will probably be able to exert some pressure on him. The other letter is from B.

April 19, 1946, Friday

It is Good Friday. I spent it reading, teaching, and relaxing. In Greece the Royalists got the government in their hands, and on the question of Spain, the Allies have split: Russia, France, Poland, and Mexico want the UN to sever diplomatic relations with Spain, while England, Holland, and probably the United States advocate a hands-off policy. Under both situations lies the fear of England. The communists have expanded to the shores of the Mediterranean, and as a result, poor Greece is going to be saddled with a good-for-nothing king and get a reactionary government. And the unfortunate Spain is going to be ruled by a Fascist dictator imposed upon her by Hitler and Mussolini. According to the British, a King and a dictator are good for Greece and Spain as long as their interests are protected, and yet millions of soldiers from all races and nations sweated, bled, and died with the hope that the scourge of kings and dictators might pan away from the face of the

Earth. But a Mikado, a Franco, and a Chiang are kept in power by us and the British, and any person who advocates their removal is branded a red communist, or at least radical.

This is the first Easter I'm spending as a civilian. I spent the last three in the Army: the first at Camp Robinson and the others at Camp Crowder. Even the holidays didn't seem like holidays when one has lost freedom of action and motion. The Army always allowed three hours in the afternoon for religious observances, but I never availed myself of the opportunity. I stayed in the barracks and read a book and probably went to the motion pictures. The Army chaplains never impressed me as either sincere or ardent Christians. It was pleasant and profitable to be an officer and live comfortably with so vague and undefined duties that almost amounted to no more than an hour's service on Sunday. They were supposed to help the poor soldiers, but their power and intention was limited by the authorities. They were just tolerated by the Army because the American public would not hear of an Army without chaplains. The fact that their sons, husbands, brothers, and even sisters were carefully trained in the art of killing did not bother their conscience at all. But to have no chaplains to bless them and comfort them was too much for them.

May 10, 1946, Friday

Exactly one year after V-E-Day, almost every soldier and sailor is back home, but the Allied leaders are disagreeing in Paris, and the nation is nearing industrial paralysis on account of the coal miners' prolonged strike. Our civilization is indeed very flimsy if a few thousands of workers can disorganize and paralyze it. What will happen if not only the coal miners but also the railroad and factory men strike? The world is desperately in need of social justice at home and peace on earth! And yet most men are pursuing their own petty and insignificant affairs, forgetting that they build their houses on the sand if security and peace are not first. It is like building a roof without first building a wall or beams to support it.

May 14, 1946, Tuesday

I spent the day teaching, reading, and correcting papers. It has cleared and turned warmer. I was driven to town by a man who four years ago traveled to Little Rock to the Reception Center with me. He stayed in the Army only five months. Felix Olin has also been discharged from the Army. I saw him in civilian clothes, walking down Main Street, but I've not talked with him yet. It is the first glimpse I've caught of him since the memorable day he left Camp Robinson for a Georgia camp. He later became a transport officer and crossed the Atlantic 17 times. Now that the war is over and almost everyone is back home, the Army life seems like a thing of the past and unreal.

May 20, 1946, Monday

Yesterday I went to chapel. Dr. Brown preached a baccalaureate sermon. Daniel, who refused to obey man, obeyed God and was thrown into the lions' den, but the lions did not touch him. I rather like the explanation given by the Negro preacher in "Ol' Adam and his Chilun" that King Darius liked Daniel very much, and, therefore, he fed the lions before he cast him among them. But Dr. Brown said that Daniel at that time was ninety years old. I don't blame the lions for not spoiling their appetite by devouring a ninety-year-old man.

Today I received a registered letter from Wad-Medani, Sudan, Africa, where my eldest sister lives. She also sent me three pictures of her six-year-old daughter. The girl looks pretty and neat, and from the reading of the letter I concluded that both the parents worship her. I'll look up Wad-Medani, Sudan, on the map tomorrow. It is curious how my sister lives in a town whose name she'd never heard of. I hope that someday she will return to Cyprus. I must thank God for taking such wonderful care of my brother and sisters.

May 25, 1946, Saturday

Yesterday it rained heavily all afternoon. Some damage was inflicted by the storm on some neighboring towns. The railroad strike is the subject of the day. President Truman threatens that he will order the Army to take over and run the railroads of the country. It is a vain threat. The Army can't run anything when the labor men don't consent to cooperate. It is also a dangerous threat. The time may come when the Army will refuse to take over the mines, plants, and railroads. And that will be the end of the government. The best plan is nationalization of the mines, railroads, and other utilities. It is time that public service, and not private profit, must become the guiding principle of the business of this nation!

May 27, 1946, Monday

Exactly one year ago today I was discharged from the Army. At the end of my first year of freedom, I really have nothing worthwhile to show. I saved about 1,000 dollars. I read about 50 books. I tried to write two or three novels. I ate many meals. I taught and lectured, but the total sum of my activities almost equals zero. A man must be judged not by what he does or earns but by what he creates. And I have created nothing tangible, neither a book nor a baby! But there is no reason, nor excuse, for despair. Slowly, painfully, I'm groping toward self-expression. My philosophy of life is becoming a kind of religion. I want to spread it among my fellowmen. I want them to share my desire for peace of mind, peace on earth, unity of mankind, pursuit of knowledge, and practice of virtue. My insight into human nature is deepening and widening; my knowledge of forms of literature is becoming more intimate and inspiring. If I don't weaken, if I keep on working cheerfully and courageously, I shall realize my aspirations. This being my week of vacation between terms, I'm enjoying myself, reading on the porch, eating good meals, and taking walks. My world-lust powerfully urges me to travel, but I must resist temptation. There is no use in going somewhere for four or five days. What I need is a two-month vacation to do some reading and replenish my mind with new ideas about the subjects I teach.

May 28, 1946, Tuesday

The railroad strike is a thing of the past, but the coal miners' strike is still on. It is expected to end today. It has lasted about 45 days and literally paralyzed the nation. Some are supporting the President's stand, but others are still in favor of the labor unions. I guess the politicians got scared about their precious political careers. They know that the unions are strong enough to defeat any politicians if they bend their effort toward that end. Democracy is a good country to live in, but it is a hard country to run. It requires infinite patience, insight and, above all, spinelessness. I'm, of course, in favor of the unions and the workers, but I have been their friend since childhood, and I'm likely radical or red on account of my siding with them. I have everything to lose and nothing to gain by taking sides. I must be impartial, and then my criticism may be both penetrating and disturbing. Life is short; art is long.

May 30, 1946, Thursday

Today we, the Americans with our banks bulging with money and our atomic bomb, sneer at the efforts of other nations. We must be able to help others and profit by the efforts of others! I started walking up the Hill; the sky, however, looked threatening, so I walked in town for a few minutes and returned home. Well, I'll read a while and then go to bed. This is my vacation week. I must take it easy and relax. I must think more and read less as I advance in years! Above all, I must develop the habit of writing. My future depends on writing.

I have not yet developed a theory either of life or art. I'm not an original scholar. I'm simply a repeater and a digester. In politics I have reached the conclusion that I must work for the brotherhood of nations and the unity of the human race—the one-fold, one-shepherd idea. In private life I've reached the conclusion that I am here to improve myself and to serve God and others. As a way of life I embrace plain living and high thinking. I esteem leisure, health, and freedom as the most precious treasures a man can possess. Leisure must be used for play and learning. Freedom enables one to say what he thinks, to be sincere and never practice moral cowardice and intellectual dishonesty. I believe in creative work, work that improves me and serves others at the same time. In dealings with my fellow men, I seek to love everybody and have no prejudices. Regarding sex, I believe that marriage as it is practiced today is compatible with neither contemplative nor adventurous life. Celibacy, however, has no joys, and burning is just as bad as providing for a family. These are some of the ideas that underlie my philosophy of life. Will it fit everyone because it fits me? Of course, each one must build his own rock. I can only point the way.

June 1, 1946, Saturday

It is cool and partly cloudy. It is ideal weather for working and walking. I ought to have written some letters this week, but proverbial procrastination got the better of me. I owe a letter to my brother and sisters and one to Dr. Martin. I guess some afternoon next week I'll buy some paper and envelopes and answer those letters. Sometimes I'm ashamed of my aversion to letter writing. It is both painful and difficult writing letters to a brother and sisters one has not seen for 26 years! How time flies! It seems like yesterday when I left Nicosia on May 14, 1920, and started my trip to America! Time and space make fools of us all!

June 3, 1946, Monday

It is registration day. Like a fool, I rushed to be on the Hill before 7 o'clock to be told that registration would not start until 8 a.m. I put on my new gray suit. I felt clothes-conscious and uncomfortable. Well, everybody has seen me in my new suit, and the ordeal is over. Tomorrow at noon I'm invited to talk to the Rotarians. I'll tell them some things about the Russians as recorded by W. L. White in his book, *A Report on the Russians*. I also have to meet my class at 1 o'clock, and that makes it very awkward; but I told Miss Sh. to tell the students to wait for me. I'll take my time and give a good report.

June 4, 1946, Tuesday

I spoke to the Rotarians at noon today. I told them briefly about the size, population, farms, factories, diet, government, and schools of the Soviet Union. I got most of my information from *Report on the Russians* by W. L. White. They said they liked it. I frankly don't care. I'm not an entertainer. I enjoyed the meal and the companionship and shook hands with many old, prominent men of the town. They are the salt of the earth and the light of the business world. They are successful men; they are in business and have homes, shops, cars, farms, and bonds. The late poet Robinson once remarked that the successful men of the country do not live at all. Of course, they consume good food, they wear expensive clothes, and they distribute goods, but their esthetic, mystic, and, I am afraid, moral sense are not developed. I doubt if they can read a newspaper intelligently. They are practical men with their eyes on the ledger rather than on heaven, even the preachers who attended the meeting. They looked like successful businessmen.

June 7, 1946, Friday

I wish I could get hold of some great books. But the city and the college libraries are pitifully poor. The city library gets only popular books, i.e. dead books for men and women who fear to live. The college library has ceased to buy any books since before the war. The present library building is not fireproof, and the new library building is not yet on the architects' blueprints. Meantime, I'll reread all the famous plays and novels of the present and lay the foundation for a vigorous and fruitful advance!

June 28, 1946, Friday

Tonight I met Dr. Swann by accident at Brownie's Café. He was in a communicative mood. He had bought a shirt at the Pyatte's and spent seven dollars for a ten-minute talk over the telephone with his wife in Virginia. He told me that his wife is awfully jealous, although she had no reason to be, and that she was at the point of breaking the contract with JBU and not coming to work here. Nietzsche said that a married philosopher belongs to comedy, and here is a philosopher saddled with a jealous wife and two grown-up girls, trying to be the light of the world. A philosopher and a professor must at least have a rest from the things of the day. Every time I talk to Dr. S., I call to my mind Dr. Hale. He is over 65 years old and has neither wife nor children. He is a confirmed bachelor.

July 3, 1946, Wednesday

I felt for the first time the effects of the removal of the OPA ceilings on food. A meal that three days ago cost me only 45 cents tonight cost me 67. The price of milk went up to seven cents a pint. Well, I hope that the prices don't begin to skyrocket. We will then get inflation, a boom, and then a bust. People's greediness is still the most powerful social motive or agent. Everybody in the country is fairly prosperous; but, of course, the merchants could not be satisfied with moderate profits. There were no shoes, no shirts, no suits of clothes, and no cars on the market. The manufacturers simply refuse to flood the market with goods; the prices were too low for big projects. They created scarcity and black markets. They forced the administration to repeal OPA ceilings; the President vetoed the bill. This orgy of profiteering may put an end to this profit system; it may usher in a new age: not profit but service should be the watchword. Meantime, the poor salaried people will suffer, and worries will sour the disposition and digestion of millions.

I saw Dr. Wills, who promised me that there would be no high school teaching for me by next fall. I hope that he abides by his word. I don't particularly like the idea of teaching high school youngsters. Their minds are on play and sex. Well, I'll undress and go to bed. I need rest and sleep. I usually get up at 4:30 a.m. That's much earlier than I used to get up in the Army. The early bird, however, is supposed to catch the worms if not the germs.

July 5, 1946, Friday

I spent the glorious Fourth reading Goethe's *Faust* and visiting Sh. and the Cooks. After a good chicken dinner, Dr. Cook gave us a ride to the lake newly formed by the building of the dam. The county looked green and clean. I returned home about 9:30 and immediately went to bed. Today I taught as usual and started reading Huskins' *Education of Freedom*. I'm in thorough agreement with him regarding liberal education and the division of the educational process with six years of elementary, four of high school, and four of college. He also advocates giving a B.A. at the end of what we now call the sophomore year. His plans will get rid of the students who come to college for a B.A. degree at the age of 18 or 20 and devote more time to the few students who care for university training and are prepared for it. I also agree with him in condemning the vocational informational system now prevailing in all institutions of higher learning.

July 11, 1946, Thursday

A few clouds and a 10-minute shower have broken the terrific heat that had tyrannized over us since the Fourth of July. I've just finished Sinclair Lewis' *Elmer Gantry*. I read the novel about twenty years ago. At that time I did not have the slightest idea of the religious life of America with its Baptists, Methodists, Presbyterian Evangelists, and whatnot. My interest in religion has always been extremely mild. But since 1939, for good or ill, I've been teaching English in an institution that advertises itself as "decidedly evangelical," and necessity has compelled me to come in touch with preachers, the so-called ministerial professors, and soul-savers. The book seems to have been written after very careful study of the religious activities and delusions of many Americans. The hero, Elmer, is a scoundrel; he is a conscious hypocrite, suffering from intellectual dishonesty and moral cowardice. But as usual, ignorance and imprudence have made him notorious. As the story ends, he is on his way to New York City to assume the pastorate for a very rich church and the presidency of an association, the aim of which is to suppress vice. At the bottom of the success of such a scoundrel lies the undeniable faith that the masses are ignorant and superstitious. They are not educated enough to distinguish a villain from a saint. As a matter of fact, the decent and sincere preachers suffer on account of their candid and straightforward utterances. This novel best exemplifies the theory that American civilization is hostile to pleasure and art; it is essentially moral and puritanical. It also points out that the worship of monetary success has extended the church and turned our preachers from servants of God into servants of Mammon. Hence the eagerness of the average preacher to own a car, a home, and a beautiful wife and to spread enslaving dogmas. In the noise of the choirs and the splendor of the buildings, the Christianity of Christ has been entirely forgotten and neglected. Churchgoing and ritual have taken the place of good deeds and brotherhood of man. The pillars of the church are in many respects the exploiters of the poor and the enemies of progress.

July 22, 1946, Monday

I've not written in this diary for some time. The summer's dry heat has taken away all ambition for walking, doing bending exercises, or even eating. Nothing unusual or extraordinary has happened. Bitzer phoned from Tulsa that he was coming to Siloam for a visit, but somehow he could not make it on account of his plane connections. Sh.'s sister and family have been in Siloam since Saturday. They are on a camping trip.

Yesterday and the day before, I fulfilled the duties of the chaperone. The task of the chaperone is as easy as it is boring. He sits in the California building lobby and waits for the silent, slow hours to go by. He occasionally takes a walk around the campus to "beat the bushes" and stops at the Coffee Shop for a cold drink or a cone of ice cream. At 5:15 he takes his supper consisting of the remnants or the remains of the noon meal, and he reads a paper or magazine and waits for the 7 o'clock evening service, which is conducted in the open air of the Guest House Lawn.

August 5, 1946, Monday

Yesterday, Sunday, I rode with the Ingrams and Sh. to Fayetteville and Fort Smith. On the way, we stopped at Mount Gaylor. It has been some time since I've taken a long trip. On our way back, we deposited Sh. at the Ye Ark Hall, where she will stay for fifteen days, attending what we call "the workshop." We had a little difficulty in locating the hall; it was not really a hall but apartments over a theater and the University Cafeteria. It was rather late when I reached my room. At noon yesterday, I attended chapel. Dr. Brown preached a sermon entitled "Little by little, I will establish you."

August 12, 1946, Monday

It is Monday morning, cool and cloudy. I'm sitting on the swing on the porch of 1005 Wright Street. A problem that has been long bothering me has become a little clearer to me. I often wondered why most people drink, smoke, go to the motion pictures, play games, gamble, and make noise. These are "make-believers." They are either unable or unwilling to find pleasure or happiness in the solid things of life. They can't see beauty in nature or in real art (literature, music, painting, sculpture), and that's why they rush to these "make-believers." Another source of their misery is selfishness. They are either unwilling or unable to serve others, to spread sweetness and light around them. They are egocentric; they are no fellow workers of God in building the Kingdom of Heaven on Earth. The best way to banish the social evils from the face of the earth is to educate men and women for enjoyment in nature and art and in self-sacrifice rather than selfishness. People will then have plenty to do: hiking, traveling, flying, and examining plants, animals, and minerals. They will have a good time reading great books, seeing shows, and listening to glorious music. They will lose themselves in taking care of the children, the sick people, and the aged; they will simply have no time to waste on cards, wine, or even love.

August 19, 1946, Monday

The weather is still hot and clear. It has not rained since the Fourth of July, and the grass is withered, the creeks are almost dry, and the paths and streets are dusty. It reminds me of the long, dry summers of my native island. I kept on teaching and reading. I'm planning to take a ten-day vacation, God willing. I'll probably spend it in a big city like Kansas City, shopping, eating, sleeping, and going to the shows. I also want to do some reading, but it is impossible to do a decent amount of reading in ten days. Besides that, my eyes get tired easily when the type is small. The valley across from the Guesthouse has been filled with homes for the members of the faculty. Everybody seems surprised that I did not buy one. I am simply not going to tie myself to houses and women. My aim has always been, and still is, the pursuit of knowledge and the practice of virtue; one can't afford to be either wise or virtuous when burdened with houses and women. By virtuous, I don't mean theft and adultery but instead intellectual honesty and moral bravery.

September 2, 1946, Monday: Labor Day

Summer session ended last Saturday, August 31. It was a rather funny session. I taught mostly high school English. My college classes were too small to meet more than two or three times a week. Anyhow, I drew the salary and saved a few dollars for a rainy day. I'm at present on vacation. I intend to take a trip to Kansas City just for shopping, seeing one or two shows and consulting the library catalogue for new books on my subject. I don't expect to do any reading. Dr. Brown's health has been the subject of many discussions, rumors, and fears. It is rumored that he suffers from diabetes and gallstones and that the doctor cannot operate for gallstones on account of the diabetic condition. One must remember only one thing: One must not prophesy about one's health.

There was unusual activity on the campus during the last two weeks: the dusty, stony paths are paved, new housing units have been erected, new apartments for GI's are in the process of being built, and the work on the Cathedral has advanced considerably. Even the enrollment of both college and high school students is unusually big.

September 3, 1946, Tuesday

Today I read in the papers that the Greeks voted to restore

the monarchy. The Royalists, backed by England, won the elections. It is an anachronism in the days of democracy and communism, but England, of course, is afraid of the spread of communism to the shores of the Mediterranean; therefore, the Greeks must love a king and the Spanish, a dictator.

It has been cool and clear. It was a joy sitting on the porch. I'll probably take a trip to Kansas City next week just to break the monotony of reading, walking, and sleeping. I have grown so fond of comfort that I'm averse to undergo the petty inconvenience of a five-hour railroad trip. And yet three years ago at this time, I traveled under miserable conditions with the German and Italian prisoners from Staten Island to North Carolina and back and from Staten Island to McAlester, Oklahoma, and Little Rock.

September 7, 1946, Saturday

As a professor of English, I'm blissfully ignorant of the noble art of reading. I read masterpieces of English literature for information rather than understanding. I ask my students superficial questions, which they answer easily and creditably. I stuff their minds; I don't enlighten them. Most students don't even bother to read the assignments. They take some notes, and on the quizzes and tests they simply repeat my own words in a slightly altered fashion. I feel flattered and honored; therefore, I give them a passing grade. I must at least teach my students how to read, i.e. how to derive profit and pleasure from the printed page. My colleagues are ardent evangelists; they preach salvation and redemption. Why don't I become an ardent evangelist of the art of reading—the best way toward self-development and profitable leisure? I love reading; I ought to infect others with my love. I must be able to interest and inspire them. Late in the afternoon I took a long walk in town. I walked to the railroad station and then down to the new Millsap "Foodliner" and back home. The town has been enriched by half a dozen decent buildings recently: The Ozark Pasteurizing Plant, the New Theater, the T.H. Machine Store, the Jones Store, the Wer Ford Store, etc. The town is assuming the airs of a city, but still behind the houses are the inevitable chicken coops, and the grass lines the sidewalks of many an unpaved street. The town with its Twin Springs and hilly landscapes resembles my native village Cythred with its famous "fountainhead," issuing from the bowels of the Five-Fingered Mountain. This town is much cleaner. It has all the convenience and comforts of civilized life, while Cythred is without waterworks, a sewage system, hospital, high school, etc. It's more picturesque with its orange, lemon, and olive groves stretching from the plain to the slopes of the mountain. It needs only modern plumbing to turn it into an earthly paradise. No wonder Venus, the goddess of love and beauty, used to haunt its groves and streams. In the ancient times, with its white marble temple, spacious baths, and stadium, the place ought to have been a pleasant abode for gods and men.

September 15, 1946, Sunday

I spent the last week (to be exact, from Monday, September 9, to Friday, September 13) in Kansas City, Missouri. I stayed at the Plaza Hotel, room 907. I paid two dollars a night. I explored the vast metropolis of the Midwest by riding streetcars and busses. I visited the immense stockyards, the spacious Swope Park and its zoo, Kansas City, Kansas, Independence, and the library. I ate at cafeterias and vast drugstores. I saw three good shows: *The Notorious, Monsieur Beaucaire,* and *Anne and the King of Siam.* I got a list of books from the library. I hope to get Dr. Wills to order them for our library so I'll then be able to increase my knowledge at the expense of the school. My income is too small to allow me to buy the books that I need. I also visited the campus of the University of Kansas City. It is too small a campus to be compared with the mighty campuses of the University of Minnesota, Columbia, Harvard, or Princeton, but it is a much larger campus than that of our John Brown University.

.Last night I attended the charivari given by the faculty and students to Dr. White, who at last married the woman with whom he was going during the last ten or twenty years. A bevy of pretty girls brought him (with his bride) to the flagpole with rope around his neck. They intended to hang him, I guess, for not marrying earlier. Then they made him trundle the bride in a small low-wheeled vehicle to the Home Economics building, where Mr. Springfield performed a mock wedding with many jokes and allusions to White's weaknesses and pet ideas. After the mock ceremony, the newlyweds were presented with a cooking vessel and a reading lamp—both good, expensive presents.

September 16, 1946, Monday

It is clear and cool. It seems that winter is around the corner. We are starting the fall semester next Wednesday. We are expecting a large enrollment. We moved houses from Pryor and almost formed a new village between highway 33 and the Oak Land Cemetery. I must never lose sight of my goal in life. Otherwise, I'll lose my way also, and I'll drift instead of steering and live in hell rather than heaven, for as G. B. Shaw remarked, "to drift is to be in hell, and to steer is to be in heaven."

September 17, 1946, Tuesday

I walked up the Hill about 2 o'clock. I was supposed to go with my colleagues to the Baptist Assembly Grounds for a picnic. On account of the weather, the picnic was called off at noon. Mr. Haley drove me to town. I ate a fried chicken sandwich at 75 cents.

Today is my last day of vacation. Tomorrow I have to report for a faculty and staff meeting at 8 o'clock. As the new semester starts, I pray to God that I'll be given health, happiness, and success in my efforts to spread sweetness and light. Literature ought to be the backbone of the education of the Democratic man. Most people today are practical rather than idealistic. They want to learn a trade in order to earn a comfortable living, marry a girl, and lose themselves in the worries of the family life. Sex and food, or rather, love and hunger, play havoc with the education of the modern man. These desires ought to be satisfied without the sacrifice of the higher life. They are the needs of survival; by this time, they ought to give way to the needs of fulfillment.

September 25, 1946, Wednesday

We registered about 400 students and started classes last Monday. My schedule is both light and easy. I start working at 9 a.m. Three afternoons I finish at 3 p.m. I'm offering English Literature, Shakespeare, Milton, American Literature, and High School English IV.

My intention is to become one of the best teachers of English literature on this continent. I've always envied Kittredge, Lowes, Thorndike, Phelps, and other great professors. All of them except Lowes are dead. Some of us must step into their shoes and carry on the fight for the perpetuation of knowledge of the masterpieces of the American and English writers.

September 27, 1946, Friday

For a change, I took a nap at noon. It was rather hot, and I was literally worn out after three continuous hours of lecturing. It seems that I don't have the stamina and the bodily strength I used to have six years ago. At that time, I used to teach for four consecutive hours without even going to the toilet room for natural needs. Well, I guess I have to slow down. I'm no longer in my thirties. I'm in my late forties. At the same time, I don't like to acquire the habits of old age. In some ways I feel that, just now, I'm beginning to live the experience of getting an education and securing a job; serving the country as a buck private lies behind me.

September 28, 1946, Saturday

Today being Saturday I taught three hours and loafed the rest of the day. It seems that I've developed a knack for killing time. I no longer read "a hundred pages" a day. I browse among magazines and newspapers and like to gossip. That represents a desire for death. I must pull myself together and get down to work. It does not become an educated person to waste his time and energy in simply doing nothing. My program is light, my classes are small, I'm still young, and I don't see why it should be an abatement of effort. I must be true to myself; I must still be cheerful and courageous and try to realize my aspirations!

September 30, 1946, Monday

Yesterday I chaperoned with Sh. I did not overexert myself. I walked around the campus in the warm sunshine. After a meal at the dining hall, Dr. White and Mrs. White walked with me to Dr. Hale's "air-castle," as he calls the GI house he bought for about 2,000 dollars. We found Dr. Hale at home and inspected his not-so-clean rooms; the bed was unmade, the silver was lying on the table, and soot was mingling with the sugar in his uncovered sugar bowl. A bachelor who keeps house, like a married philosopher, belongs to comedy. After the inspection of his house, he joined us in a visit to the apartments that are being built for the GI's who attend our university.

When I walked to town, I was saved from stepping on a snake crawling across the highway by the headlights of an approaching car. Yesterday being a rather hot day, the snakes were out. I saw three or four during the afternoon. They were crushed by the speeding cars, apparently while seeking the roadbed for a sunning bath. After eating a dish of ice cream at Chandler's, I walked home and went immediately to bed. I slept soundly till 6 o'clock. I got up, shaved, bathed, and walked up the Hill. I taught for three continuous hours and spent the afternoon reading *Abraham Lincoln*. He was really a great man. Poor humanity is very rarely blessed with such a kind and capable man. As a rule, our capable men are either ruthless or hypocrites, ambitious, or downright scoundrels. They are not meek, humble, or kindhearted. Lincoln is a perfect example of right and might combined, of kindness and ability united, of wisdom and goodness mixed in good proportion.

October 2, 1946, Tuesday

Last night I attended a faculty meeting. We discussed all kinds of subjects from membership in AEA to closing the windows and turning off the lights of the classrooms. I was appointed chairman of the Library Committee. I don't have the slightest idea what kind of duties or responsibilities this "honor" involves. I returned home about 9:30 and immediately went to bed. Today I attended chapel. Dr. Brown talked about plans for improving the food and facilities and about building two magnificent buildings in addition to the Cathedral of the Ozarks. Of course, he also talked about raising half a million dollars.

October 4, 1946, Friday

I received a new contract. My salary has been raised to 225 dollars a month, a most unexpected and agreeable raise. This is the highest salary I've ever earned. Dr. Brown, however, indirectly gave me to understand that I have to attend the famous Wednesday evening prayer meetings at the Blood Memorial Building. He approached me this noon and playfully said that out of the eight doctors on the staff, I was the only one cutting the meetings. Well, I guess I've got to imitate my friend Dr. Hale and go there occasionally, even if the affair is not very agreeable to me.

October 5, 1946, Saturday

It is a warm, balmy, but somewhat dusty day. I spent it teaching, reading, and walking. I sat on the porch and read *A Yankee From Olympus*. I had two interruptions. Bernice—or rather Mrs. Dunwoody—happened to pass by and visited for a few minutes. She looked enlarged but not aged. She and her husband are running a store in the lobby of a hotel. They had just bought a new house, and she had come for a visit to her parents. Miss Reese also visited me. I saw her early this morning and promised to buy a pound of Oleo for her at the U. store. Unfortunately, I could not get it, but when she called for it, we had a talk about Atlanta and Georgia. There was a crowd in front of the Millsap store this morning. They were anxious to secure some steaks or chickens. According to the papers, the country is suffering from an acute meat shortage. In this small village, however, the restaurants serve steaks, chicken, and oysters. I ate a nice steak sandwich with French-fried potatoes at 35 cents and washed it down with two glasses of ice-cold pasteurized milk. It was a very satisfactory meal and cost me, including the sales tax, exactly 50 cents.

Today the *Threefold Advocate* appeared for the first time this year. There was an item about me. According to the piece, the new professor of modern language, Dr. Floyd, was dying of curiosity to be introduced to Mrs. Panage at the recent faculty reception. She said that she had "met everybody except Mrs. Panage!"

October 11, 1946, Friday

It is the first night I'm spending at home since Monday. On Tuesday evening I visited Sh. On Wednesday evening I attended the faculty prayer meeting. Last night I took Sh. to supper. It is a cold, clear night. I lighted the gas stove and intend to put on my winter underwear tomorrow. Today I was shivering. It is about time I learned to mind my own "private affairs." I worry too much about my teaching. I go to school early, I'm always ahead of time, and I get upset about almost nothing.

October 16, 1946, Wednesday

At the faculty meeting Dr. Brown announced that he got a new manager of the store and that he is worrying over the finances of the institution. He said that the income is 20,000 dollars a month while its payroll is 21,000 dollars. He also mentioned the protest of three or four preacher boys who didn't like the motion picture that was presented to the student body last Saturday evening.

In the afternoon I read President Truman's speech concerning the meat shortage. It is a good speech; it blames "the few" for the wrecking of OPA ceiling prices. It is funny how the *Tulsa*

World, an avowedly Republican paper, announced that the popular opinion swept restrictions. Well, I hope that some day these gentlemen who own the papers and their hirelings who edit and write them will find that they don't represent the people. They represent the vested interests and are masquerading under the term of free press. Their aim is to perpetuate inequality of property and opportunity. They are not the mouthpieces of the people; they are its secret and insidious enemies.

October 21, 1946, Monday

I taught two hours and spent the rest of the day reading and dreaming. I attended Chapel yesterday afternoon. Dr. Smith preached a rather remarkable sermon for a Christian. He said that he had certain convictions or, better, certain habits, like not going to the movies and not visiting bathing beaches, but he did not think that a person who did those things was less Christian than he. It is about time the Christian world came to the conclusion that the better policy is to live and let live.

October 25, 1946, Friday

Today I talked with Miss Monks, who proudly wears a diamond engagement ring. She will marry a GI who, at present, studies dentistry at a Kansas City college. I tried to tease her by telling her of the dishwashing, dusting, cleaning, and cooking that are in store for her, but she bravely and proudly answered that "housekeeping is preferable to school teaching." I probably made her a little mad, so I'll make a point of being exceedingly nice to her next time I meet her. I also repeated the argument against marrying to Sh., whom I took to dinner at the Cozy Corner last night, and she also seemed not to appreciate my arguments against marriage. Well, let them marry! More power to them. I always maintain that it takes a brave man to stay a bachelor, but whether he marries or not, one must keep on improving himself and serving God and man.

October 28, 1946, Monday

It is still nice and warm, and I spent the afternoon reading on the porch. There were clouds, but the winds have scattered them, and tonight it is clear with the new moon like "a silver bow new bent in heaven."

October 30, 1946, Wednesday

Last night I took Sh. to supper at the Cozy Corner, and then we attended the faculty meeting at 204 Memorial Building. We elected a secretary, Mr. Montgomery, and an assistant, Mr. Wayne. We decided how many will go to Little Rock for the AEA meeting and listened to a report by Mr. Cox, who spent about four weeks last summer at a workshop study at Chicago University. I ate a good noon meal at the University dining hall and then returned to my room and spent the afternoon reading on the porch overlooking the lake. The temperature being nearly 80 degrees, I perspired in my winter underwear, but just the same I'll keep it on since no one can tell what the unpredictable weather of Arkansas has in store for us. I'm trying to return more to sincerity, silence, and solitude. Above all, I want to read 100 pages every day. Sometimes I don't read even twenty. I must never forget that self-improvement is the cornerstone of one's success.

November 2, 1946, Saturday

In the evening I walked the streets of the town up to the

"famous" Millsap "Food Liner." Everybody was shopping, including my friend Mr. Wootton. Married life must indeed be a pleasant condition since most of the married men spend most of their time earning money to buy groceries to feed their families. At the Youree I ate fried fresh trout. The trout was a very tiny piece, but it tasted good and seemed to be fresh. It cost me 60 cents. In the good old times, I used to eat a piece of cod, a trout in Boston, 10 times bigger in size and 10 times tastier for 25 cents. One of the privileges of living in a mighty country like the United States is that when salaries go up, prices go up, and when prices go down, salaries go down. It seems the height of folly to earn more and spend more. This is called "crash," or depression. In both cases the wage earners are in the same predicament. Owing, however, to the immense capacity of this country to produce, one can get plenty to eat in both cases, provided he is gainfully employed.

November 15, 1946, Friday

During the 11 days that have elapsed since I wrote in this diary, I've been to Little Rock, Arkansas, where I attended the Teachers Convention. I spent two delightful days there, loafing and roaming. I roomed with Dr. Wills at 256 W. G. Street, Park Hill. It was an excellent room with venetian blinds, soft beds, and modernistic fixtures and lights. Last Wednesday Dr. Wills, Miss Sh., Mr. Olney and I traveled to Pittsburgh, Kansas, where we visited the library of the Kansas Teachers College. The college buildings are spacious and majestic; the campus is as large as a village, but I noticed that the seats in the classrooms were not comfortable and that the classrooms themselves looked cheerless and bleak. There was a great number of Negro students of both sexes behaving like ordinary college students. We returned to Siloam Springs at 6:30 p.m. after a pleasant and uneventful ride through Neosho, Noel, Gravette, and Gentry.

November 18, 1946, Monday

Today the thermometer went down to 29 degrees. It was clear and cold, and for the first time this fall I put on my heavy winter overcoat. It felt good in the morning. In the afternoon the thermometer registered 70, and I had to carry my overcoat over my arm. These variations of temperature influence the character of the inhabitants of the country. They swing like pendulums from one extreme to the other. Their winters are icy cold; their summers are scorchingly hot, their mornings are chill; their afternoons are hot. No wonder a person who lives according to the golden mean has great difficulty understanding them.

November 20, 1946, Wednesday

This world of ours is a strange world. As things stand now, I don't know of any position or profession that can tolerate that rare virtue called intellectual honesty as integrity. Long ago Emerson said that a genius is a person who tells what he thinks and feels; i.e. he is sincere—be damned conformity and consistency, but today the verdict seems to be this: Be sincere and starve; be a conformist, i.e. a yes-man, and you will prosper. Economical insecurity has made cowards of us all. In the medieval times, within the state and the church, the policemen and the priests made cowards of men; today, after immense sacrifices of time, effort, and blood, we have declared our independence of church and state to find ourselves slaves of economics. With the same ease with which a rebel and nonconformist was sent to the stake in medieval times, now he is sent home to die of starvation. One by one our institutions—state, church, and schools—have succumbed to the power of economics. The noble men have simply been replaced by the financier; the serfs have become wage-slaves.

November 22, 1946, Friday

At 6 o'clock I supped on Italian meatballs and spaghetti at the new restaurant that opened last week, bearing the romantic name "Southern Grill." It is by far the best restaurant in town. The food is good, the service is prompt, and the atmosphere is clean, elegant, and rich. For some of us who have no home, the new restaurant is a blessing. This town has not been built for bachelors. There are no decent apartments for them to occupy. Until last week there was not even a decent restaurant for them to eat; they can't go out with a lady without being thought to be engaged to her if not secretly married. It seems that modern civilization is built on the proposition that all men must marry and support a family. For the few who are dedicated to a contemplative and adventurous life, no provision whatever has been made. They are looked upon as nomadic on the face of the earth, with the exemption of monks—who live solitary, studious lives. People feel sorry for them, and they feel sorry for people.

November 27, 1946, Wednesday

Today is Thanksgiving Day's Eve. It is clear and not very cold. I walked all the way from the Hill to the town with my overcoat on my arm. During the last week I attended service and faculty meetings. Everybody talks about the coal miners' strike. Our interest in the strike is academic. The village depends on natural gas for heating and cooling. I think only the Pet Milk Company uses coal. Even the train that connects the village with Kansas City and

New Orleans is diesel engined. Most of the people are in favor of the government or the coal mine proprietors and operators. I'm on the side of the strikers. I wish them success. They dig the coal for the comfort of the white nation. Without them, schools, trains, factories, and mills can't function. If they are as precious and as indispensable as the papers maintain, then we must pay them well and keep them interested. If they are not indispensable, let us dismiss them with scorn and jeers, the same way we scorn the teachers. Our civilization is indeed in a very bad condition. It can live without teachers, but it can't live one single month without coal miners. Coal is more indispensable than knowledge or wisdom.

November 29, 1946, Friday

Yesterday being Thanksgiving Day, I spent it reading and visiting at the Wills' and at Sh.'s. I ate a nice chicken dinner and then drove to the JBU airfield, where I saw Dr. Wills' father take his first air ride in a shining Encoupe. Mr. Jim Reed, the famous ace who had 50 flights over Germany to his credit, was at the controls. Mr. and Mrs. Cook and their aged mother joined the party later in the afternoon.

About 3 o'clock I went to the JBU Hospital to visit my friend Dr. Hale, who, according to some reports, had a stroke yesterday. The nurse told me that he'd already left the hospital, although as she phrased it, "He ought not to have left it." He is quite an old man and suffers from high blood pressure. He is undoubtedly overworking for his age and physical condition. He ought to work half time and take it easy and relax. As somebody says, "old age itself is a disease."

November 30, 1946, Saturday

A cloudy, warm day. I taught as usual and loafed in the library, poring over magazines and newspapers. I met Dr. Hale on his way to his home. He was unshaved, wore no tie, and looked unkempt and unwashed. I simply told him to go back to bed and stay there until he'd gained complete recovery. Mrs. White was much concerned about him, but I don't see what we can do about a stubborn, eccentric old man. On my way home, a coed walked with me to town. She is the daughter of a man who is at present studying agriculture at the University of Arkansas. To my surprise, she asked me to lend her two dollars to buy material for a formal dress. I told a white lie to get out of the delicate situation. I don't mind lending money, but lending money to coeds is likely to get one into trouble. Everybody will put a wrong interpretation on the affair.

December 6, 1946, Friday

I'm curious to know how the coal miners' dispute is going to be settled. The coal miners have been fined 3,500,000 dollars and Lewis 10,000 dollars for contempt of court. The other labor leaders are supporting Lewis. If they back him by declaring a general strike, then the politicians who talk glibly about repealing labor acts will know that they are in power simply because the workers of this nation are either unwilling or unable to take the reins of the government. The workers produce all the goods we consume and use, dig our coal, and run our railroads, busses, planes, and ships. Without their cooperation, the products of the farm will rot in the country, and the factories will close. I think the government erred in siding with the operators against the miners. It's been made a tool of big interests, and in the eyes of the people it appears to be the oppressor of the poor miners who never share in the great prosperity of this country. As usual in cases like these, the labor leaders are pictured as anti-American and enemies of order and law. Underneath all this struggle about shortening the hours of working miners lies the vicious and well-planned strategy of the Republicans to break the union and abolish the privileges they had been accorded during the liberal administration of the late President Roosevelt. We are still a long way from solving the problem of social justice. We are still thinking too much of ourselves rather than the general good. We have not yet transformed ourselves from competitive to cooperative creatures. We are still ruled by the "law of the jungle."

December 11, 1946, Wednesday

It was announced today at Chapel that the Christmas vacation starts at noon, December 21, and ends at noon, December 30. It is a rather generous vacation as far as JBU is concerned. I don't plan to do any traveling. I'll get three or four great books from the library and spend my vacation in my room reading, resting, and writing. Winter is not the time for traveling. Once I traveled to Minneapolis, hit sub-zero weather, and was glad to return to the mild temperatures of Arkansas.

Meantime the coal miners' strike ended by Lewis' ordering the men back to work last Monday. By knowing when to retreat, Lewis showed that he is a great leader. The reactionaries, however, greeted his gesture as labor's defeat and are now pressing for legislation to curb the so-called dictatorial powers of the unions. I'm not at all surprised that the leisure money classes are not averse to limiting the privilege of the unions. What grieves and puzzles me is listening to workers or poor farmers declaring that Lewis ought to be placed before a firing squad. The task of the teacher and the uplifter of the masses is not only opposed by the big interests but also by the stupidity of the masses themselves. They are like sheep without a shepherd; they are easily led astray by patriotic and religious slogans. They can't think effectively; they can't discriminate values; they are likely to crucify and stone their own friends and protectors. As the years go by, men and women who are willing to sacrifice themselves for the uplifting of the masses get fewer and fewer. It takes noble and brave souls to undertake such a thankless and onerous task!

December 13, 1946, Friday

Last night I went to bed late. I attended a party at Sh.'s. The Fredericks were about one hour late. They told me that they usually go to bed after midnight. I took leave of them about 10 o'clock under the pretext that my landlady might lock me out since I did not notify her and had no key for the door. Mr. Frederick came from Minnesota as a new addition to the faculty. He teaches business courses. Mrs. Frederick is at present taking courses at the University of Arkansas toward her master's degree. Since there is a great scarcity of English teachers, she was assigned a section of freshman English. She wanted to consult Sh. on procedure and methods, and that's why Sh. invited her to her apartment.

December 18, 1946, Wednesday

On Monday evening by chance I met Mr. Olin, who invited me to his newly built home for a steak dinner. Exactly four years ago, we traveled together to the Reception Center to start our military career. He is married to a charming girl and has a charming little baby girl. He and I are the only alien corn in Siloam Springs.

He is a Jew; I'm a Cyprist. He married a Christian girl, so in a way he has been adopted by the natives.

I received two cards—one from Mildred Pool, who used to teach chemistry at JBU in 1941, and another from Dr. Mort, who used to live in Siloam. Both of these young ladies are at present studying osteopathy at a college in Kerrville, Kansas. It was very nice of them to remember a confirmed, aging bachelor. I guess on Friday I'll buy a few cards and mail them to my few friends.

I received a bundle of papers from home. Nothing memorable has happened to the quiet island of Cyprus. England has promised them a new constitution, and it has given amnesty to all the exiles who were expelled from Cyprus on account of the 1931-1936 rebellion. Poor Cypriots are too poor, ignorant, and unknown to receive justice or even claim justice. They are still chained by the past. Church and country alone imposed on them a kind of thinking and acting that's inimical to progress. They certainly need popular education, science, and industry to pull them out of the slough in which they have been wallowing since the fall of the Roman Empire. Malnutrition and a lack of sanitation have undermined their health; their leaders fail them. They look up and are not fed. They ask for bread and are given stones. Over all waves the British Flag, covering a multitude of iniquities, sins, and misery.

December 25, 1946, Wednesday, Christmas Day

It is a clear, sunshiny, warm day. I got up at 7 o'clock, put on the blue suit I bought in Kansas City last September and went to the Southern Grill for breakfast. I ate scrambled eggs and drank a cup of coffee. I returned to my room and conducted my regular mental exercise of reviewing some notes I've gathered from my miscellaneous reading. I'm now sitting in the window overlooking bare trees and brown gardens and scribbling these lines. Somehow on Christmas days one feels like indulging in recollection. I particularly remember my first Christmas in America in the distant year of 1920 (26 years ago), in Lynn, Mass., where I was teaching at the community school. I was still attending the Salem Normal School, boarding with an American family in Salem. I was in love and most miserable and wretched. They lie about youth; it is neither happy nor healthy. I was then tormented by passions I could scarcely control and by ambition that a century could not suffice to realize. I also remember my Christmases in Atlanta and Minneapolis. I also remember my three Christmases in the Army, two in Camp Robinson, 1942 and 1943 (one with the famous M.P. 766 and one with M.P. Headquarters) and one at Camp Crowder, Missouri, as a mail clerk for the famous B-31st company in 1944. How fast time flies! What grieves me is not the swift passing of time but instead my inability to achieve something mighty and sublime to conquer time!

December 30, 1946, Monday

Last day of Christmas vacation. It is one of the coldest days I've ever experienced in Arkansas. I stayed in my room with windows closed and stove in full force and read William Faulkner's *A Rose for Emily and Other Stories*. I also read two acts from Sh.'s *Measure for Measure* and reviewed my notes for my lectures tomorrow. Coming out of the Southern Grill, I met Dr. Mort. She looked pretty in her new hairdo and her fur coat. She will finish her studies next August and establish herself as a D.O. (Doctor of Osteopathy) in Siloam Springs. We used to correspond while I was in the Army but discontinued our correspondence because we did not want to hurt Sh., who roomed in the same house with her. I guess I'll go to bed early tonight and get up tomorrow rested and refreshed.

January 1, 1947, Wednesday

It is New Year's Day. I taught three hours in the morning and spent a quiet afternoon in my room reading the January edition of *Harpers' Magazine.* At 5:30 I went to the Southern Grill for supper. It was already dark, and snow began to fall rapidly and densely. After my supper I took a short walk through the snow. Before I reached home, one inch of snow was on my hat. If the snow continues to fall all night with the same velocity, we will have to dig ourselves out. For the New Year I want to keep two resolutions I picked up today while reading Milton's Sonnet "On My Arriving at the Age of Twenty-Three" with my high school seniors:

(1) I'll do everything I have to do in the best way I can.

(2) I'll behave as if the Lord were looking at me every moment.

Above all, I liked and dwelt on the verse: "Who best bear His mild yoke, serve Him best." This year by reading Milton's *Comus, Paradise Lost* and *Paradise Regained* with the college students and some sonnets with the high school students, I've become almost Miltonic. He is a kind of Jewish Greek who writes in English. He is a lover of beauty, and at the same time he pursues truth and practices virtue. Addison must have had Milton in mind when he created his new ideal gentleman made of the virtues of the Puritan and the culture of the Cavalier. He scorned delights and lived laborious days. Such must be the life of the average man. Today the average man tries to get the maximum of comfort with the minimum of efforts. He pursues delights and shuns labor.

January 3, 1947, Friday

It has been cold and snowy since New Year's Day. I had to phone for a taxi both today and yesterday to take me to the U. The streets are slippery, and it is extremely cold. Just now it is 13 degrees above, and according to the weatherman, it will fall to five or six degrees above before tomorrow morning. On account of the "foul ways," I get my supper at 4:30 or 5 o'clock so to be back in my room before dark.

I've finished William Faulkner's *A Rose For Emily and Other Stories.* The stories are good, especially the "Odor of Verbena," "Delta Autumn," and "Barn Burning," but the material is as morbid and depressing as it can be. It is death, revenge, and shooting. It is material too deadly to be raised to the level of beauty even by a consummate artist like Faulkner. The stories stink of the decay of the South. They deal with frustrated, narrow, and provincial characters. Faulkner, in spite of his art, remains a local-color writer, sensational and theatrical like Bret Harte. The difference between the two is their differences in manner and matter. Bret Harte is old fashioned. He is a mere onlooker, not a sympathizer. Faulkner describes the action of the character, and by these actions the reader gets an insight into the soul of the character. In life one sees a person laugh or cry and has to guess at the motive that prompted that laugh and cry. Bret Harte's characters are the cheerful seekers of gold; they are gamblers and bigamists. They are extroverts, they are active, and they look out, not in. Faulkner's characters are the decayed persons of the South living in recollection rather than anticipation. Bret Harte's men let the part go; Faulkner's characters live in the tombs built for them by their forebears. They seem to be unable to forget. They are conservative, not progressive. It seems that in literature, as in industry and science, there are some materials that cannot be transmitted into forms of beauty and perfection. Choice of matter is as essential as choice of manner. Certain stories like the stories of the house of Pelops, Thebes, or Troy lend themselves to artistic treatment. Countless writers turned that material into beautiful literature. It seems that the essential quality of good material must be its capacity to express or represent the universal by the particular. Oedipus' marriage to his mother, Electra's love for her father, and the respect both the Greeks and the Trojans have for Helen are universal aspirations, hopes, and, to use a psychological term, complexes. To write a masterpiece, one must carefully choose his subject, his audience, and his method of presentation.

January 8, 1947, Wednesday

I sold my two pairs of military shoes for 3.50. It was like giving them away. The shoe salesman said that it would be hard for him to resell shoes of my size. They are long and narrow, and very few people in this part of the world have such feet. Well, I could see through the argument, but at the same time I didn't have any use for the shoes. They have been lying in my closet accumulating dust and deteriorating.

January 10, 1947, Friday

Everybody has learned with great pleasure that Mr. Frederick, who got fired, found a nice teaching position at Mississippi State. He also told me that the U. of Arkansas needs a Ph.D to teach Anglo-Saxon and Chaucer. I could teach both subjects, but just now I don't contemplate a change. I can't yet speak clear, correct, and accent-less English. I must however begin to think seriously about a change. To stay in a place too long is to freeze, crystallize, and be bound in a mold.

January 16, 1947, Thursday

Mr. Wills told me that Sh. has resigned and that she is going to teach at the University of Arkansas. Of course, I already knew about it, but I pretended semi-ignorance. He also told me that another teacher has already stepped into the shoes of Sh. I guess with Sh.'s going, I'll be really insulated and isolated from the rest of the faculty. She was the link that connected me with the Wills and the Cooks. But it will be good for her. She has already stayed too long at JBU. The salary will be 220 a month, and she will be connected with a stable institution that pensions off its teachers and promotes them according to ability over years of service.

January 20, 1947, Monday

Last night I supped at the Cook's. The most pleasant moment was when their fat cat came in and Dr. Cook took him in his arms and petted him and called him Pinkey. The cat seemed so pleased and proud. I also received another invitation to dine on Wednesday evening at the Whites. They are, of course, giving this supper in honor of Sh., who is leaving for U of A next week, and they feel honor bound to invite me also.

January 25, 1947, Saturday

Last night the Cooks, the Wills and I celebrated Sh.'s birthday a little prematurely. Her birthday is on Monday, January 27, but since the Wills could not attend the celebration that day, we held it last evening. The Cooks contributed chop suey, the Wills brought rice and bread, Sh. and I, the beverages and the cherry tart. It was a good social affair. Sh. is leaving for Fayetteville next week.

Yesterday I saw Mr. Frederick off to Winona, Mississippi. He was in high spirits since he sold his house for a profit of 500 dollars and his furniture at a profit of 300 dollars.

On Wednesday the Whites had Sh. and me at supper in their newly bought, furnished, and painted home. The meal was the best I've ever tasted since Frances and I parted company.

January 29, 1947, Wednesday

At noon I was introduced to Mrs. Bean, the new English teacher who will replace Sh. The new teacher is a short brunette in her early or late thirties. I hope she is faithful and efficient so that I may be relieved from worry and work.

February 1, 1947, Saturday

I taught three hours and read a bundle of Cyprus papers mailed to me by my brother. My fellow Cypriots are still sending emissaries to London. They are still having trouble with the students and the faculty of their high schools, or gymnasiums, as they call them. Life seems to be expensive on the island; rents are high, and food still seems to be unobtainable. Anyhow, Cyprus is better off than many war-ravaged countries. The population has increased to 451,000, and the number of students has also increased proportionally.

February 3, 1947, Monday

In the afternoon I visited Sh. The Cooks were already there. When they left and she began to prepare the evening meal, in came Mrs. Frederick, who lingered till 7:15. She had scarcely left when in came Mrs. Rapp. So we did not have any time to ourselves. Since she will start teaching at the U of A this Thursday, yesterday was the last Sunday we had to spend together, and it seems everything and everyone conspired to spoil it. The Cooks were in a visiting mood, Mrs. Frederick was feeling lonesome with her husband away, and Mrs. Rapp was feeling like gossiping.

February 5, 1947, Wednesday

Last night I took Sh. to the Southern Grill for supper for the last time. She has left today for Fayetteville. After the meal we went to her apartment—it was a scene of disorder: books, boxes, clothes, etc., were strewn about and scattered on chairs, the table, and the floor. About 7 o'clock the Waynes dropped in with their little boy, Billy. They stayed until 7:30, and when they left, Mrs. Frederick came to spend the night with Sh. because the pipes of the "Cottage" froze and the place was cold. I was sorry to hear Mrs. Frederick discontinued her studies at the U of A and resigned from her teaching position because she got two C's in her semester exams.

February 7, 1947, Friday

I went to Chapel at 11 o'clock. R. Stewart from Scotland talked about the suffering and woes of the poor Europeans. He had been in a German prison camp for five years. He told about the wholesale murder of the Jews in Budapest and Poland during the German occupation; and yet he referred to the Russians, who sacrificed hundreds of thousands of men to free those countries of the Germans, in bitterness not only unbecoming a Christian but also a man. His reference to the iron curtain was insidious and calculated to blame the Russians for the suffering in Europe.

February 11, 1947, Tuesday

Last night a fire started on the roof of the Mechanical Building No. II over the woodwork shop. It soon spread over the whole building and two small neighboring buildings. In one hour it burned them to the ground. The fire hose could not function because of a lack of pressure and perhaps a lack of water. Everyone tried to save the equipment and records. A great deal was saved, but much more was burnt. Everybody stood around and, somehow, enjoyed the awesome spectacle. On account of the fire, my classrooms have shifted to the basement of Alvin Brown Hall and the Alumni Building over the laundry.

February 13, 1947, Thursday

Today I taught in Alumni Building Room 3 for the first time. It is hot even now in February; it must be an oven in summer. It is above the laundry and has only two windows toward the east, and its ventilation is poor. Yesterday I wrote two letters, one to Sh., who wanted to visit Siloam Springs over the weekend and take me to Fayetteville in Grandpa Wills' car, see a show, and return by the evening bus. I'm not willing to subject myself to so much trouble in order to speak to a woman. By this time I welcome and accept pleasures, but I don't seek them. I also wrote a letter to my brother in Famagusta, Cyprus, Box 82. I also enclosed about four or five not very good pictures of my precious self, taken by Mr. Wayne.

I'm really shocked and disgusted with the apathy and listlessness of my students. Neither Emerson nor Milton seems to touch their hearts or souls or minds. No amount of illustration or explanation can make them show any interest. The past has no message for the modern Americans. Emerson's sanity and shrewdness, Milton's majesty and nobility leave them cold and indifferent. Fed on nasty, cheap novels, listening to trashy radio shows, seeing third-grade movies and reading dirty magazines, the modern American student is like a spoiled child who prefers cake to bread and soft drinks to milk. They remind me of the saying of Oscar Wilde: "Give me the superfluities of life and I'll dispense with the necessities." And certainly our students nowadays are satisfied with the superfluities of culture and have developed an aversion to the fundamentals of culture, which are science, literature, and mathematics.

February 17, 1947, Monday

I received a letter from Sh., in which she urges me to take a trip to Fayetteville and see Dr. Jordan. I once told her that I should like to teach Anglo-Saxon, and she now tells me that Dr. Jordan is looking for a man to teach that subject. Teaching A.S. is not a very enviable or enjoyable task; it is, however, well paid, and I've taken enough courses to enable me to teach the subject. It is not like Greek or Latin. It is a Germanic language, and its weak and strong verbs and its phonetic changes have always been a puzzle to me, but one, of course, learns by teaching. Miss Lawrence told me that she will be driving to Fayetteville tomorrow morning and has volunteered to carry a table for Sh.

February 19, 1947, Wednesday

Today at Chapel Dr. Brown talked about his plans for the future. He will send the high school to Sulphur Springs, increase the number of students to 600, finish the buildings, give monthly home leaves, etc.

February 24, 1947, Monday

Yesterday I rode on a bus to Fayetteville. On my arrival I walked all the way from the bus station to 527 Storer Street, where Sh. lives. It was cold, and I almost collapsed crossing the large, windy campus of the University of Arkansas. About 1:30 Sh. and Mrs. Fred and I went to a cafeteria for lunch. After the lunch Mrs. Fred went home to pursue her studies, and Sh. and I went to a motion picture house called U-Ark, where we saw *The Al Jolson Story*. The theater was overcrowded and overheated. It was the first show I'd seen since my trip to Little Rock last November. About 5 o'clock, when the show was over, we dropped into a restaurant and talked about our friends and our affairs. She looked thinner. I hope she does not diet in order to appear younger than her years. At 6 o'clock I took the bus for Westville and Siloam Springs. It was a rather crowded bus, reminding me of the war years. At Westville I waited for the Siloam Springs bus for half an hour. The road from Westville to Siloam is unpaved, dusty, and bumpy. At 8 o'clock I stepped out of the bus in front of the Chandler's store and then walked to Brownie's Café for apple pie and a glass of milk. At 9 o'clock I was in bed. Taken all in all, it was an enjoyable day. It broke the monotony of the routine and brought to my mind the heroic days of my life when I used to hasten all the way from Boston to New York to see Lucille. At that time I was certainly not governed by reason but by passion. There I was, a poor, shabby, ill-fed and ill-housed teacher-student, wasting my time and money on long trips to get a glimpse of a lady who did not particularly care for me. Every man has had his days of folly. They are good days because sometimes above the logic of the head is the feeling in the heart. I only thank my stars Lucille turned down my proposal. She did me the greatest service in the world. After twenty years I'm still untainted and optimistic and still take immense pleasure in taking trips and escorting unattached ladies to restaurants and shows. Above all I'm free. I'm not tied to houses and women and children. I've not yet anything to show for my freedom, health, and leisure, but much greater men than I did not achieve success before 45 or 50, and I'm only 47. I had to acquire the mastery of a new language and adapt myself to a foreign environment. Just now, only my accent betrays my foreign origin.

February 28, 1947, Friday

It snowed lightly last night, and today is wet and cloudy. I taught three hours in the morning and then went to lunch. Dr. Swann told me that he, his wife, Mr. Wayne, and Mrs. Wayne have been notified that their services will no longer be needed after May 31. I was both surprised and chagrined that four members of the faculty had been discharged. I really don't know why they would be discharged. All four were conscientious workers and attended Sunday school, prayer meetings, chapels, and faculty meetings very faithfully. My opinion is that they were rather costly. All four cost the U. at least 700 dollars a month in salary, room, and board. Well, I don't know yet what is in store for me, but I'll follow the advice of Sh. and get acquainted with Dr. Jordan of the University of Arkansas. He is just now in dire need of professors with Ph.D. degrees, and it is good to have two strings in one's bow. Life is not as sweet as it used to be. Strictly speaking, I have no friends to whom I can reveal my private sentiments. Dr. Cook and Dr. Wills like me and I like them, but neither our interests nor our backgrounds make for close friendship. We are merely polite acquaintances. As for Dr. White, I don't dare even be serious with him. He might take me for a red or a radical. As for the female members of the faculty, they are either too young or too old for me to associate with them. I would like to get better acquainted with Dr. Woodland, but she is of the Eve type—a cool, calm, and collected scientist who will either consider a man as a future husband or not at all. All romance and feelings seem extinct in her. It seems that chemistry, biology, and mathematics kill all poetry and romance not only in men but also in women.

March 1, 1947, Saturday

Of course, the main topic on the Campus is the dismissal of the members of the faculty. Neither Dr. Cook nor Mr. Haley liked it, but as far as I can see, there is nothing one can do about it. We, the professors and teachers, regard it beneath our dignity to be organized in unions or brotherhoods, and we are therefore underpaid, unproductive, and insecure. Just now, teachers in different cities of the country are on strike, demanding higher salaries. Some of them had to strike since prices have been soaring because the OPA ceilings have been removed and they have been unable to make both ends meet.

March 2, 1947, Sunday

I spent the afternoon in my room reading. About 5 o'clock I went out for supper. Since the Southern Grill is closed on Sundays, I ate at the Youree, which at present is patronized by people who are either transients or newcomers into town because they are utterly unknown to me. They also seem not overly clean. It seems that the man makes the place. As long as the restaurant was under good management with a decent standard of quality, service, and cleanliness, it was patronized by the best people. The same rule holds about schools, churches, and shops. Good service and good materials help to build an institution. Even countries deteriorate with the decay of their inhabitants. Man is still the measure of things.

March 6, 1947, Thursday

I received a card from Sh. with the information that the department of journalism is understaffed, and therefore it might have an opening for Mr. Wayne. I ate a chicken-fried steak with a few French fried potatoes, a glass of milk, and three slices of canned peaches for 87 cents. That dinner used to be 35 cents four or five years ago.

March 7, 1946, Friday

At noon Dr. Swann told me that he is at least certain that he'll be teaching at a Baptist College in Mississippi this summer. He was jubilant. Even Mrs. Swann shared his high spirits. Mr. Edwards told me that he was going back to his hometown on the border of Mexico. He said that he could not stand loafing and that he had been loafing during the year for lack of equipment and material. I walked to the dining hall with Mr. Montgomery, who told me that yesterday he drove to Fayetteville and bought a suit of clothes for 54 dollars. I never paid so much money for a suit of clothes. The highest I ever paid was 45 dollars, and it was the first suit I bought on this side of the Atlantic. It was an oxford gray and did not fit me well. I cashed my check, deposited 40 dollars in my bank account, wrote a 20-dollar check to my life insurance company, and renewed my subscription to the newsletter of the C.E.A. Tomorrow I intend to pay 7.50 of my medical fee and give about three dollars to the fund for a gift to Dr. Brown on his birthday.

March 8, 1947, Saturday

It is a fair spring day. I taught and read all day long. I drove to town in Mr. Montgomery's car. The thing that surprised me was that he carried his lady dog on his lap. He told me that once a week he gives her a bath and that her hair is free from vermin. He is a married, childless man, and both he and his wife are attached to their pet. I really can't understand people who take care of dogs, cats, and birds. Time must hang heavy in their hands, and their affections must be starved. Besides wasting their time on feeding and washing animals, they endanger their health, for dogs, no matter how often they're washed and brushed, must carry germs!

At noon I talked with Miss Monks, who told me that she was going to quit teaching at the end of the semester and marry. She is a short, graceful young lady from Ohio. She will marry the uncle of Mrs. McCurdy (the former librarian) and settle in Kansas City, Missouri. As she has been very kind to me, I wish her good luck!

March 11, 1947, Tuesday

I went to school as usual about 8 o'clock in the morning. I was told that a meeting was scheduled at 8 in Chapel. Mr. Whaley announced that there would be no classes for the day and that we would clean up the Campus and its buildings. Dr. Cook and I were given four students and told to clean outside the Memorial Building. We provided ourselves with four rakes, and the boys worked hard and cleaned up the mess. After the noon meal I waited for them to turn up for work, but since all of them were day students and GI's, they thought it more expedient to stay in town. Since my workers did not turn up, I knocked off at 1:30 and returned home. I was also expecting Sh. to turn up, but apparently the cloudy weather made her change her mind. I ate at the Southern Grill. There were a few students dressed in their best and dining in style. It must be quite a change for them to eat at a restaurant once in a while.

March 14, 1947, Friday

Mrs. Haley drove me to town. She asked about Miss Sh. I told her that she is well and having a very good time. Mr. Edwards had both his hands burnt and bandaged today. The big political problem of these days is the problem of helping Greece and Turkey in order to succumb to the so-called tide of communism. The Russians, of course, called it imperialism, and we called it safeguarding the freedom and independence of the small nations. I would like America to help the Greeks—they deserve help—but to use them as pawns in power politics is neither moral nor profitable. The Americans may become as hateful to the Greeks as the British are at present. Meantime, let us hope that Russia is as weak as she's pictured to be and as unwilling to fight as we desire her to be. Since the end of the war, the Americans have been indulging in baiting the Russians and Iran in Spain, Greece, Turkey, Palestine, China, and everywhere they see Red agitation and Red influence on the increase. Some of them are even willing to restore Germany and turn her against Russia. Racial, religious, and ideological differences, instead of being smoothed over, are exaggerated and magnified, obsessed and dwelt upon with a malicious reiteration. It seems that the war has changed the temper and disposition of the Americans. Their equanimity is somehow disturbed by the fact that the French know how to manufacture the A-bomb. Joliot Curie, in an article in the *United Nations World,* has hinted at this fact. I really wish for peace, prosperity, and happiness for the whole world. I'm not afraid of ideas; I welcome them. If we can learn anything from communism, let us, by all means, do it. If they are ignorant, let us teach them. Reviling and fighting have never settled anything. They only make things worse and lead to confusion of minds and destruction of bodies. Emerson once said that imbecility is the key to all ages! It is certainly the key to our age.

March 17, 1947, Monday

I spent Sunday in Fayetteville visiting Sh. Mr. Dill drove me to Fayetteville in the morning, and I returned by bus about 8 o'clock in the evening. After talking for one or two hours in her room at 527 Storer Street, we went to lunch and then to the U of A theater, where we saw *The Razor's Edge*. It was a very faithful and successful version of the novel by W. S. Maugham. Today I taught three hours and then returned to my room. Dr. Brown is back on the Campus and has announced that at 3 o'clock two or three nurses will be in the lobby of the California Building and that anyone who can spare a dollar may receive an injection or shot that will guarantee immunity against flu. This morning there were about eight or nine students absent from my English IV class, but I don't know whether they were sick or relaxing and taking it easy on account of the day. But the newspapers report that many towns have closed their schools for flu. That reminds me of the days of my childhood in Cyprus. We also used to close the schools on account of meningitis, typhoid, or whatnot. Cyprus being not a particularly clean island, it was visited every year by malaria, typhoid, and other diseases. We youngsters used to enjoy those enforced vacations with fear and trembling. Ignorance, filth, and superstition conspired to instill fear and terror in our souls!

March 19, 1947, Wednesday

I taught one hour, gave a test in Word Mechanics, attended Chapel, and then after eating lunch at the dining hall, I returned to my room for study. I'm reading *Abraham Lincoln: His Speeches and Writing*, edited by Roy Bassler. In spite of the valiant efforts of the admirers of Lincoln to raise him to the stature of literary artist, he is, in my opinion, a literary thinker like Pericles, Dr. Webster,

Cicero, etc. An artist's aim is to delight and to deepen our insight, lift the encumbered soul, and create beauty. Indirectly, he might improve and inform readers. But a statesman's aim is primarily to inform, improve, and entertain. If he occasionally reaches the heights of literature, that does not entitle him to a place among the artists. In American literature, we have quite a number of literary thinkers: Jonathan Edwards, B. Franklin, Thomas Paine, Jefferson, Hamilton, Henry Adams, William James, etc. They express their ideas in memorable prose, but they are not artists in the strictest sense of the word. They ought to be separated from the literary artists and studied carefully by those who intend to become historians, statesmen, and political writers. They now appear in the books of American literature. They don't receive the attention they deserve. In some respects the literary thinkers are far more important than the literary artists. Thomas Paine, Jefferson, Hamilton, Franklin, Lincoln, James, and H. Adams have greatly influenced our histories and institutions. The ideal would be to study these literary thinkers as background for the American humanities. This will enable the students to better understand Hamilton, Thoreau, Emerson, Melville, Poe, and Whitman. To these literary thinkers we may add the great historians like Parkman, Prescott, and others who at present receive very scant attention from the average student of American literature.

March 22, 1947, Saturday

Yesterday I drove to Fayetteville with the Waynes. Mr. Wayne is trying to get a job since he was discharged from JBU. He interviewed with two or three department heads and was told that a lack of money prevents them from hiring new professors. Of course, we stopped at Sh.'s, and she took us around the campus. I also met

Helen Brown, who used to be a waitress at the Youree in the years before the war. She looked collegiate with books in arms and this earnest face. I guess she was flattered when I introduced her to Sh., using her correct name. We also met Mrs. Frederick, who rooms with Sh. About 4:30 we picked up Mrs. Wayne and little Bill, who stayed at the new Laundry where Bendix Machines wash the soiled linen for the housewives, and after a cup of coffee and a piece of pie at the Blue Mill, we returned to Siloam about 5:30 p.m. Mr. Wayne did not get a job, but at least he was weaned of the hope of getting one at U of A and could turn his attention to some other institution. When Sh. comes to Siloam Springs for Easter, I'll have the Waynes, the Whites, and the Cooks to supper at the Southern Grill. My impression of the U of A is that of a chaotic institution; it is much larger than JBU. Its enrollment is about 5,000 while JBU does not even boast of 300 college students, and some of us have to teach high school in order to be fully employed. Sh. wanted to introduce me to Dr. Jordan, but since I made up my mind to stay at JBU, I did not see the necessity of getting acquainted with a man whom J. E. Brown does not like since he opposed the admission of our institution in the North Central Association.

March 25, 1947, Tuesday

Today the restaurants of the town have hiked their prices almost 10 percent. The senators are still debating whether or not to help Greece and Turkey. At Moscow the Big Four are debating the fate of Germany and disagreeing on everything.

March 30, 1947, Sunday

I went to Chapel. Rev. Schimpff preached a sermon on the fifth and sixth petition in the Lord's Prayer. I ate a chicken dinner at the University dining hall and then returned to my room to read and study, but somehow I feel listless and apathetic. It seems that in my preoccupation with the things of today, I've lost sight of my goal in life and have lost my way. I must never forget that my aim in life is not simply to become a good professor of the English language and literature. That's my vocation; that's the way of earning my living. Far more important is my avocation, or the minding of my own private affairs. This includes the sharpening of my ability to write, to express myself and to know people. The progress in self-expression has been pitifully slow. As for knowing people, I've ceased to be interested in them. Like Hamlet I can say that neither man nor woman interests me. I've no friends; perhaps it is my fault. I have no "sweetie." They want to marry me, and marriage will put an end to all my hopes and aspirations. It will complicate my life; it will add worries and work. It will not add even one pleasure since by nature and education I regard casual conversation to be not a pleasure nor a passion but merely an unhygienic habit. I must renew my faith in literature and philosophy.

April 4, 1947, Friday

It is Good Friday, but business goes on as usual in this holy town. No bells are tolling, no processions and marches, no ceremonies are held. It may be that the more religious the people are, the more they can dispense with ceremonies. We start a three-day vacation. I'll stay in Siloam and spend most of my time reading and resting. Sh. is staying with the Cooks. Last night I took her to supper at the Kay-June Restaurant, and then we walked all the way to the other end of the town where the Cooks stay. Today I saw her in school. Most of our students have already left for home. During the week I pinch-hit for Mr. Bean, who had been ill with flu. I spent many long hours keeping the freshmen busy. Consequently, I neglected my own reading. It is now 72 degrees, and I'm sitting in my room with the windows open and the gas stove unlighted. The branches of the trees display their first tender leaves, and the earth begins to cover its nakedness with green grass. Some birds are singing, and the clouds are sailing over the hills. One can't help but be influenced by nature. Today while I was drinking my morning chocolate at the coffee shop, the waitress reminded me of Gussie, so young and so virginal and so untouched. And to use a poetic expression, it much grieved my soul to think that during the seven months we were going together, owing to the fact that she was always driving, I never kissed her lips. I've not heard from her in five or six years. I wonder what became of her. She is probably happily married, and, to use a poetic expression again, she is "suckling fools."

April 5, 1947, Saturday

Since today is the first day of the Easter vacation, I spent it reading and resting in my room. I well remember the time when Hitler was threatening our very existence. At that time we praised the Russians to the skies, minimized their failures, and rejoiced at their successes. At the present time the Russians are the worst enemies of freedom, democracy, and progress. The Germans are the poor victims, and the Turks are angels of purity and innocence. It takes a sincere man to rise above the prejudices of his time and country. Selfishness, vanity, and greediness shall dominate the human heart. Truth is sacrificed to expediency. God help us in this world of ours. We have forsaken truth and sincerity; we worship falsehood and profit. It is almost impossible to learn the truth about the simplest things, such as the condition of the water we drink, the quality of the clothes we wear, and the health of our community. Men are afraid to face facts; they wallow in illusions, fiction, and dreams, and yet only "truth shall make us free!"

April 7, 1947, Monday

Last day of vacation. Yesterday afternoon I dined and supped at the Cooks, where Sh. stayed. After the meal we drove to Nicodemus. We were too late for the service. We heard only the end of the sermon.

Today I drove with the Cooks to Fayetteville. The weather was ideal. We took Sh. to her home, they shopped, and then we drove back to Siloam. It was a nice drive. At the Southern Grill I met Rev. Schimpff. He told me he had just returned from Fayetteville. The telephone strike is on; the dispute about the mine continues; the help of Greece has not yet been voted on; the Big Four are still quarreling in Moscow. The wise man should study and teach and mind his own private affairs.

April 10, 1947, Thursday

It has been an unusually stormy and rainy day. Between 10 and 11 o'clock it poured so heavily that it flooded the Campus and filled the creek that flows through the town to overflowing. To increase the hardship of the rainstorm, the lights were out on the Hill for two or three hours. We ate our lunch in a dark dining hall, the candles on the tables scattering a dim and sinister light. About 3 o'clock the rain stopped, and I walked to town along the highway, on both sides of which streams of water were still running. It is now 6:30, and the sun is setting behind golden clouds in the west. The evening newspapers, however, carry the headline that at least 152 persons are known to have been killed by a tornado that struck at Woodward, Oklahoma.

The *Threefold Advocate* carried as a headline, "A New Dean was Named." That's, of course, Dr. Dorothy Woodland, the head of the chemistry department. According to the newspaper item, she was born in Ohio and got her Ph.D. at Ohio State University. She has already taught for 14 years. She is a tough nut to crack, and I wish her all the luck in the world. It was also announced by Mr. Storm Whaley at the dining hall that Mr. Brown and Mrs. Brown escaped unharmed from the wrecked train that was carrying them from California to Arkansas. Of late, there have been many accidents both on land and in the air!

April 13, 1947, Sunday

Last night I attended the Founder's Day banquet. About 50 or 60 alumni attended the banquet. Mr. Springfield acted as a Master of Ceremonies and managed to bring into the halls of learning the cheap and coarse humor of the Rotarians. Two or three alumni made brief speeches, in which they attributed their success to the training they received on the Hill. One was a preacher, another a singer, and the third a gardener. At the end Dr. Brown repeated his theory about trained hands. I guess it is perfectly all right to possess trained hands, but above all one must possess a trained mind, and one must be able to think. This emphasis on vocational training seems to be an escape from actual mental training. Four centuries ago men insisted on the study of humanities (literature, philosophy, history). About 70 years ago, they started stressing the study of sciences (chemistry, medicine, etc.). As of a few years ago the tired men of our age are avoiding the study of the humanities and sciences and are ready to surrender to the learning of trade and profession that will increase the earning power at the expense of their initiative, intelligence, and imagination. It is much easier to learn a trade or a vocation than to master literature or a science.

April 21, 1947, Monday

Yesterday in spite of the cold and cloudy weather, I drove with Mrs. Dill to Fayetteville in order to visit Sh. We talked in her room, ate at the university grill, saw *Magic* at the U Ark theater, and walked the streets of the town. Short trips break the monotony of life and return one to his job rested and refreshed.

April 23, 1947, Saturday

My landlady sent me a newspaper clipping with the news that Dr. D. D. Aris will sail for England and Cyprus very soon. I remember the first time I saw him in the University restaurant. He had come to study dentistry. He took his degree one year before me and had a fellowship. He opened an office and began to prosper when the Army drafted him. He almost lost one of his eyes, but he was released from the Army. He went back to practice and has prospered since he stays in the Oak Grove Hotel and will travel in luxury to England and home. I am afraid two things will ruin his career. First, marriage, and second, nostalgia. He has been looking for a rich wife since I've known him, and he has always dreamt of Cyprus as an earthly paradise. Cyprus is still wallowing in superstition, party strife, race conflict, ignorance, poverty, and fear. No great soul can thrive in such an environment. Even the fairest flowers die for lack of air and light. With the British repressing every sign of progress, with the church persecuting every free thinker, with the rich exploiting the worker and the peasant, the Island of Aphrodite has become a place of suspicion, hatred, and superstition! Aris will probably sell his birthright for a mess of pottage.

May 5, 1947, Monday

The trouble with mankind is neither too much thinking nor too much doing, but instead sheer ignorance. Mankind errs by his lack of knowledge and insight. Men are still weak and wicked because they are ignorant. What was true in the days of Socrates is still true in our day. Virtue is knowledge, and vice is ignorance. Our misery is the result of the lack of information on our heritage, social system, and science. Someday we might know why we suffer, and then the knowledge will cure us of our complexes, our illusions, hopes, fears, and wants.

I donned my summer underwear yesterday and started going out bareheaded. By next month I'll go out in shirtsleeves.

May 7, 1947, Wednesday

I ate a good supper at the Southern Grill. Mr. Hurley delivered a sermon in which he compared the game of baseball with the game of life. He related an episode of how in 1932 he caught the ball hit by Babe Ruth. After the sermon I took the ball in my hand and read Babe Ruth's signature. It was a rather unusual sermon, but the importance of preparation, concentration, and cooperation in baseball was stressed as important in the game of life. At noon I sat at the table of Miss Monk and Miss Wendelken. I had a better time than I would have sitting with the Swanns. The young ladies still stimulate me.

May 8, 1947, Thursday

Sometimes I think that the best way of teaching literature is the one practiced at Princeton. Let the students read a book or an essay or a poem and repeat it to the class. By this way the average student masters the technique of gathering material and presenting it in an orderly and interesting way to his classmates. It also relieves the professor of the necessity of lecturing. I'm afraid it will not work at JBU because the students spend three or four hours a day in vocational work and have little time to devote to the reading of books and preparing of papers. Very often they come to the classroom without ever reading their short daily assignments.

May 13, 1947, Tuesday

Last Sunday I rode in the Dills' car to Fayetteville. I dined at Sh.'s room, and then we went to the U-Ark theater, where we saw *The Lady of the Lake,* a mystery murder case. After the show we walked to the Blue Mill restaurant for pie a la mode, and a cup of coffee. At 6 o'clock I took the bus for Westville and Siloam. It was a cloudy, cool, perfect day for traveling. Last night I attended a faculty meeting in No. 204. We discussed our graduates and our plans for commencement exercises and summer school.

I learned that three high school students have been arrested for breaking into the Spot Theater and stealing money and tickets. Two of them are in my English IV class. The other is the son of a missionary who is in Africa at present. The high school students have always been successful in giving a bad reputation to John Brown Schools. Some of them are worse than the Greek-American boys I used to teach in my pre-college career.

May 18, 1947, Sunday

I became a professor of English simply because I was born in a British colony and perhaps because, when I was a baby, my grandmother carried me to the homes of the British officials for whom she cooked and cleaned. Also at my time, the environment of Cyprus was saturated with talk about philosophy and literature, both Greek and European. Even my predilection for philosophy and utopian literature can be traced to the first books that I happened to have read and enjoyed. One was *Utopia*, and the other was a short pamphlet expressing the theory that after death one's soul mingles with the elements and disappears. My interest in labor problems and social justice stems from the fact that I am the son of a carpenter who was unemployed during the winters, and I was reduced almost to starvation. My championing of the oppressed race is the result of being a native of an island governed by the British. My religious tolerance is due to the fact that I grew among Mohammedans, Catholics, Armenians, Protestants, Arabs, and Jews. Even my accent, which is still plaguing me, is due to the accident that I was born in Cyprus and didn't come to the United States until I was 20 years old. So there must be causes for the professions and trades of other people. What we are is the result of our past, and what we will be will stem from the present. "What we will be we are now becoming." If we waste time now, time will waste us later on. For everything that's given, something is taken. Thus upon casualty and compensation turns not only the life of the individual but also the life of a nation and of the whole earth. What a man sows, that he will reap. We are now engaged in sowing seeds of hatred toward certain classes of people and toward certain nations, and we are sure to reap a nice harvest of class struggles and international wars. It seems that we are unteachable. We forget easily and learn the hard way. Is pain or suffering the only efficient mnemonic? God help us!

May 20, 1947, Tuesday

It rained at noon, but now about sunset it is cloudy and cool. I put on the suit I bought in Kansas City last fall. Somehow I don't think it fits. I guess it needs pressing or else I'm not used to it. Anyhow I still go through acute suffering whenever I put on a new suit of clothes or a new hat. It must be the result of the environment in which I grew. I was so poor that a new suit was a great event in my life. Sometimes those homemade clothes did not fit, and people probably made fun of me. I'm still carrying the traces of that fear. It is unthinkable for me to change suits in the middle of the year or wear a different suit every day the way most people do. As a result, I decided to buy an expensive suit that I can wear a whole school year without looking shabby. I know it is unreasonable. I'll try to get rid of this endymatophobia.

May 23, 1947, Friday

Yesterday I was Officer of the Day. I went to the dining hall at 7 o'clock, at noon, and at 5 in the afternoon. From 5:30 to 9 p.m. I was in the administration building. Mrs. Wayne left little Bill in my care while she attended a senior class meeting. Bill behaved nicely till he wanted to go to the bathroom. Since he did not know how to take care of himself and I did not understand the special dialect by which he tried to convey to me his discomfort, he fouled his pants and filled the office with an offensive smell. Luckily enough, some girls were passing by and I sent one to call Bill's mother, who came in a hurry and cleaned Bill and the bathroom! That's a lesson for me!

May 24, 1947, Saturday

I received a letter from my sister Corinne. She is worrying about her son Byron, who has failed to pass his mathematics and ancient Greek exams. She also sent me a picture of him and one of herself. She also wrote that all my uncles except Lavithes have died and that my nephews and nieces are thriving and multiplying!

May 28, 1947, Wednesday

Two years ago I was honorably discharged from the Army at Camp Chaffee, Arkansas. At 2 o'clock I had my eyeglasses checked by Dr. Hardin. It took him one whole hour to examine my eyes and prescribe new glasses for me. Optometry is getting more and more complicated. I guess it is because of my age. I really need a good pair of eyeglasses to get the strain off my eyes and enable me to read fine type.

May 29, 1947, Thursday

I spent the day reading *The Well of Loneliness*. I ate three good meals (price of the three, $1.05) and took a good walk to the railroad station and back. I saw two or three well-kept lawns and hedges. But still one meets unpainted, tumble-down frame houses nestled between newly painted houses. I dream of writing a novel called *The Soulsaver* with Bill Potter as a hero. I'll start the story with his walking up the Hill, his conversion, his country preaching, his marriage, his Neosho work, his Mississippi work, and his return to Siloam Springs, from which he plans to save the entire nation by evangelistic campaigns. I don't know whether to make the hero a conscious hypocrite, a bigot, a fanatic, or self-seeker. Until now he has been successful in a material way, and one can't argue with success. It always means that God has blessed one's work. But, of course, there is a cause for his material success. The war has created many demands of all professions, including preaching and teaching. He is still young, and he is a good talker and moves in what we call the "Bible Belt." There are, and I guess there will always be, people who like to hear about sin, salvation, Paradise, Hell, etc. In small towns people go to the revival meetings out of mere boredom. Besides that the evangelists are always entertaining. They seem to possess an unlimited supply of anecdotes and tall stories. In some respects they are the descendants of the narrators who used to entertain the pioneers with anecdotes and tall tales. They also condemn some sins like gambling and drinking, which the poor listeners cannot indulge in for lack of money and opportunities. They save souls, but they are afraid to even mention social and political evils. They usually support the employers and the rulers; therefore, they are allowed to preach unmolested. They are emphasizing dogmas. They are against communism and unions. Railroad companies give them passes, and industrial magnates occasionally send them their checks. They serve the existing social order by diverting the attention of the masses from social evil and world affairs to spiritual sins and heavenly mansions. Whether they do it wittingly or unwittingly, it is hard to say. But there is no doubt that they help Mammon to perpetuate his hold on the poor and ignorant. Many people serve Mammon while they think they serve God. Under the banner of the Prince of Peace they preach class and national hatreds. At this time Russia attests the fact that it is a communist state (and therefore champions the cause of the workers), and a mighty nation has become the focus of religious and social attacks. Christians and capitalists are in alliance; the liberals and the workers are the enemies of Democracy and of the country!

June 2, 1947, Monday

Yesterday I drove with Mr. Hurley to Fayetteville. At 10:10 I dropped in to see Sh., and at 12:30 we dined at the Blue Mill. We ate a nice chicken dinner (It cost me $1.94). Then we walked to U-Ark Theater, where we saw a picture called *The Two Mrs. Carrolls* with

Bogart, Barb. Stanwick, and Alexis Smith. There was a grim humor in the way the husband, who was a painter, got rid of his first wife to marry the second one, and then he tried by the same method (giving her poisoned milk) to get rid of his second wife. But he failed, and she married the adorer and lover of her youth. Her husband very nonchalantly walked with the policemen to his punishment.

June 4, 1947, Wednesday

Today I put on my bifocal eyeglasses. They are a pain in the neck. One has to move either his head up and down or his eyes up and down. The doctor said that in time I'll get used to them. Of course, I will. Everybody does! I'm still reading *Peace of Mind*. I somehow got my classes organized, and I'm settling down to the routine so dear to the heart of the average professor. Summer is at last here; it is clear and warm, and I'm glad I don't have any afternoon classes. I'll eat more ice cream and drink more milk in order to increase my vitality and be able to teach and study. I think I'm still the slave of some fears engendered in me during my cheerless and unhappy boyhood.

June 7, 1947, Saturday

I am faced with a problem. In my senior English class I have two students who apparently intend to be mere attendants in the classroom without paying attention or reading the assignments. If I get tough with them, I'll probably create trouble for myself; if I let them alone, it would be condoning their bad habits and doing them injustice. I'll try all kinds of tricks with them. Sometimes a teacher wonders whether he is wise to bother about students who have been miseducated beyond hope. During their school career, those boys apparently "sat out" their classes because teachers were either too tired or too indifferent to make them work. Now they have reached the senior class and expect just to attend the classes and get a credit and a diploma and go home, having acquired neither knowledge nor good work habits.

June 11, 1947, Wednesday

This morning Mr. Barnes, the owner of the Southern Grill, drove me to school since I could not get a taxi and since it looked like a rainstorm. At Chapel we had an officer of the Salvation Army as our speaker. He spoke of the social and religious aspect of the organization. I think the whole church ought to take more interest in social problems, especially those of social justice, war, disease, family, and ignorance. I don't mean by this that the church will tell the people what to believe and what to think and what to do. I mean that the church ought to help men to secure the good life and teach them how to think, how to work, how to love their neighbor, and how to acquire peace of mind.

Sh. dropped into the Chapel today, and I walked with her to town. She was invited to lunch at the Cooks, so she went her own way, and I ate a good meal at the Southern Grill.

June 13, 1947, Friday

I taught till 10 o'clock, and the Cooks and Sh. picked me up at the University Store and took me first to Lake Wedington, where we ate a nice lunch under the trees consisting of shrimp salad, macaroni, potatoes, deviled eggs, cake, and coffee. After that we drove to Fayetteville, and after washing at Sh.'s place, we drove to town and then to Mount Sequoia, from which we looked at the valley and the surrounding hills. It was cool and partly cloudy, but the view was glorious. After deporting Sh. at her apartment, we drove back to Siloam Springs, which we reached about 5 o'clock. I returned to my room, and after washing I went to the Southern Grill for dinner. I ate a cheese sandwich (25 cents), a glass of milk (7 cents), pie a la mode (20 cents)—the whole meal, 53 cents!

It is now about 7 o'clock, and the sun still pours its beams into my room. Last night I took Sh. to dinner at the Southern Grill, and then I walked with her to the Cooks, where she was staying since she came from Fayetteville last Tuesday. Dr. Cook tried to focus his huge telescope so we could look at Jupiter, but somehow he could not manage it, and after that fruitless effort I walked home.

June 17, 1947, Tuesday

Last night I took Sh. to supper at the Southern Grill, and then we visited at the Davis's. Miss Davis, who is a Ph.D. in home economics and a professor at the U. of Chicago, was home for a short visit. Her mother said that she was going to marry an advertising man from Tulsa, Oklahoma, next September. Sometimes I think it is a frightful waste of time, energy, and money to educate a woman, and then have her marry and keep house for a man.

Mr. Snider drove me to the Hill in his new car, a Stylemaster Chevrolet. He sold the old car at 275 dollars. It once belonged to Mr. Regan, and Bitzer taught me how to drive in it. Of course, I never mastered the technique of driving a car, but the car always reminded me of my efforts in that direction.

June 24, 1947, Tuesday

I spent the day lecturing in the morning and reading in the afternoon. I mailed two books to my brother for the son of his employer. I received a letter from Linda Swann. Dr. Swann has secured a job as head of the department of English at Pembroke College, North Carolina, at 3,600 dollars for nine months. His dismissal from JBU proved after all to be a blessing in disguise.

The circus is in town; it has attracted a good number of Indians who shun Siloam Springs because it is a dry town.

June 25, 1947, Wednesday

I discussed the Labor Bill with the young Campbell. Although he himself is a worker who is employed almost at a starvation salary at JBU, he violently attacked the unions and the workers. He thinks that they are overpaid and always in the wrong. It is really a sad and depressing fact to meet so-called educated men who do not know what is good for them and the country. I noticed that, with a few exceptions, it is very fashionable to condemn any labor movements and regard even friends of labor as communists, radicals, or scoundrels. At the same time, I blame the labor men for not sticking together and getting the government in their hands. Then they could tell the so-called big bosses and magnates that if they don't like the country, they may go elsewhere!

June 27, 1947, Friday

I spent the afternoon reading O'Casey, *Juno and the Paycock*. It was really sad reading the plight of the Irish, till they got rid of England. It is like the plight of Cyprus under the British; the energy of the inhabitants is spent in quarreling with the government and each other. Instead of creative activity, we get the perennial accusations, recriminations, and frustrations. Indeed good government is not a substitute for self-government. Colonial empires must be abolished, and then all the nations must be left alone to solve their own problems to the best of their abilities. The wiser, richer nations must act like brothers to the younger nations, helping them, not exploiting them.

July 2, 1947, Wednesday

I finished O'Neil's *The Great God Brown,* and now I'm reading Kaufman's *Of Thee I Sing.* Twenty years ago, while I was in New York, I took Lucille to see *The Great God Brown.* It is remarkable how little I can recall from this play. Only the fact that the actors wore masks stuck in my mind. Yesterday I received a package of newspapers from Cyprus. Poor Cypriots. They are in the throes of electing an Archbishop, and they are so stupid that they will probably elect one that is neither born nor bred in Cyprus! The paper also contained news about Pyrron and Fosco, two old friends of mine. They are still in New York, acting as secretaries of the Cyprus Club. It is pitiful how people fail to outgrow their environment. On the contrary, it is deemed a high honor and rare distinction to continue to be a Cyprist even in America. Priests, teachers, lawyers, and physicians encourage the resistance to the so-called foreign environment. Their bread and butter depend on the immigrants sticking to the native country's ideals and customs. Vast sums of money are spent on clubs, associations, brotherhood, newspapers, and whatnot. What we really need are immigrants who absorbed the American civilization so they can transplant it or at least adapt it for foreign countries. America is by no means an ideal place, but in its sanitation, plumbing, organization, education, religion, etc., it leads the world.

July 10, 1947, Thursday

I spent the day teaching in the morning and reading in the afternoon. I attended a faculty meeting. Dr. Brown talked about his plans to move the high school to Sulphur Springs and complete the building in 60 days. He also said that we are financially stronger than ever and at the same time that we need 100,000 dollars to move equipment and finish our buildings. Meantime, the teachers must remain unpaid! He urged everybody to work with all his might and never spare himself. Work never hurt anyone!

July 18, 1947, Friday

Tomorrow I expect to give exams to my students in English Lit. and American Poetry. Giving exams is an easy task. It is correcting papers that bothers me. I'll try to correct all my papers by tomorrow evening so I can visit Sh. on Sunday in a happy spirit. Sh. has returned from a visit to Ohio last week, and she is going to start teaching next Monday. Rev. Hurley promised to give me a ride to Fayetteville; the bus does not leave Siloam till 10:45 a.m. and does not reach Fayetteville till 12:10, which shortens my visit by two or three hours.

September 15, 1947, Monday

I have not written in this diary since July. To start with, during the last two months it has been terribly hot and dry. For days and nights the temperature hovered around and about one hundred, and I felt faint, listless, and apathetic. I managed to survive by keeping out of the sun as much as possible, drinking milk, and eating ice cream and light meals. Above all, I was lucky in having my classes meeting in the mornings in Room 204, which is a very cool room. I also took trips to Fayetteville to visit Sh., and we usually went out for lunch, a show, and a walk. The only thing that greatly chagrined and disturbed me to the very depth of my soul was the news that my brother Takis was killed in an automobile accident early in August. It has been about 27 years since I heard of my father's death, and this news almost stunned me. That is the reason I did not feel like keeping up my diary. But life must go on. We honor the dead by becoming more useful to our fellowmen, by serving mankind, and by becoming nobler and better. Death is a fact, to which we must adjust ourselves.

On September 4 I took a trip to Kansas City, Missouri. I stayed at the Plaza Hotel, Room 404. I rode the buses and street-cars and saw three shows, *The Variety Girl*, *The Bachelor and Bobby Soxer*, and *Mother Wore Tights*, all of them of secondary interest. I returned to Siloam on Sunday, September 7. Last week I ostensibly helped Mr. Cook move his equipment and books to the new science building. I loafed to my heart's content. One can't do work at jobs he does not like. Anyhow, it is fun and gives me change of occupation, and that's rest. Today we worked for a few moments at the sawmill, and it was fun having the sawdust and the shavings cover me. In the afternoon I sat on the porch, and since it was chilly I put on my coat and read George Eliot's *Romola*. I read that novel about 27 years ago and don't remember anything at all!

September 19, 1947, Friday

I received a letter from my nephew or cousin Byron. He describes his family life as a constant fight with his parents. Well, I shall not worry about youngsters who are spoiled to the marrow of their bones by indulgent and foolish parents. He is lucky he has plenty to eat. In my time we went to school hungry, dirty, and scantily dressed. We shivered and fainted from hunger, and yet we wallowed in pleasure reading the masterpieces of all literature, taking long walks, and cherishing far-reaching dreams. Today's children are well fed, warmly dressed, properly housed, dreaming of becoming engineers, salesmen, and businessmen. I am afraid they will soon find out that, without noble dreams, there will be neither building, nor selling, nor buying. Man can't live by bread alone. He needs beauty and idealism. Great art and literature can give the esthetic sense, but they have neither patience nor inclination for greatness!

October 11, 1947, Saturday

The weather being ideal, I enjoyed my work immensely. Last Sunday I visited Fayetteville and took Sh. to dinner and the show. The dinner cost me $2.25, and the show, 90 cents. Both were not superior in quality. The talkie was *The Fox of Harrows,* a historical romance about a gambler who married the proud daughter of a Louisiana planter. They managed between themselves to make a mess of the married life by causing the death of their child and by uniting before the grave of this child. Mr. Williams drove me to Siloam about 9 o'clock.

October 20, 1947, Monday

Yesterday I visited Fayetteville and Sh. We dined at her room with Miss Renner as our guest. She is an instructor of mathematics at the U of A, about 50 years old, with white hair yet well preserved and not bad to look at. I talked with her rather freely about JBU, and Sh. later hinted that I was rather indiscreet. Her opinion was that Miss Renner might get a bad impression about our working for such an institution as JBU. It is hard sometimes to steer clear between offending a person and mental lying.

October 30, 1947, Thursday

I spent the whole day doing practically nothing besides

teaching. To become immortal, one must make constructive use of his leisure. A few years ago I made the point of reading at least one hundred pages a day, but of late I don't read even thirty. There are many reasons for my backsliding. To start with, I get up later than before. Since I don't have classes till 10 a.m., I don't get up before 6 o'clock. Once I used to get up at 5 o'clock. Then I acquired the habit of reading all the magazines from *Atlantic* to *Life*. I ought to read one or two good magazines well and not many superficially. Since Sh. moved to Fayetteville, I've spent one or two Sundays a month in trips to and from Fayetteville. When I was young and ambitious, I used to spend my Sundays reading and studying. I used to grudge the time I had to spend in church. But I must pull myself together. I must never forget my great goal in life—immortality, i.e. being remembered to posterity.

November 6, 1947, Thursday

Today I read in the *Harper's Magazine* that Darwin never worked more than three hours a day! I guess one can make a comfortable living if he works hard for three hours a day at teaching, preaching, and writing. S. Maugham applied this Darwinian habit to his writing. Every day, no matter what happens or where he is, he spends the hours between 9 and 12 o'clock in writing. I can't devote three hours every day to writing, but I can at least give it 10 or 15 minutes. Just now I don't seem to have any ideas or feelings worth recording. But I'll form the habit of writing at least a page every day. It will ultimately give me a tool by which I may open the door of immortality. One needs work; one needs never despair.

November 7, 1947, Friday

Yesterday I happened to mention to Dr. Meadows that

Mr. Watts, a GI student that lives next to Mr. MacKinney's, was from Memphis and that he would probably travel to that city at Christmas. This statement made Dr. Meadows desirous of meeting Mr. Watts, so I had to take him to the mechanical building and endeavor to locate Mr. Watts. Of course, Mr. Watts was not there, but I inspected the annex to the main building that is the former gym for the first time. It is a square, wooden building with a cement floor and rails in the front and four dilapidated cars, on which the students are supposed to practice. This is indeed an industrial age. Motors and engines, parts and tools, are everywhere, and the younger generation plays with these gadgets the same way I used to play marbles and "knuckles." Our ancestors used to spend a considerable amount of time cleaning and feeding horses. We spend our lives and energy in taking care of machines. Engines are good servants but, unfortunately, have become our bad masters. I hope they will not destroy mankind either by killing it or by weakening its brain and muscles.

November 8, 1947, Saturday

I drove with the Cooks to Fayetteville. We started at 10:15 a.m. and reached our destination, i.e. Sh.'s apartment, at 11:15. After visiting awhile, we drove to Washington's Hotel Restaurant for dinner. We ate four one-dollar dinners; that was all on the menu. Today one-dollar dinner is almost the cheapest a person can get. It consisted of tomato juice, salad, fried chicken (one leg and one unidentified part), a small dish of beans, coffee, and ice cream. A few years ago such a small meal would have cost only 50 cents at the best restaurants. After dinner the ladies did some shopping, and then we returned to Sh.'s apartment for a half-hour visit. Mrs. Cook talked about her aged mother (83 years old), who persisted in cooking for their family and bossing her daughter. About three o'clock we started for Siloam. The weather was ideal for motoring. It was clear and cold, and the trees were brilliant.

November 14, 1947, Friday

Last night I was a guest at the Olins. They treated me to fried chicken, southern style, but both my hosts and I were tired and had scarcely stamina and courage to entertain one another. Gracious hospitality requires leisure. Mr. Olin showed me his little baby son, who was lying asleep in the bed with the pip of the milk bottle in his mouth. In the warm room, clad in his clean clothes, with his clean, smooth face, this baby looked like a satisfied animal in sleep.

November 17, 1947, Monday

Yesterday I spent the day correcting papers. About 7 o'clock I walked down to the Community Building and attended the rally of the Drys. Dr. Brown was the main speaker and was very effective with his illustrations of saw-mill, cotton-mill, grits-mill, and gin-mill. The three first ones were supposed to house, clothe, and feed mankind while the last one was supposed to deal with innocent boys and girls and destroy their lives. Tomorrow is the day of voting on the question of dry or wet county. Since I paid my poll tax and still have the receipt in my envelope, I'll vote for the first time in Benton County, and, for that matter, for the first time in America. Being a foreigner who is engaged in artistic and intellectual activities, I have been very unwilling to take active part in politics. But since I was discharged from the Army, I have become aware of the vast issues both domestic and foreign, and the least I can do is to cast my vote.

November 19, 1947, Wednesday

About 3 o'clock Mr. Spivey drove me to town and told me that Mr. Barnes, who owns the Southern Grill, had a stroke this morning. Everybody is talking about the results of yesterday's voting. Benton County has voted 2-to-1 to remain "dry." That's a smashing victory for the Dry Forces, which were led by Dr. Brown, who has already left for Washington, D.C.

November 21, 1947, Friday

I noticed that they changed the number of the house that I'm staying in from 1005 to 203 South Wright Street. The last number was much easier to remember.

November 28, 1947, Friday

Yesterday being Thanksgiving Day, I took a trip to Fayetteville and was a guest of Sh. at a dinner at Washington Hotel. Turkey dinner this year cost $1.50 a plate. Sh. paid three dollars for both. After the lunch we went to the show, where we saw Reagan and Shirley Temple in *That Hagen Girl!*. The sufferings of a girl in a small town where gossip thrives were exaggerated to impress the people with the importance of an unimportant subject. Of course, in small towns, "what people will say" causes more misery than ignorance, neuroses, or even wickedness. After the show we went to the Blue Mill for a cup of coffee and then to the station, where I took the 6 o'clock bus for Westville and Siloam. The night was cool, clear, and moonlit.

November 29, 1947, Saturday

It is clear and warm, but the streets are littered with sere leaves, and the town is enveloped by smoke rising from the piles of burnt leaves. The shops are displaying their selections of Christmas presents, and some buyers, like the early birds, are trying to catch the best. I don't think I'll buy any costly presents this year. I'll concentrate on candy and chocolates. They are by no means cheap, but they are easy to buy and appropriate to give.

November 30, 1947, Sunday

Today is the last day of Thanksgiving vacation. It is only 20 days before Christmas vacation. I wonder whether or not the students and the faculty will be able to get down to work. Men can't work without vacation, and yet vacation either past or anticipated unsettles them. This is due to the fact that most of us live not in the present but indulge in either recollection or anticipation. Since I've no place to go and I'm not willing to travel in discomfort and pay exorbitant prices at hotels, I can wait for the Christmas vacation with patience. One thing is certain: I don't make wise use of my abundant leisure. I ought to devote at least part of it to creative activities, such as writing either fiction, criticism, or essays. It is about time to give the world something to be remembered by.

December 1, 1947, Monday

I read the December *Literary Digest*. A man thinks that only a miracle can save Greece from civil warfare, government corruption, and public inertia. Perhaps his opinion is pessimistic, but Americans indulge in exaggeration. They rush from one extreme to the other. They have their ups and downs. Frankly speaking, what people need nowadays is "rest from the things of today." The newspapers, the radio, the magazines, the leaflets have turned the attention of the people from things eternal to things contemporary. The headlines scream the news; the commentators talk glibly about it; the politicians exploit it; the people worry and fear. The loss of perspective gives disproportionate importance to everyday occurrences.

December 4, 1947, Thursday

It is clear and cool. I got a haircut and taught three hours in the afternoon. I received two letters, one from Cyprus, written ostensibly by my sister, but really by my brother-in-law, and one from Mr. Bitzer, who is at present at the Ward-Belmont School in Nashville, Tennessee. He complains about how we still record some of the courses he initiated or created in the JBU catalog. I don't know why a person should be so solicitous and anxious about things like that.

December 5, 1947, Friday

I do not have the newspaper today, so I don't know what is going on in this stupid world of ours. Strikes are going on in France and Italy, meetings in London, riots in Palestine, discussion about prices and aid in the United States, runs on banks in Russia, etc. It is a pity that men can't apply reason and logic to their social and political affairs the same way they do to their farms and factories. A little fine thinking and a little love, and men's troubles will come to an end. It is so simple and yet so hopelessly impossible to solve mankind's troubles that now the majority of the people have resigned themselves to defeat and failure and fatalistically wait for new wars and devastations. Mankind suffers from inertia of the will; strong will, good will, and intelligence are missing from mankind. Is this because they were born like that or because they are not properly fed, or because they are not properly educated? Emerson said to be cheerful and courageous and try to realize your aspirations. Plato said to cheer up; there is nothing in the whole world that cannot be set right. I state their optimism, but it is hard to believe that men are getting better, nobler, wiser, and stronger.

December 10, 1947, Wednesday

Yesterday I received a packet of newspapers from Cyprus. Poor Cypriots. It took them 10 years to elect an Archbishop, and he died of typhoid only 36 days after he assumed office. So they were at their old game once more with invectives, speeches, stabbings, riots, and whatnot. My childhood was spent during the struggle of the election of Archbishop between the Kyrenians and the Citians. I think the Almighty God delights in afflicting the poor Cypriots with Archbishop elections.

December 12, 1947, Friday

It is by far the coldest day since summer. There was a very heavy frost not unlike thin snow. Pools of shallow water were frozen solid, and the little pupils of JBU's teacher training school slid on the smooth surface with infinite delight. I put on my heavy overcoat and felt comfortable enough. Instead of the usual lecture for my English Lit class, we had the motion picture *Hamlet*. It was silent, and the overacting of the actors was really funny. The students seemed to enjoy *Hamlet*, although most of them did not grasp the full meaning of the story. For a brief space of time Dr. Wills, who was operating the machine, fell asleep and the machine went haywire. The extraordinary behavior of the machine wakened him, and he set everything right. Dr. Wills seems to have never had enough sleep. He is likely to fall asleep at Chapel, meetings, and whatnot. One time while he was driving to Fayetteville and I was sitting beside him, I noticed that the wheel was moving unsteadily, and I looked at him and saw that his eyes were half closed. In the back seat were his wife and his son Paul. I started an argument on purpose in order to keep him awake and thus save my skin and that of his family.

December 15, 1947, Monday

In the morning we had a slight snow and heavy frost, and for a moment it seemed that one could not venture out on the steep streets of Siloam without endangering life and limb. By 10 o'clock the sun came out, and the cold and crisp breezes added zest to life. I had my chest x-rayed with all the students and faculty of JBU. It was much less troublesome than I thought. One does not even have to take off his shirt. One removes his overcoat, coat, and vest and steps in front of a machine, puts his chin on a prop, takes a deep breath, and in the twinkling of an eye his picture is taken. The X-Ray Unit Car was parked in front of the store; a young man and a young lady were in charge of it. I wish that the island of Cyprus had one or two X-Ray Unit Cars of the sort.

December 18, 1947, Thursday

I taught three hours in the afternoon. The weather is ideal for walking and hiking. I received two or three cards from different members of the faculty. I guess I must begin dispatching cards. I must be awfully tired because I have developed all kinds of fears. Next to my nose, just below where the glasses press my nose, I have a kind of pimple or swelling, and it scares me to death. In my imagination sometimes I think it is cancer. I also fear tuberculosis simply because four days ago the TB unit visited the campus and X-rayed all the students, teachers, and workers. Such fears poison one's life and are sure to appear when one has been overworking. For years in Boston, Massachusetts, while I was teaching, going to the University and giving private lessons, I suffered from autophobia. I was scared of being run down by cars. In New York City while I was working from 4 p.m. to midnight, reading in the

New York Public Library, taking courses at Columbia University and worrying about my finances, I suffered from the fear of being suspected of every murder committed in the metropolis. I'm glad Christmas vacation starts next Saturday at noon. I'll take it easy and relax. There is nothing that compares with one's peace of mind and health.

December 20, 1947, Saturday

Today at noon the Christmas vacation started. It will end on January 3, exactly a fortnight from today. Last night we had the annual Christmas Carol Candlelight Service in the Cathedral building auditorium. It was a very impressive service with candles burning, decorations, exalted singing, and playing. Today at 11 o'clock we had a special Chapel. Dr. Brown announced some changes in the management of the vocational department. He also said that he told the North Central Association to hold everything in abeyance till he had completed his campaign of raising 80,000 dollars and put the production department on a business basis. I knew that something like that was in the offing. He wanted to use the application for admission to the North Central Association as an argument lever for raising money. I guess everybody heaved a sigh of relief for, as strange as it may seem and sound, many members of the faculty and the administration are not very keen on entering the North Central Association. They prefer the good old leisurely way of doing things. Supervision and the keeping of standards will vex and unnerve them. As far as I'm concerned, I don't care at all. My aim is to teach and collect a salary. Whether the school is accredited or not does not affect me at all. I'm teaching not for prestige but for enlightening the people.

December 22, 1947, Monday

I spent the day in writing and mailing Christmas cards to my various friends and in reading the December issue of *Harper's Magazine,* which I borrowed from Sh., whom I visited yesterday in Fayetteville. The weather is clear and crisply cold. It makes one feel like walking and eating. I ate at noon at the U. dining hall. I sat at a table with some students, and after getting my mail I returned to town. Some of the articles I read present a very gloomy picture of the United States as well as the world. In the United States the military is getting more and more influential, and abroad the Communists are gaining ground in the Balkans, Czechoslovakia, and Poland. In Greece the American aid is likely to fail to achieve rehabilitation for the nation since 75 percent of the 400 million dollars was spent to equip the Army, which one day may establish a dictatorship, either Communist or Fascist.

December 23, 1947, Tuesday

I received a card from Dr. Swann. In the message attached to my card to them, I made a mistake. I spelled wholly with one *l.* I noticed it after I sealed the envelope, but I was too indifferent to correct the mistake. It might give the Swanns the idea that I don't yet know how to spell the most common words in the English vocabulary. But who does?

December 24, 1947, Wednesday

I walked up and down the Hill for exercise and to get my mail and my noon meal. I bought four boxes of candy, two for the Wills children and two for the Clines, for three dollars. Those three dollars, together with the five I spent on Sh., are my Christmas contribution to the Christmas commercial racket. Of course, I spent about one dollar on cards and postage. I guess the average person in the United States must contribute about 10 dollars to the buying and selling business. It helps stimulate commerce and create aimless activity. Sh. is in town. I met her in front of Sisco's store, and she was going to stay at the Wills'. I gave her the package to carry to them. Since tomorrow I'm supposed to be the Officer of the Day, I'll spend the afternoon on the Hill and probably copy some of the notes I've accumulated during the last two months into my scrapbook.

I remember the three Christmases I spent with the Armed Forces: two at Camp Robinson, one with the 776 MP Bl and one with the Headquarters Co., and one at Camp Crowder in 1944. There was snow on the ground, and it was cold and Prv. Williamson and I had hard time "getting the mail out."

December 27, 1947, Saturday

I spent the day resting and loafing rather than studying. Yesterday about noon I experienced a very bad attack of giddiness or dizziness that scared me out of my wits. It was either the result of acute indigestion, fatigue, or bad posture. Anyhow, I soon got over it, and last night with fingers crossed, fear, and trembling, I attended a party at the Wills'. The Cooks were there and also Sh. We had a good meal and then played games on biblical names. I guess those games must be good for the children, but for adults they are weaknesses of the flesh. I personally prefer conversation to games. But since I was the guest and not the host, I had to play ball with my hosts. Dr. Cook drove me home about 9:30, and I went immediately to bed.

I also saw two of our former students, Mr. and Mrs. Storm.

The man looked stout, sleek, and prosperous, and the lady, elegant and neat. Somehow I ignored the lady and paid a compliment to the man. I don't know why, but I always make the mistake of ignoring the ladies. That's neither polite nor politic.

December 28, 1947, Sunday

Last Sunday of the year. I spent it reading at home and walking in the warm sunshine. It was so warm that I walked up the Hill for lunch without my overcoat. Everything on the Hill was upside down on account of the wedding of Mr. Smiley's son. There were also many outsiders who came for the 40-cent meal, which, like today, proved a free meal since nobody bothered to collect any money or punch the tickets. Being lazy and on vacation, I have developed a taste for daydreaming. Today I dreamed that somebody whom I had advised sent me a 10,000-dollar certified check as a token of gratitude, and I, being very generous, announced to my classes that I would finance certain students through college! This kind of reverie, if disciplined, will help writing fiction, but otherwise, it shows signs of a wandering mind.

December 31, 1947, Wednesday, New Year's Eve

Since this is the last day of the year, and since I've both time and paper, I'll try to sum up some of the great events that took place during the year.

First, I thank God that I spent the year without illness, accident, or other personal misfortune. I enjoyed good health, and only once or twice during the unusually hot and dry summer did I show signs of physical weakness.

The two most important events that affected my life were

first, the death of my brother, who was killed in an automobile accident early in August while motoring from Necosia to Famagusta, Cyprus. The second was Sh. moving from Siloam to Fayetteville. That made it necessary for me to take one or two trips every month. The trips were short and pleasant and afforded change from routine.

As usual I taught and read books, walked, and attended Chapels, prayer meetings and faculty meetings. But I've failed to write a book, make a friend, or grow nobler, stronger, wiser, or better. As a matter of fact, I'm encouraging myself to grow larger, stingier, more cynical, and more skeptical. I must get down to work and begin writing that book by which I'll live in the memory of future generations. Immortality and fame must be won; otherwise, this life of mine has neither value nor meaning. Being the descendant of a noble race, being nourished with the best literature both ancient and modern, having suffered and endured, I ought to be able to communicate some of my thoughts, feelings, and fears to my fellowmen. We live at a time when men must do their best to bring about social justice to the nation, peace on earth, and mental and physical health to the individual. Only wholly developed human beings who organize wholly free from fear, indulgence, jealousy, superstition, and resentment can organize a world state and achieve the unity of mankind. As things are just now, with the guerrillas invading Greece, the Reds occupying Manchuria, the Americans financing Marshall Plans, and the Russians counteracting them, the world is far from being a harmonious whole. It is divided against itself, and a house divided against itself can't stand.

As for myself, I'll try to work hard and behave, to keep an eye on my health and an eye on my budget, improve myself, and serve others to the best of my ability, so God help me!

January 5, 1948, Monday

At 4 o'clock I attended a motion picture at the projector room. Its name was *Atomic Power*. It showed how the scientists, alarmed by the progress they were making in the construction of the Atomic Bomb, got together and split the atom and built this A-bomb that I'm afraid will cause numberless woes to the sons of Adam.

I received a letter from Bitzer, whose appetite for news I whetted with a short postscript in my Christmas card. Of course, I'll not write to him since his only interest is to hear gossip and news about the members of the faculty. The weather is ideal for walking and idling. I've not read the papers today, so I don't know what is going on in the whole wide world, but I'm afraid not much to gladden the soul of a sane and sensible man.

January 7, 1948, Wednesday

I received a fanciful poem from an unknown lady offering herself to become my wife (this is a leap year, and according to tradition ladies may tease bachelors by proposing to them).

January 9, 1948, Friday

Mr. West gave me a book, *The Art of Plain Talk* by R. Flesch (Harper Bros.). The author aims at popularizing the rules for plain speaking and plain writing. He makes the same mistake that the other writers of composition often make. They fail to realize that speech and writing are generated by thinking and that unless one can learn to think effectively, he cannot communicate his thoughts clearly and simply. Logic must precede rhetoric and composition. His rules, like getting rid of "empty" words (i.e. modifiers and independent elements) and sticking to the word order (S. V. C.), are helpful, but they will not change the mental process of the reader. How one can train students to think effectively so they can write and speak simply and clearly, I don't know! My teachers in Cyprus used to explain that clarity and simplicity of the Athens prose was due to the fact that the Athenians used honey instead of sugar and syrups. Honey, they maintained, clears not only the digestive system but also the brain. I wish some institution would try to serve honey instead of butter and sugar. I guess the Athenians were born clear thinkers and then developed into clearer thinkers by arguing and debating all day long. After all, the slaves used to work for them, so time was not money to them; time was leisure to them, and leisure was turned into thought and expression.

January 10, 1948, Saturday

I received a bundle of newspapers from the island of Cyprus. I skimmed through them and then cast them into the wastebasket. My fellow islanders are, on the one hand, quarreling with the British about constitutional rights and self-government and, on the other hand, are quarreling among themselves about their church leaders. Life is never dull in Cyprus. The feverish activity, however, prevents them from thinking of education, sanitation, production, or distribution. The American people lose sight of the needs of fulfillment by playing with mechanical toys; the Cyprists forget the things of the mind by chasing illusions or shadows. It seems that something always prevents men from becoming realists, i.e. seeing life clearly and seeing it whole. They are unable to think straight and clearly. They are embracing shadows; they fall foul for toys.

January 11, 1948, Sunday

This morning while shaving and bathing, I indulged in

daydreaming. I imagined myself making a speech to my fellow islanders, under the title "Be Good Cyprists." The gist of this imaginary speech is that the Greeks think of Greece, the Turks of Turkey, the British of England, the Armenians of Armenia, yet nobody thinks of Cyprus. My advice to them would be "Love Cyprus first; be good Cyprists. Think in terms of the happiness and prosperity of the Island. Greece, Turkey, England, and Armenia are not your real mothers; Cyprus and only Cyprus is your mother." As an illustration, I would introduce the American habit of thinking of America first and then of the different states. I'd also point out that to not think of one's country first is a sign of decay. Greece has always thought of England, France, or Germany. Now it thinks of the United States or Russia. Europe lies in ruins simply because her children think of states first and Europe second. And I'd point out that our whole planet Earth must claim our first care and love and then our own country. Otherwise, we get a divided world with its usual wars, devastation, misery, disease, and famine. So my advice to Cyprists is this: First, be good Earthlings; second, good Cyprists; and then be Greeks, Turks, English, or Armenians. A house divided against itself cannot stand. In the same way, the Earth, the nation, and the individual will fall when not harmony and unity but discord and disunity take hold of them.

January 17, 1948, Saturday

I started reading Tennyson's *The Princess*, a story I read about 20 years ago when I took a course in Twentieth-Century Poetry at Harvard under Professor L. Lowes. How fast the years fly! At that time I was teaching Greek at the Cambridge Greek School two blocks off Central Square and the sentence "I grate on rusty hinges here" appealed to me. Indeed, that time I lived by faith.

And just now, I need faith.

January 19, 1948, Monday

Yesterday I took the bus and drove to Fayetteville. At 11:30 I met Sh. at the Station, and we went to the Blue Mill for dinner. We ate a very good meal. Canadian Bacon, vegetables, coffee and ice cream for 95 cents each. On leaving the dining room of the Blue Mill, Sh. insisted on introducing me to a young man, Mr. Poindexter, an instructor of English at the U of A. She told me later on that the young man seems to be in love with her. He eats with her at noon at the Union, and she did not know whether or not it looked right.

January 22, 1948, Thursday

The poet often laments the fact that many Greeks lost their lives and that the proud Troy was destroyed because of a phantom! Did he mean that all our wars are really quarrels about phantoms? History seems to agree with Euripides! Wars are fought, men are killed, cities are razed to the ground, famine sweeps the globe, and all this for causes that are as insubstantial as the thin air. We fight about abstract nouns, the referents of which we are unable to find! We fight about Democracy, Communism, Fascism, and whatnot while almost all of us do not and cannot define those terms! Are we better than the Greeks and the Trojans who fought for 10 years over a "phantom Helen"?

January 26, 1948, Monday

Yesterday I was guest at Dr. Williams' house, where Sh. was visiting. At noon they entertained us at home with nice roast beef and fried potatoes, coffee, and dessert. In the evening they made arrangements for Sh. and me to dine by ourselves at the new hotel called Hacienda Espagnola. We were the only customers, and we received the undivided attention both of the cook and the waitress, who is the daughter of the owner and a high school student. We ate a nice chicken dinner consisting of tomato juice, salad, fried chicken, mashed potatoes, and string beans. Since I was not too hungry, I concentrated on the chicken and the dessert. After the meal, we returned to the Williams' parlor and were left to ourselves.

Today I bought oranges and bananas and intend to spend the day in my room reading and resting. The snow-covered streets and roofs, the frozen pond, and the bare trees remind me of the years I spent in New England. By nature I'm chill blooded and thrive better in the South than in the North. Thank God, it snows only once or twice a year in Arkansas.

January 31, 1948, Saturday

This is the last day of January, and I hope it will be the last day of the bad weather that has plagued, pestered, and frozen us since last Saturday, January 24. There is still plenty of snow on the ground, and the wind is cold. Today, while correcting papers, I felt like writing a novel beginning as follows: "On the western part of Siloam Springs, the Queen of the Ozarks, is situated the world-famous J.B. University. To this famous institution arrived one hot September afternoon Dr. John H. Panage in order to take up his duties as the head of the Department of English. This new and valuable addition to the faculty of the University was a bespectacled, bald-headed, tall, thin, stooping man in his late thirties who spoke English with a most obvious accent, which he brought with him from his native island of Cyprus, the inhabitants of which speak only acquired language, having no native language of their own. This new doctor was justly famous because not only could he not speak good English but he also never wrote a book or published an article. His first duty on arriving at the station was to take the taxi and ride to the Campus, carrying all his treasures in two cheap, black cardboard suitcases, which he bought at a downtown store in Minneapolis previous to his starting on his trip to Arkansas. The taxi man, after listening respectfully for a few minutes, at last understood where the doctor wanted to be taken and drove him through the main streets of Siloam Springs to the Hill, on which the wooden University buildings reared their unpainted walls, etc."

February 2, 1948, Monday

The greatest news of the last few days was the assassination of Gandhi, the great Indian leader. It is hard for us, the Westerners, to understand the minds of the East. Gandhi seemed queer to us with his loincloth, his vegetarianism, his fasts, his civil disobedience, and his triumph over the British. He died trying to reconcile the Muhammadans and the Hindus. He certainly did for India more than George Washington or Lincoln did for the United States, and he succeeded by relying on spiritual rather than material strength. He has proved in an age of materialism the power of spiritualism!

February 11, 1948, Wednesday

It has been drizzling all day; it is both wet and cold and reminds me of the cold, wet days of Boston. I taught one hour in the morning and two in the afternoon. My students are extremely sleepy; they yawn and can scarcely keep their eyes open. It can't be the effect of my teaching since they begin yawning long before I start talking. It seems that they are neither properly fed nor properly rested and refreshed. They are on the go both day and night, every day of the week, including Sunday. They are in the same predicament I was in the Army, where I used to be on the go from 6 o'clock in the morning 'till 9 in the evening. But at least once a week, even in the Army, one had a day off. It is no wonder our students do not study and do not care about anything except credits, grades, and the degrees. The beautiful goddess Minerva and the graceful Muses lie buried under formalities, schedules, bulletins, credit hours, tests, exams, and whatnot. O, for a Hercules to clear once more the stables of learning! O, for the brave days when learning and wisdom were beloved for their own sake and not for the use they were likely to be put to! But as a professor, I must keep myself like a pure flame or bright light burning in a world gone mad over machines, wealth, sex, comfort, and food!

February 14, 1948, Saturday

I got a letter from my brother-in-law with a statement about the property of my deceased brother Takis. According to the statement, I am heir to 56 English pounds. I also received a letter from Sh. this morning. She wants me to take more frequent trips to Fayetteville. Sunday is my only day off; it is really semi-off because I sometimes have to go to Chapel. I hate to spend it on buses, in stations, and in walking to and fro with her. It would be pleasant if we were young, but both of us being in our late forties, it seems, smells, and sounds ridiculous. This has also been the Missionary Conference Week. Dr. Harvey Farmer, a robust man of 80, delivered all the addresses. I admire the zeal and the self-sacrifice of the missionaries. From them I might learn how to spread the gospel of good books and inspire love of literature, philosophy, and refined pleasures.

February 20, 1948, Friday

It has turned cold and cloudy since yesterday morning. I read an article *in Harper's Magazine* (Feb. 1948), "Too Many People," in which the writer points out that, in spite of wars and famines, the world population is increasing too fast for the production of food and that, unless the UN tackles the problem in a comprehensive way, malnutrition and its evil consequences will be chronic. The problem is how to strike a balance between food and population, how to produce more food and fewer children. I became painfully aware of this population-food problem in my native island of Cyprus. The soil, impoverished by 3,000 years of cultivation and unchecked erosion, could not produce food enough to feed the population. The result was a deficient diet for most of us, with tuberculosis reigning supreme among the peasants, a lack of initiative and energy, migration, epidemics, and whatnot. Scientific birth control ought to be taught to women, and each family ought to be small, well housed, richly fed, and warmly dressed. Fewer and healthier individuals are better off than many who are sick.

March 1, 1948, Monday

I borrowed *East Side, West Side* by Marcie Davenport from the lending library. The novel starts leisurely. It takes about 10 pages to get the heroine, Jessie Bourne, out of bed. Sometimes I wonder if there is not a way of telling a story without so many minute details both about the outside and inside world. Not only are the room, the bed, the view, and the breakfast menu described but also what is going on in the mind of the heroine. This minute analysis of mental states and minute description of furniture and clothing interfere with the readability of the novel. Details must be added if they have any bearing on the story but not merely to fill pages and create a sort of environment in which the reader loses track of the characters. I've noticed that women writers are inclined to indulge in this furious accumulation of details, most of them unnecessary and irrelevant. Sometimes I wonder whether or not it is worth my time and effort to read novels, even if they are acclaimed as bestsellers and masterpieces or penetrating and whatnot. My only excuse for reading novels is that since I'm a teacher of literature, I cannot ignore them without becoming outdated and outmoded. Johnson's advice to read what people around you read is a sound one!

March 5, 1948, Friday

I am still reading *East Side, West Side,* a rather slow novel full of reminiscence and recollections. I can't see why a modern writer can't tell a straightforward story beginning either in the middle or at the beginning. It seems that confused chronology and the intermingling of recollections and actions are fashionable ways of telling a story. They really confuse the reader and interfere with the motivation of characters. Well, someday I'll sit down and write a novel, starting in the media res, after the manner of *Odyssey and Paradise Lost.* Just now, I keep my nose to the grindstone so closely that I scarcely feel like writing in my diary or keeping up my correspondence.

March 14, 1948, Sunday

It is good sometimes to be by one's self and get rest from the things of today. Of course, rumors about war with Russia are flying thick and fast, and everyone seems to be driven by some kind of madness toward war with Russia. It is hard to say how the anti-Soviet feeling has arisen. Three years ago the Russians were our best allies. We used to extol their contributions toward victory. We sent them food and ammunition. We were on the best terms with them. By now it has become treason to speak in favor of the

Russians. Is it fear? Is it envy? Is it propaganda? We are undoubtedly the strongest and richest nation on Earth. Russia does not even have borders with us, but we are afraid of its ideology? Already in our mind's eye, we have seen Germany, Italy, France, Greece, Iran, China, and whatnot gone red or communistic? A slight change in the government of Czechoslovakia has been termed a danger to us as enslavement of a brave people or a conquest! We are really more neurotic than the doctors tell us that we are. If we are not careful, we will find ourselves engaged in a World War III, out of which we will come victorious but either weakened or dishonored. We are really trying to provoke war since we are superior in planes, warships, equipment, and atomic weapons. God has not yet helped any aggressor nation, no matter how strong were its Army and navy. Might is not right. It is right that is might!

April 4, 1948, Sunday

I spent a miserable day correcting papers, staying at home, and eating bad meals. Since my favorite restaurant is closed on Sundays and the other ones are and look filthy, I don't dare eat my meals in any of them. So except for breakfast, I subsisted on ice cream, coffees, and Hershey's. It may be that it is good for my system to get a rest once in a while from heavy foods. I am sure that there are billions of human beings on this planet of ours who did not taste one-third the amount of food I consumed today.

Last night I attended the banquet in honor of Dr. and Mrs. Brown. Mr. Cox introduced me to Dr. Johnston, who visited our University on behalf of NCA. He was a Minnesota man, and we talked awhile about JBU. With him was a young professor of English from Stephens College who showed unmistakable signs of not understanding me on account of my unusual accent. He seemed puzzled and nonplussed. I hope they don't report that the head of the English Department of JBU is a person who does not even speak English!

April 18, 1948, Sunday

On Friday and Saturday I went to Fayetteville, ostensibly to attend the CEA of Arkansas meetings at the University of Arkansas. I attended only one meeting, but that was a good excuse to take a nice, long weekend vacation. The meeting I attended was held in the Blue Room in the Student Union. Dean Nichols gave a short welcome address, and then there was a discussion about communications and trends in teaching literature. At the tea hour, I talked with Sh. and then left to catch the 6 o'clock bus for Westville and Siloam. At 4:30 I attended a special faculty meeting in the home economics building. Dr. Furrow, the coordinator for the North Central Association, gave us some of his observations on higher education. He has already visited 20 colleges this year and marked some trends. He praised our University for the effort it is making to harmonize liberal and vocational education, but he indirectly criticized our isolation and insulation. People said they do not know what we are doing or trying to do at JBU. I am afraid we've got an idea, but the idea either refuses or cannot become reality. Neither the vocational, the academic, nor the Bible division cooperates or coordinates. Each is functioning as a unit by itself. Some departments do not have any definite aim. They simply offer various courses, when and if they get the students and the teachers. The proportion of vocational, academic, and biblical learning that each student should absorb has never been worked out. We simply keep our students busy in the shop, the classroom, and the laboratory, but we rarely know where we are going. The lack of goals in the individual's life leads to drifting and failure. The same may be said about an aimless or goal-less education.

April 27, 1948, Tuesday

It is good to live, learn, and teach. Self-improvement and service still keep me busy day and night. With the election in Italy over and the Berlin situation dormant, the situation in Palestine is now in the news. The Arabs are preparing to invade Palestine, and the Jews are determined to defend their homes, while the UN is planning to send a police force and the British are departing. What a terrible mess! It seems that the statesmen of this glorious planet of ours are enjoying getting in one quarrel after another. By those constant quarrels, they keep the minds of the poor men on destructive goals instead of constructive ones. Instead of peace and prosperity, we have "Cold War," inflation, and taxation for armaments. They make men live on borrowed time!

April 29, 1948, Thursday

Yesterday at Chapel, Mr. Whaley talked on the differences between communism and democracy. He, of course, defended democracy, but he did not fail to point out that the dynamic energy of communism is promising for not only political but also economic equality. He was sure, however, that communism can't work! Well, 200 years ago, they used to say that democracy couldn't work. But it has worked!

May 2, 1948, Sunday

I spent the day on the porch, reading three short stories from *The Portable Russian Reader*, edited by B.G. Guernes (Viking Press). The third story and the most significant is by Dostoevsky, "The

Grand Inquisitor" from *Brothers Karamazov*. The argument of the inquisitor is that Christ, by increasing man's freedom of choice, increased man's misery. Christ rejected Miracle (He didn't turn the stones into bread, didn't come down from the cross, didn't jump down the pinnacle), Mystery, and Authority (He turned down riches and wealth and the kingdoms of the Earth). According to "The Grand Inquisitor," men dread freedom and can only be led by Miracle, Mystery, and Authority.

I didn't go to Chapel, but while waiting for dinner at the administration building, I listened to the sermon over the radio. Rev. Schimpff was saying that women must be subject to their husbands, that the husbands be subject to Christ, and that Christ be subject to God. About 6 o'clock I drank a chocolate milkshake and bought two bags of Tom's peanuts.

May 4, 1948, Tuesday

Tornadoes over the weekend through yesterday have been destroying lives and property in Texas, Oklahoma, and Kansas. We had our share of torrential rains, lightning, and winds. The Jews and the Arabs are still fighting in Palestine while the British, as usual, are playing a double game. They want to establish one of their Arab Quislings in Palestine so as to have control of the oil and the country without the expense of money and men. Meantime, they have succeeded in involving the United States and Russia in a feud over partition and trusteeship. Poor Cyprus, my native island, is used both as a concentration camp for the Jews and as a base for British forces. Someday the innocent islanders will suffer from bombs and rockets for the simple reason that the island is strategically placed in the Suez Canal and the Near East. All the Mediterranean countries near and islands have suffered for being the lifeline of the British Empire. Let us hope that someday the Empire will be liquidated and the lands around the Mediterranean will cease to be battlegrounds.

May 15, 1948, Saturday

On Thursday I received a letter from the Socony-Vacuum Oil Co. Inc., Cairo, Egypt, informing me that I was the sole beneficiary of my late brother Takis. The sum to be paid to me in monthly installments of 22 pounds is 499 pounds. They notified me that 198 pounds have already accumulated in Cyprus, and I wrote them to pay it to my brother-in-law.

The Jews proclaimed the State of Israel today, and President Truman recognized it as a de facto government. The Arabs and almost everybody else were surprised beyond measure. The United States was not supporting partition. Of course, the Arabs will try to invade the new state, and the Jews will defend it. Only God knows how far this little war may spread. Palestine is of strategic importance, and its ports are the mouths of long and costly oil pipes.

May 24, 1948, Monday

Today is the day off both for teachers and students since this is examination week. I stayed at home and had my suit pressed for the first time since Christmas. It looks decent. It is a great marvel and mystery to me, my aversion to wearing new clothes. It seems that from my boyhood, I've worn old suits for so long that a change is an event that attends such attention that it scares me out of existence. Well, I'm not a boy any longer and can afford nice suits of clothes. At least I ought to look prosperous since in this country they gauge a man's worth by his coat! Well-dressed men are supposed to be wise, witty, and good.

September 15, 1948, Tuesday

I taught all summer, three hours a day. I attended Chapel every Wednesday at 11 o'clock and every Sunday at the same time. I read books, newspapers, and magazines; and two or three times I rode to Fayetteville to see Sh. My classes, although larger than ever (in Advanced Grammar, I had 28), were cooperative. I stopped teaching on September 4, and after Labor Day, which fell on September 6, I took a trip to Fayetteville first, and then last Thursday, September 9, I took a trip to Kansas City, Missouri. I stayed at the Plaza Hotel (Room 206), rode the streetcars, and saw two motion pictures, *The Good Sam* and *Red River*. I traveled with Mr. Springfield, who paid for both my meals on the train. He told me not to mention it, that JBU's expense account would take care of my meals. I ate roast beef for $1.75 and beef stew for $1.50. For the record, the price of meals was higher in Kansas City than in Siloam Springs. I returned from Kansas City last Sunday. I immediately went to the circulation library at the *Dixie News* and borrowed *The Naked and the Dead* by Norman Mailer. It is a great book, and the astonishing thing is that it is written by a young man, almost a boy. I marvel at his command of language, his insight into human nature, and his ability to identify himself emotionally with his various characters whether they are Jews, Boston Irish, Texas hunters, or Montana hobos. It is an unusual performance for a young man. I guess he must have suffered and loved and learned much.

September 20, 1948, Monday

I walked up the Hill about 9 o'clock. Dr. Wills got hold of me and informed me that he and I were supposed to get in order or shape up the four upstairs classrooms of the Memorial

Building. Since I was dressed in my best, minus a coat of course, I did not overextend myself. But, as Dr. Floyd phrased it later on, the administration ought not to ask the faculty members to do janitor work. I stayed on the Hill for my noon meal. I sat at my usual table. The Whites, Dr. Meadows, and Mr. Montgomery were missing. Only Dr. Floyd shared the table. I was so mad that I let the old lady fetch not only her own coffee but mine also. She will probably think me very impolite. But simply by nature and nurture, I'm averse to waiting on ladies. I've not yet become Americanized to the degree of becoming a woman's slave or servant. At 1 o'clock I returned home and spent a peaceful and quiet afternoon reading *Tomorrow Will Be Better* on the porch.

October 4, 1948, Monday

Yesterday I went to Fayetteville by bus. Sh. met me at the bus station, and we went to dinner at the Blue Mill. We ate broiled ham with pineapple, salad, soup, ice cream, and coffee, all for one dollar each. At her apartment, she introduced me to a very attractive girl who teaches economics at the University of Arkansas. We talked about classes and our reactions to students. At 3 o'clock we went to the U-Ark Theater, where we saw Betty Grable in *The Lady in Ermine*. It was a good show as shows go today, i.e. romantic, war, songs, dances, happy ending, all very loosely blended.

After a cup of coffee and a piece of pie at the Blue Mill, we went to the station. She left before the arrival of my bus. I spent the time talking with her landlady, a charming young lady called Miss Hackett. She is short, plump, attractive, blonde, and much interested in Presbyterianism. She is a very earnest, devout, and capable lady. There seems to be no romance in her life. Her religion is her substitute for a sex life, the outlet of an energetic personality that cannot express itself in song, poem, or story.

At the Westville bus station, I met Miss Connie Baker, one of the JBU graduates, who at present teaches at the Farmington High School. She was on her way home from a visit to JBU. There was something virginal and untouched about her. She is healthy, and sex appeal sticks all over her.

Today I rather loafed. Mr. Seal fixed my florescent lights this afternoon, and the room is flooded with a soft bluish light much resembling daylight. The lights cost 13 dollars, of which I'll pay 10 and my landlord will pay the rest.

A young couple, a preacher and his wife, moved into the apartment downstairs. The husband will conduct some kind of services at the Community Building for three months. In spite of the fact that they are evangelists of a sort, they are abundantly blessed with the things of this world. They travel with their own car, loaded with dresses, overcoats, and suits of clothes; and they brought with them in a truck their own Frigidaire and furniture. It is a far cry from the first missionaries who went out barefoot with a walking stick in hand and a bag on their back. Imagine the first Christians traveling about in cars, escorted by trucks transporting their iceboxes and furniture.

October 10, 1948, Sunday

About 3 o'clock Mary who runs the Shop of Style dropped in to see Mrs. Cline. Since she could not see Mrs. Cline, who is on a visit to Little Rock, she visited with me. Mary is a lady in her late forties, rather plump, with graying hair, large blue eyes, and a soft, gentle voice. She is like an overripe fruit ready to spread and soften. As I understand it, she married once, and she is now either a divorcee or a widow. Anyhow, she came to Siloam about the same time I arrived, and she started a millinery shop that is apparently prospering. She does not seem to care for men.

October 18, 1948, Monday

Today I visited for about 15 minutes with Miss Brooks, who had just returned from the island of Cyprus. It is almost unbelievable that she walked the streets of Nicosia and talked with my sister, brother-in-law, and nephew. She flew all the way from Cyprus to Kansas City, Missouri, through Athens, London, and New York. She is a very attractive young lady and must have kindled inextinguishable desire in the hearts and bodies of my very sensitive islanders.

October 19, 1948, Tuesday

Of late, I've developed a habit of talking about myself. Today, for example, I made three personal remarks. First, I told the students that I've been reading *Sir Gawain and the Green Knight* every year since 1918. That was an overstatement. It ought to be since 1939. Secondly, I told them that I developed five diseases when the Selective Service Board drafted me to illustrate the point that one like Gawain might lie to save his life. Third, I told my grammar classes that I once commanded a boy to shut down instead of shut up. In all these cases, I deliberately lied. I have to stick to TRUTH, to the bare statement of facts. From now on, I must resist the temptation of making personal remarks. One must be neither personal nor petty; the moment one begins to speak about himself, he becomes a bore!

October 22, 1948, Friday

I taught only one hour, from 1 to 2 o'clock, and returned home about 2:30 and, the weather being clear and warm, I continued my reading on the porch. About 7:30 I walked to Chandler's to purchase one pint of ice cream. On the way I met a goat dragging its rope. For a moment I thought it must be a huge dog and picked up a stone and feigned at throwing it at him. But the goat stood still, unable to make her mind up. The neighborhood dogs, however, rushed out barking furiously, and the poor goat rushed by me with all the speed she could command. Her owner, whoever it might be, will have great difficulty in locating her. By this time she is probably beyond the city limits and on her way to either Fayetteville or Tulsa.

October 25, 1948, Monday

Yesterday I took the bus and traveled to Fayetteville in the company of Mr. Haley, who happened to go my way. He said that he was satisfied with his new position and that his duties were both light and delightful. He also added that he had heard from neither Dr. White nor Dr. Meadows. I reached Fayetteville about 11:30 and walked to 527 Storer Street, where Sh. is rooming. It took me about half an hour to negotiate the distance between the bus station and her home. It was crisp and cold, but I felt hot and late and developed a headache that lingered with me 'till late in the evening. We dined in the company of Miss Hackett, Sh.'s landlady. Miss Hackett is a short, plump young lady with ample bosom and round hips. She is all that Sh. is not. Sh. is small, dainty, almost breast-less. Somehow the conversation was dull. We talked mainly about preachers, churches, and religion. It seems that by a tacit agreement, we avoided the vital questions that agitate our civilization. It was the conversation of people who are afraid to live, afraid of reality, of people, and escape from life into religion and art. Miss Hackett is a religious worker, and Sh. and I are teachers of English literature who have never yet given up our ambition to produce great literature.

Yesterday was my traditional birthday, at least according to the old almanac. Anyhow, just now I'm 49 years old, and I thank God for the health and happiness and success I've enjoyed until now, and I earnestly pray that the same good luck, good health, and success continue 'till the end of my earthly sojourn.

October 29, 1948, Friday

A very warm day; partly cloudy. The trees were in their full glory. I taught one hour and loafed the rest of the day. At 2:30 I got a haircut and finished in time to see the elementary school children parading in their Halloween disguises. Neither the spectators nor the paraders and their escorts showed great enthusiasm for the affair. The teachers were a little ill at ease, having to parade through the heart of the town wearing small, silly hats. The schoolchildren were too conscious of their hats and costumes, and the spectators simply gazed because they had nothing else to do. I returned home about 3 o'clock and spent the rest of the day reading *Inside USA*. I'm about to finish it. The book has given me a vast amount of information about the country in which I've been living since 1920. One thing is very prominent in Mr. Gunther's discussion of politics. The people are still exploited by the Church, by the big corporations, and by the politicians. Everywhere there is prejudice against a certain group. Sometimes it is the Negroes; sometimes it is the Jews; sometimes it is the Catholics; sometimes it is the Mexicans. It seems that equality of opportunity and advancement by merit, not by prejudice, are far from being achieved. Democracy is really a camouflaged exploitation.

November 3, 1948, Wednesday

Everybody is really astonished. President Truman won the election by carrying 364 electoral votes. And yet there is nothing surprising about it. Commentators, prostitute writers, and Gallup publishers only told people that Dewey was certain to win. Some even thought that the Democrats ought not to even contest the election. The only man who refused to admit defeat was President Truman, and in the end he won. The Republican dreams of cutting income taxes, putting teeth into the Taft-Hartley Law, and silencing all the liberals faded into thin air before the determination of a small, graying man from Missouri. He is neither so intellectual as Dewey nor so brilliant as Wallace, but he went to the people and pleaded his case, and the people responded. Not only did he win the presidency for himself, but he also won a Democratic House of Representatives and a Democratic Senate, which means a smoother administration for the country than the one we've enjoyed during the last two years. In 1946 the arrogant Republicans captured the Senate and the House and fought tooth and nail against every progressive measure initiated by President Truman. They showed that they were conservative, old-fashioned, selfish, and greedy. The people, in spite of their drawbacks and stupidities, discovered their inadequacy and voted them out of office. President Truman's victory is really the victory of the people, i.e. the workers and the professional man.

November 6, 1948, Saturday

I finished the week in high spirits. Two events have raised my spirits: The Democratic victory of last Tuesday's election and Sh. finding an apartment. During the last few days I've been undergoing great sexual stirrings. This may be due to the prime physical condition I now enjoy, thank God, or to the crisp, cold weather that has followed five months of hot weather or from the anticipated pleasures from Fayetteville. Anyhow, I must realize that I'm almost 50 years old and that love-passion upsets both my stomach and my nerves. I thought that I'd outlived my passions, but even a hint that opportunities will be available for expressing them turns me into a burning volcano. Anyhow, I'll take it easy; passions and emotions must be controlled by reason. Even in passion, a wise man should be calm, cool, and collected. They buy passion too dearly who buy it by restlessness and agitation. Let us be calm! Let us enjoy God's blessing in peace and humility. Let the beast in us behave! One has occasionally to behave like a beast, but one must not let the beast in him govern him and take his attention from things that add to his own happiness and the happiness of others! Let us work out our salvation with fear and trembling, yielding to flesh only those things that are necessary to health and efficiency.

November 11, 1948, Thursday

Today being Armistice Day reminds me of the first Armistice Day in 1918. It was my first year of teaching. I took my Chemistry class to the forest by St. Anthony's Gate, and while standing in front of the boys sitting under the eucalyptus trees, I explained the production of the qualities of either Oxygen or Hydrogen. I remember that I interrupted the class at 11 minutes past 11 o'clock for five-minutes of silence and meditation. That was about 30 years ago! How time does fly! Meantime, a new war has been fought and was one I took part in. Today while reading Chaucer's "Pardoner's Tale" with my English Survey class, I remembered my Chemistry class under the eucalyptus trees in distant Cyprus.

November 19, 1948, Friday

It is cloudy, windy, cold. Flurries of snow have been whirling in the air since morning. I put on my heavy overcoat and felt quite comfortable in spite of the fact that I'm still wearing my summer underwear. Today I did nothing except correct papers, give tests, and waste my time and energy. I met Mr. Brooks at the corner of Central and Broadway; he is the man who had been to Cyprus and met my sister and brother-in-law. He is much shorter than he appears in the pictures. He is shorter than I, but he towers over my brother-in-law and nephew. It seems that I have forgotten how short my fellow islanders are. As a matter of fact, I was taller than the average Cyprist, and that is the reason I don't appear diminutive among the Texans and the Arkansans.

November 21, 1948

(Editors Note: The following entry was written not in Greek, but in what Dr. Panage calls a "phonetic alphabet." Dr. James Blankenship, Assistant Professor of Biblical Studies, translated it.)

I went to church. Doctor Brown preached a sermon on Colossians; after the service he waved his hand to me, and he told me that he appreciated the fact that I work at such a small salary. He promised to increase it, and I hope he will do so.

I returned home about 1:30, and I began to read *The Epic of America* by James T. Adams, but soon my mind began to think of making sexual love. I was so greatly seized by sexual desires that I reread the chapter on First Union in *Sane Sex Life*. It is curious how often a man can think he is safe from sexual desires and then all of a sudden feels the things of the flesh.

About four o'clock I dressed and went to the Southern Grill for a cup of coffee and a piece of pie. I returned home and resumed my reading.

I think from now on I will write in phonetic alphabet. It will make this diary unreadable to the average person, and it will help to impress upon my mind the correct pronunciation. Fear has left me very insincere, and I'm in danger of becoming intellectually dishonest.

November 27, 1948, Saturday

Yesterday I took a trip to Fayetteville. I dined at Sh's, and then we went to the U-Ark Theater. To tell the truth, I was not in high spirits. It seems that Sh. discussed my prospects and abilities with Dr. Carter, at whose house she was a guest at Thanksgiving. They both came to the conclusion that I was wasting my time teaching at an unaccredited university and that my chances of teaching English at an accredited university are very slim on account of my foreign accent. The argument with Sh. grew more animated because of a letter from Arkansas Polytechnic College, asking me to teach Latin and Greek and Latin Literature in translation. The offer sounds good, but it stinks. It will take me clean out of the English Department and the teaching of English, for which I've been preparing the last 20 years. I never taught Latin, and I'm too old to review what I learned almost a quarter of a century ago. Of course, Sh. thinks that I ought to get out of JBU, but JBU seems to be created especially for my training in teaching English. I may butcher the King's English, and I may mispronounce many words, but the fact remains that I've been teaching English these last seven years—if not perfectly, at least satisfactorily. I must go forward. Retreat is death. Teaching English is the hardest job I can undertake in the United States of America. But the difficulty involved in it will bring out my best qualities. It is like following a hard God. People die following easy gods. I must persevere; I must face obstacles, overcome them, and rise to magnificent achievement. God gave me an opportunity. I must avail myself of it, even if I have to endure scorn and loss of money. I must not forget that, nine years ago, I was teaching elementary school. With a little more patience, the victory will be mine.

November 28, 1948, Sunday

I answered a letter I received from Miss Lillian Massie, head of the Deptartment of Language and Literature at the Arkansas Polytechnic College. She asked whether or not I was interested in teaching Latin and English. I answered that I was decidedly interested in teaching junior and senior courses in English, American, and World Literature but not in teaching Latin to sophomores and freshmen. After all, I'm a Ph.D., and the head of a division in a university. I don't expect to hear from her again.

December 2, 1948, Thursday

I read an article in the December *Mercury* about fresh-water colleges. The writer classifies Bob Jones as a hillbilly type of fresh-water college. Of course, he doesn't mention JBU simply because it is too small a college to be known outside the county or at least outside the state of Arkansas.

December 8, 1948, Wednesday

Last night I attended a faculty staff meeting at the home economics building. Mr. Jackson drove me home. He said that he had received many compliments about my work, but just the same I've not gotten a raise these last two years. My salary is 225 dollars a month, the lowest paid of the Ph.D.'s and lower than the salaries paid to many members of the faculty who joined the University only lately and have neither my degrees nor my experience. Somehow I have to eat humble pie since I've not yet succeeded in getting rid of my foreign accent and since there are not many universities that will tolerate a chairman of the Department of English who does not even speak English fluently, correctly, and without an accent. Sometimes I think I'm lucky to be employed as a professor of English since it is the subject I most like to teach and apparently less fit to teach. It is easy to conceal one's lack of knowledge, but it is not easy to conceal one's accent. To be tolerated as a teacher of English in an English-speaking country, I must become very preeminent in the fields of American and English Literature.

December 9, 1948, Thursday

It was a cool, clear day, and I spent it teaching and reading monthly newspapers and magazines. I got up rather late, about seven o'clock. It was dark and cold, and lying warm and comfortable in bed, I planned on writing a novel. It will start with the description of a small town like Siloam Springs with its Main Street, JBU, Pet Milk Co., its many churches, and poor hotels and restaurants; and the provocation will be marked by the arrival of a young man at the Station from Kansas City, Missouri. The young man will be myself, of course, glorified and beautified, and his adventure in love, teaching, and writing will be mine. It will be autobiographical, although I am aware of the fact that an artist must practice absolute objectivity or impersonality. But somehow, I have not yet reached the point of thinking and writing in strictly esthetic neutrality. I am subjective; I must become objective. I must try to understand other people's feelings, thoughts, hopes, fears, and aspirations. I guess this subjectivity, which psychologists might call narcissism or infantilism, is the result of the solitude and isolation in which I live. My life is narrow; it deals only with eating, sleeping, walking, reading, teaching, and writing. It is not the rich and full life of a person who abounds in vitality and reacts fully to life.

December 13, 1948, Monday

I received two long letters from Sh., simply about nothing. I suggested that it would be easier for me to visit Fayetteville on a weekday rather than Sunday, but the suggestion seems to interfere with dental appointments and whatnot. Women certainly have a knack of complicating life. She wrote that she would phone this evening, and I'm still waiting for the call.

December 16, 1948, Thursday

Last night I attended the annual Christmas Carol Candlelight Service. I watched Dr. Woodland, who directed the little ones in their efforts to light and extinguish the candles. She looked girlish, virginal, and untouched, although she is 40 years old.

Today I ate a cheese sandwich at the Dodson's Luncheonette, and while the young lady was making the sandwich, she handled money. That made me imagine an invasion of germs. Sometimes ignorance is bliss. Since I've become "germ conscious," I've ceased to drink water at the restaurants. I worry about cracked cups. I shudder at hairs I occasionally discover in the plates or in the coffee. I wash my hands as often as I can. I gargle hospital mouthwash twice a day, and I'm even afraid to touch animals or humans. When I was young and ignorant, I used to literally wallow in dirt. I used to take baths only once in a blue moon. I drank water from open creeks. I ate fruit, candy, and vegetables, on which flies had feasted. I slept in beds abundantly blessed with bugs and other vermin, but now I have grown so fastidious that the very sight of dirt strikes terror into my heart. Sometimes I dream of taking a trip to Cyprus to see my sister and her family, but when I think of the unsanitary conditions prevailing in the island, I change my mind. Cyprus has probably made some progress in cleanliness and sanitation, but I refuse to believe it. America, with all her sanitary equipment, is not clean and sanitary enough for me. I think that without hot water, soap, and daily baths, the world will come to an end. It is strange how the poor human beings are victims of habit and the environment!

December 18, 1948, Saturday

We started Christmas vacation today at noon. Tomorrow I plan to take a trip to Fayetteville. The weather tonight looks cloudy and snowy, but the weatherman promises a clear Sunday. I'm not only worrying about the weather but also about what sort of clothes I'll put on. I'm the kind of man who, having once put on a suit, wears it 'till it's shabby. In many cases, the suits are far from being shabby, but somehow I don't have the physical, moral, nor mental stamina to wear them. I guess tomorrow I'll put on my second-best suit and hope I'll not feel clothes conscious.

I have not yet bought the inevitable Christmas cards and presents. I'll have to buy about half a dozen presents. Of course, I'll have to write a letter "home." It is one of the things I keep putting off. It is a thing of profound wonder to me how small things annoy me. When I think of the trouble and responsibilities of others who have children, wives, mothers-in-law, pets, and whatnot, I really feel ashamed of my little worries. It is an act of Divine Providence that I have not burdened myself with family and great affairs.

December 22, 1948, Wednesday

Last Sunday I visited Fayetteville. I dined at Sh.'s apartment at 608 Storer Street; then I went to the U-Ark. Theater, where I saw *Embraceable You*, a love affair against a background of violence. I returned home by way of Westville about 8 o'clock. Last night I attended a party at Doctor Wills' house; he was celebrating his 44th birthday. He showed pictures of his trip last summer from Siloam Springs to San Diego and back. I spent a delightful night talking with Dr. Woodland (who came dressed in a sleeveless gown), Miss Oieson, Mr. Hoke, Mr. Cox, and the many youngsters who literally overran the place. Mr. Cook drove me home. Today I spent the day reading Giesseppe Bertos' *The Sky is Red*. Just a few minutes ago, the "old gramma," aged 93, the mother of Mrs. Cline, at whose house I'm staying, died of heart failure. It seems unbelievable to me that only hours ago I heard her voice while she was mounting the stairs to her room. They are now preparing her body for the undertakers. Margaret McKinney, the nurse who lives next door, is helping. Dr. Bloav has just left. We are indeed such stuff as dreams are made of, and our little lives are surrounded with sleep.

December 23, 1948, Thursday

About eleven o'clock I met Mr. Brooks, and we had a nice, long talk at the Dodson's Luncheonette. We talked about Cyprus. Then he drove me in his new Cadillac to the Hill. I ate dinner on the Hill and then walked home. I didn't read very carefully because I was still thinking of the sudden passing away of "grandma." The house is full of relatives who have come for her funeral, which will take place tomorrow at 2 o'clock at the Methodist Church. Sh. wrote that she is coming tomorrow from Fayetteville by the noon bus, and I guess I'll have to meet her at the station and talk about the trip to Fort Smith that Mr. Cook wants me to take next Tuesday and stay there overnight. I don't quite like the idea. I rarely sleep well outside my own bed.

I bought three boxes of candy: one for the Sniders, one for the Springfields and one for the Stones (the couple across the hall). Each box cost 89 cents. I still have to buy presents for Dr. Wills and family and my landlady. Thank God, Sh. understood to buy her own present and charge me the price.

December 24, 1948, Friday

About 11 o'clock I walked or, rather, drove up the Hill, carrying two packages of candy, one for the Sniders and one for the Springfields. At 2 o'clock, after waiting in vain for the Fayetteville bus to arrive, I went to the Methodist Church for the funeral of "grandma." It was a very quiet, dignified affair. The old minister preached a very good sermon about a "good life," Mr. Melesky sang a song, and then the pallbearers brought the casket to the carrier. I drove with the McKinneys to the cemetery and witnessed the interment. It was cold and drizzling, but the words of the old preacher sounded full of promise and peace, and I thought of Socrates, that "these things are fated and therefore must be well." I returned home and started reading *Leaves of Grass* by Whitman. About 5:30 Sh. phoned that she was at the Cooks and that after supper they would drive to the Wills', where I'll meet her tomorrow at dinner.

This is the fourth Christmas I'll celebrate as a civilian. I feel sorry for those in uniform. I know how they feel.

December 26, 1948, Sunday

Yesterday I got up at 6:15. It was cold and dark. The water

was lukewarm since my landlady had left for Tulsa and had lowered the gas. I was almost chilled getting my usual morning bath. After dressing I ventured out in the cold wind in search of a restaurant to get my breakfast. All the restaurants were closed. The Brownie is being redecorated and has been closed since last Monday. The Southern Grill is closed, as I understand, for good. The Youree is closed for the 25th and 26th. I found only the Lakeside Café open. I drank a cup of coffee and ate dry toast and returned home to complete my breakfast with Hershey's, of which I always keep an abundant supply. I read 'till noon, and then I dressed and walked in the cold, crisp wind all the way to Dr. Wills' house. Sh. was there too. I gave the presents, two boxes of candy to the children, and Sh. gave me a fine Shaeffers pencil worth five dollars. It is a beauty. Unfortunately, it can't hold the lead, so I'll take it to Leroy tomorrow to fix it. At 1 o'clock we ate our Christmas meal: chicken, biscuits, pears, corn, carrots, coffee, strawberries, cookies, and candy. It was a good meal, although the coffee was cold.

December 31, 1948, Friday

I bought a new tie, and I'll put it on tomorrow in celebration of the arrival of the New Year. In taking leave of the year 1948, I must thank God for the health, happiness, peace of mind, work, and prosperity with which He blessed me. I pray that all my years be as happy, healthy, and prosperous as this year.

January 1, 1949, Saturday

At noon I met Mr. Fred Olney, who told me that his wife was taken to the infirmary and that he was expecting an addition to his family. Like all the "expectant" fathers, he looked worried and upset. He expects a daughter since he already has two boys, and I teased him by telling him that he might get another boy. He wants boys, but his wife wants a girl.

January 8, 1949, Saturday

I taught four hours and loafed the rest of the day. I showed scenes II act III of *Julius Caesar* by Shakespeare to my students. The scenes included the two famous speeches, one by Brutus and the other by Anthony. If Shakespeare had never written anything else, his fame as a great writer would have been assured by those two speeches. One gets an idea of the power of speech; one can understand why success in life depends on one's ability to talk. The power and the glory always belong to the articulate man. A teacher must be able to communicate ideas.

January 10, 1949, Monday

Yesterday I took a trip to Fayetteville. I dined at Sh's apartment on sardines, broccoli, eggs, Jell-O, cake, and coffee. I went to the U-Ark Theater, where I saw *Berlin Express*. It was a plea for the Big Four to stick together and foil the plans of the German underground by splitting the allies. The most remarkable part of the picture was the scenes from the cities of Frankfurt and Berlin. It will take a long time before these bombed cities will be rebuilt. At 6 o'clock I took the bus for Siloam. At Westville I talked with Connie Baker, one of the JBU graduates who at present teaches at Prairie Grove. I reached home about 8:10 p.m., and after a cup of hot chocolate, I returned to my room, undressed, and went to bed.

January 14, 1949, Friday

Tonight while I was returning from town, where I bought

a pint of butter pecan ice cream, Mrs.-- stopped her car in front of 203 Wright St. and inquired about the condition of the Rev.--. As she bent, her face looked so charming and provocative in the semi-darkness of the car that I was almost tempted to stretch out my hand and caress it. Instead of doing that, I entered the car, sat next to her for one or two minutes, and talked about her children. I wondered what would have happened if habit, timidity, and prudence had not restrained the natural impulse to caress beautiful and provocative faces!

January 16, 1949, Sunday

I spent the afternoon reading Flaubert's *The Temptation of St. Anthony*. St. Anthony is almost unknown in America, but he is very well known in the island of Cyprus, and the first school in which I taught was the St. Anthony Public School. Today is the eve of St. Anthony, and without doubt the poor teachers and their scholars were made to attend the evening services in the church of St. Anthony. To me, however, the remembrance of the double holidays (January 17 and 18, the last in honor of St. Athanasius and Cyril) is associated with the green fields and sunny skies of Cyprus at this season. I remember how we used to spend the day playing in the green fields, gathering "lampsanes" and other eatable herbs and plants unknown to this country.

January 22, 1949, Saturday

Last night I was the commentator for a picture called *Palestine Divided*. I'm not very enthusiastic about either the Jews or the Arabs. Yet I ought to be—they are neighbors of my native island of Cyprus. Arab and Jewish blood probably flows in my veins. But somehow, by nurture and nature, I turned my face not to the east but to the west. Turkish and Arabic are languages, the script of which I never mastered. Greek, Latin, English, and French were easy to master. Although I'm Asiatic by birth, I'm thoroughly European and American by education and taste. The avenue by which I was westernized was the study of Greek literature, the real fountainhead of European civilization.

February 4, 1949, Friday

I taught two hours; one hour of Juvenile Literature and one hour of World Classics. I got a haircut and am now reading Louis Bromfield's *Kenny*. I begin to feel the restraints of what they call "academic freedom" here in America. One is in danger, talking about the Greek and Roman gods, to say something prejudicial or antagonistic to the Bible. One is also in danger of being dubbed a communist if he is of the opinion that the Americas can deal with the Russians and end the Cold War. It has become increasingly difficult to express one's thoughts and feelings. One sincere word may brand one either as "red" or "atheist" or to say the least, "unsound in his views." The Americans must have guilty consciences to be so much afraid of an ideology, for I'm sure that America, in air, sea, and land, can withstand assault not only from Russia but also from the whole combined world. In our fear of Russia, we support reactionary governments like the Greek, the Turkish, and the Chinese. We even flirt with France and pay our good money to bribe Arabs, Persians, and Germans. I'm sure those we feed now will someday bite the hand that feeds them. Nations may turn out to be not grateful but revengeful.

February 10, 1949, Thursday

A pleasant, sunshiny day. I took a walk along the dirt road

that leads to the transmitter. I felt so good that I practiced my phonetic exercises at the top of my voice. I also feel a little amorous. This time the object of my passionate desire is Dr. Woodland, the chemistry professor. Well, like all my former infatuations, it will pass away and leave not a wreck behind. Today we read Bacon's "Essay of Love" in class, and in explaining it I felt like Dorothy Dix. It is no use cautioning the young against the evils of love. They will continue to fall in love, marry, and repent or rejoice. It is all in life's mysterious game.

February 22, 1949, Tuesday, Washington Day

In the papers and magazines, pictures have begun to appear, including one photo of the University of Gastonia, North Carolina, where I taught in the spring of 1933 at the now-defunct Greek American College. The pictures are to show that unemployment is increasing and prices are dropping. That might mean the beginning of either depression or some disinflation. This mighty country with its immense resources and its amazing productivity is the most insecure place to live in. Booms follow busts, unemployment is always staring people in the face, banks may close and wipe out savings, and yet nothing has really been done to eliminate this vicious circle of inflation and depression. I don't think this weakness is inherent in the free-enterprise, capitalistic system, but instead is due to the selfishness, greediness, and avarice of the average citizen. With a little good will and a little common sense, this vast continent can be turned into a venerable Utopia where men would work, play, and learn like gods. Instead of the noble and free life, we live like ants, worrying about old-age pensions, raises in salaries, savings, jobs and meaningless duties.

March 8, 1949, Tuesday

Buddy Brown told me that D. Brown had fallen down the steps in the guesthouse and injured his back and spent the day in bed. I gave a bond worth 50 dollars to the Cathedral Fund. The bonds were given to me in 1941 when the school went broke and owed me about 800 dollars in salary. I've already donated most of them, and it will not be long before I get rid of them. They do not mature until 1960, and the school never intended to redeem them. They expect the owner to eventually return them to the school. I might as well do it decently and properly and get a little credit for generosity.

March 11, 1949, Friday

It is a spring day. I spent it, as usual, teaching, reading, and walking. In the afternoon I took a walk along S. Wright Street, Jefferson, and Washington down to the Millsap's Store, where I bought half a dozen oranges and a can of peanuts, then along Main and University and home. On the way, I stopped at the Dixie Store and tried to get a book to read over the weekend. I found no book worth the time and effort. I've reached the stage where I can't afford to waste my time and energy in reading novels, and stories simply to kill time. I have to economize both time and energy and, therefore, concentrate on reading a few books well, rather than many books poorly.

March 14, 1949, Monday

Yesterday I went by bus to Fayetteville. At 3 o'clock Sh. and I went to the U-Ark, where we saw *Song of India*. At 6 o' clock I took the bus for Westville and Siloam. At the Siloam Springs station I met a lady whom I rather liked, but I was shocked to hear that the red-headed boy with her was her grandson, whom she was taking to Springdale on his first bus-ride. At the station of Westville I met another teacher, a friend of Mrs. Thornton, who told me that she was also a grandmother. Both women are in their early forties and still attractive to the eye. They must have married too young. But the joke was certainly on me! Ladies whom I like turn up to be grandmothers.

March 18, 1949, Friday

Today at noon a vivacious blonde sat next to me at lunch. She was a visitor from Little Rock. She was looking for students who were willing to study one year at the expense of the state and then work two years for the Health Department. The offer looked attractive, so I could not see why she had difficulty getting applicants for the scholarships. There are some women who stimulate me. She was one of them. She made me say witty things fearlessly and frankly. The Flower used to stimulate me. Sh. does not stimulate me. I don't even express myself with clarity in her company.

March 19, 1949, Saturday

It was clear and cold. I taught five hours. *The ThreeFold Advocate* published an article about me, in which there were only two erroneous statements: one that I took my Ph.D. in French and the other that I spent my 32 months of Army life in Camp Crowder, Missouri. I'll clip the article and send it to Cyprus; a little advertising will do me no harm. My brother-in-law and sister will be sure to give it to different persons to read it, and that may come in handy some future time.

March 24, 1949, Thursday

Today about 9:30 I developed a slight headache that pestered me until late in the afternoon. It must be the result of my nervous irritation. To start with, while I was bathing and showering, somebody downstairs turned off the hot water, and I had to wait all covered with soap for the water to return. Nothing upsets me so much as interference with my daily ablutions. There was a rush at breakfast, and I had to wait about 20 minutes for my scrambled eggs. Nothing upsets me more than waiting. I really ought to learn patience and wisdom and not be upset by small incidents like these.

March 25, 1949, Friday

Today is the Greek Independence Day, the Greek Fourth of July so to speak. The celebration made us feel proud to be the offspring not only of ancient gods and sages but also of modern heroes. As I look back on those heroes of the Greek Revolution, I wonder by what standard we can judge them. They were certainly small persons with small ambitions, and while they were fighting the Turks, they did not lose the opportunity to wage civil wars. No wonder the modern Greeks, who were taught to admire those heroes, are now engaged in a civil war that has already continued for three years!

March 27, 1949, Sunday

About 3 o'clock I took a long walk in the warm sunshine. I walked up to the station, then down Main Street and Broadway. It is good to be alive in the spring, especially when one is in good health, has a good job, has a good book, and is free from pain and care. Loneliness only attacks me once in a while, but I must defeat loneliness. It is the central and unavoidable fact in life. One is lonely everywhere; women, children, friends, and parents do not cure loneliness. They simply add worries and anxieties.

The strongest man is the one who is most alone. A superior man should not only conquer fear, jealousy, indulgence, prejudice, and resentment but also loneliness. This can be done by realizing one's unity with the Divine ground and all men and creatures.

March 30, 1949, Wednesday

I spent the day teaching and correcting papers. About 3 o'clock I finished *The Grand Design*. The book, to say the least, suffers from indirection. What was J. D. Parsons' purpose in writing it? Was it to demonstrate that the New Deal ideas were abandoned in order to win the War, and the United States made a mistake in helping the Russians to crush the Germans? Can these workers find any protection except by being organized in unions, and can the unions be effective except by being radical? Our State and our Capitalists are conservative; the labor must at least be radical, and it can't be radical unless it nourishes and promotes ideas different from those of the State and Employers. Strife is good for the mortals as well as the states. A state in which politicians, employers, and union bosses get along nicely is no better than a totalitarian state. The equilibrium must be dynamic, and the tension must promote progress in moral, spiritual, and social affairs. It is easy for the comfortable to sneer at the methods by which the union chiefs lead their workers, but one must not forget that our intellectuals—writers, preachers, professors, and journalists—suffer from paralysis of will, and many of them are sold as prostitute writers. They are not conscious that they lack intellectual honesty. They are moral cowards; they have sold their birthright for a mess of pottage. The few who dare to think for themselves and tell what they think frankly and fearlessly are handled either as Reds or Pinks or Yellow-travelers and are hunted down worse than the witches of past centuries.

April 1, 1949, Friday

I'm reading the *Lost World* by Sir Conan Doyle. It is a well-written story. He really knows how to "humanize science." I wish more men would become aware of mankind's lack of scientific, sound, and historical knowledge and apply themselves to make it available to the average reader. It is said that this is the age of the scholar and the citizen, not of the scholar and the gentleman, and yet most scholars, scientists, and critics act as if they are living in an aristocratic society, not a democratic one. We either have to raise the intellectual level of the masses, or else we will be engulfed by them. It is true that they are like beasts that feed, hoard, and sleep and know neither god nor hunger for greatness and righteousness. They were taught no better. We, the intellectual, have fallen asleep on our oars. We cease to be the superior men, as Confucius imagined the intellectuals to be; we are simply his average men.

April 5, 1949, Tuesday

I'm still trying to arrange that trip to Clarksville to attend the meeting of the College English Teachers. It is the first time I've organized such a trip, writing to hotels, and trying to get a driver and gasoline appropriations. Last year the meeting was held in Fayetteville, and the trip was routine for me. It is good to get away from Campus once in a while. It is also good to meet other professors of English literature and get an idea of what they are trying to do. It also adds prestige to me. The administration thinks well of professors who attend meetings. It is supposed to keep the professors well informed and on their toes.

April 9, 1949, Saturday

I returned from Clarksville, where I attended a meeting of the

College English Teachers Association. It was held at the College of the Ozarks. Mr. Kennedy drove me to and from Clarksville. On the way to Clarksville, we had as a passenger Mrs. Parker; and on the way back, Miss Sh. rode with us to Fayetteville. The meeting consisted of simply stating the merits of the three English teachers' associations. I simply can't see the point in presenting their merits. Most of us belong to one or two of them and are familiar with the aims of all. At the banquet held last night at 6 o'clock, President Hurie of the College of the Ozarks welcomed the English teachers. He assured us that we provide an immense service to the country because we teach the youth of the nation how to read and write good English and how to appreciate great literature. Mrs. L.W. Jones, wife of the President of the University of Arkansas, spoke on her work at Bennington College. She is English born and bred, and her pronunciation still trailed with it clouds of British accent. After the banquet we attended *Life with Father* at the theater of the college. It was a creditable performance. The boy who played the father and the young lady who played the mother both acted like professionals. About 11 o'clock we drove to the Ford Hotel, where we stayed in Room 203. I slept neither long nor soundly. The noise of the traffic on Highway 71 was enough to awaken the dead. I dozed off and on, and today I felt sleepy and tired but kept on my feet by drinking coffee. The trip cost me about 10 dollars, excluding the cost of transportation (5.03 dollars) to be paid by our University. Except for the pleasure of renewing acquaintances and driving through the Boston Mountains, the profit derived from the trip was not commensurate to the effort, time, and money spent. It broke the monotony of routine and gave me some confidence in talking to men and women animated by the same ideals, fears, and hopes.

April 16, 1949, Saturday

Last night I walked up the Hill and saw a picture called *One Day in U.S.S.R.* It showed the activities of Russian officials, workers, farmers, scientists, and engineers. It showed Moscow early in the morning, at noon, and in the evening. It showed wedding parties, dancing, and Shakespearean shows. I wonder what *One Day in Cyprus* would look like. The cumulative effect of the various activities was of strength, order, and productivity. I also finished *The Young Lions* by I. Shaw and returned it to the library. A huge novel by Carl Sandburg was on the shelves, but I did not dare borrow it. Life is too short to be spent in reading novels 1,500 pages long. I'm of the opinion that a good writer can express his view of life, whether mature or immature, in a short book of 250 to 300 pages. I always think a big, long book is a nuisance. It seems that the long, episodic novels are written for the reading idlers. I spent the day at home, reading, resting, and walking. It is the first day of Easter Vacation. I'm reading *The Critical Reader,* a textbook containing poems, short stories, and essays with critical analysis attached to them. Today a fight rages between the critics who believe in analysis and those who believe simply in evaluation. One must understand a poem in order to appreciate it, but minute analysis may kill the joy one may find in a poem. My professors in the famous Cyprus Gymnasium killed all delight in the Greek historians, poets, and dramatists by dwelling on every word, metaphor, and simile. A little analysis and a good reading of the poem may help students to enjoy and understand a good poem.

April 18, 1949, Monday

Yesterday, Easter-Day, I visited Fayetteville and lunched at Sh.'s. Then we went to the Ozark Theater, where we saw *Tulsa,* a talkie about the oil and cattle conflict in Oklahoma. Today I received a letter from my brother-in-law. He wrote me that while giving a haircut to the governor of Cyprus, he gave him the clipping from *The Threefold Advocate* to read, and he said that he was greatly impressed with my degrees and position. The world is indeed full of marvels. Here comes one silly girl, one of my students, who interviews me and writes down in a silly paper two columns about me, and the governor of Cyprus reads them and thinks I am a remarkable man! Of course, my sister and brother-in-law must think that I'm a "big shot."

April 23, 1949, Saturday

Yesterday Mr. Kennedy drove me to Fayetteville, where we saw *Joan of Arc* at the U-Ark. Theater. We, of course, picked up Sh. at her apartment on 608 Stover St., and after the show we went to the Blue Mill for a steak supper. It cost me over five dollars, but I didn't particularly mind the expense since the United Sates Treasury refunded me 25 dollars from the amount I paid on income tax. My landlady put a new linoleum floor and new clean curtains in my room, and it looks clean, neat, and comfortable. I thank God for the health, happiness, and success He has bestowed on me. I must work harder and more earnestly to deserve such blessings. I must become a blessing to mankind by giving them a new message of the joy of life and beauty and by making them better, nobler, happier, and wiser. The service most acceptable to God is serving men.

April 30, 1949, Saturday

Yesterday, Friday, I gave an address to the Foreign Students Club. The audience was the smallest I ever talked to. It consisted of three members and two visitors, Miss Shaw and D. Woodland. I talked about America. I'm afraid I made a fool of myself in the presence of D. Woodland, who sat through the address with an air of elaborate unconcern. This morning D. Brown picked me up in his son's car. He told me that he raised my salary to 300 dollars a month (i.e. 74 dollars a month in raise) because he "wanted to keep me" and that the raise has started from last January. The way he phrased it was that it was the "boys' mistake." I'll certainly appreciate the raise and look forward to the next payday with pleasurable anticipation.

May 2, 1949, Monday

About 3 o'clock while I was reading on the porch, the lady across the street who runs an old people's home invited me to visit it. The patients are really very old, over 80 and 90. They certainly looked like skeletons covered with skin. I left the place most depressed in spirit. Old age is as helpless as infancy. The old patients lay in their beds, and nurses had to take care of them. For this care, the patients' children or relatives pay exorbitant prices.

The day was cool and clear after Saturday's evening storm that drenched the town with heavy rains. According to the papers, the storm damaged two or three towns in Oklahoma. Sh. wrote me that *Mourning Becomes Electra* is showing at the U-Ark Theater in Fayetteville. I should certainly like to see it, but it will cost me about five dollars, including transportation and tickets. Emerson was right when he said that we should live in or near a large town. One can borrow books from libraries, see good shows, and meet interesting people. In a narrow place, one's mind grows narrow.

May 9, 1949, Monday

Sooner or later I'm going to get into trouble for my rather

liberal ideas on politics, religion, and sociology. But one must avoid intellectual dishonesty. At the same time one must eat, especially one like me who is a foreigner, having no relatives and speaking English with a faint accent. Besides that, criticism of the Bible and society are outside my subject, and I display scholasticism and pedantry when I venture out of my field. It seems that Spinoza was right when he said that by honest teaching, one rarely makes a living.

May 13, 1949, Friday

At last I got my 75-dollar-a-month raise. It became effective since January 1949, so today I got a deposit slip for 300 dollars covering the first four months. This is the highest salary I've received to date, 300 dollars a month, i.e. 10 dollars a day. I don't value money for itself. To me it means freedom, health, and, above all, leisure. I'll probably stop working summers and devote them to study and research. I must write a book every five years at least. A few days ago, I thought of writing a story called *A Modern Medea*. The hero would be Jason Shaw, the son of my Minneapolis landlady, and the heroine would be the young typist who slaves and saves in order to help him through medical school. Then the hero, influenced by his mother and drunk with prosperity and success, plans to divorce his faithful and aging wife and marry his pretty and young nurse. His wife, made furious by his ingratitude, waylays her husband and his nurse and kills them. The jury later finds her "not guilty." She inherits the property of her husband and marries the famous lawyer who pleads her case. The place may be one of the cities I know so well, like Boston, New York, New Brunswick, Atlanta, Minneapolis, or even Siloam Springs. Such passions are universal, and the scene does not very much matter.

May 14, 1949, Saturday

I gave my measure to Dean Cox to order a cap and gown for me. This year, being the 30ᵗʰ anniversary of JBU, all professors will take part in the procession in cap and gown. I taught four hours and loafed the rest of the day. I got a haircut and bought an Arrow shirt. It seems that, now that my income has increased, my apparel must follow in suit. The wise man will save a few dollars for a rainy day and for leisure and freedom. I'll keep on living the same way.

May 16, 1949, Monday

I taught two hours. I read the *Death of Socrates* with the class. They did not seem at all aware that they were reading the noblest passage in European literature. Indeed, the insensibility of modern youth to literature is frightening. It fills one with despair and dismay. It makes one wonder what will become of Homer, Plato, Shakespeare, and Milton half a century from now. Some of us who derive our keenest and highest joy from the reading of literature seem old-fashioned, not to mention queer. We are tolerated because we teach composition, grammar, phonetics, vocabulary building, and other practical branches of literature. After all, one must write a letter, make a report, use words, and talk over the radio; and these highly desirable attainments are still in the hands of the English department. But while the utilitarian side seems to thrive, the artistic side seems to decline and decay. Even the highest flights in poetry, like the "Belle Dame," "Ode on a Grecian Urn" and "Eve of St. Agnes," cannot be enjoyed or understood unless they are related to our mode of conduct. I'm ashamed of the crimes I commit in order to make poetry palatable, but, after all, my job is to humanize knowledge, to get it across; and all means are legitimate in pursuing such a worthy purpose. The alternative is to stop reading literature in the classroom and spend the time talking about authors, books, and backgrounds. That is like talking about pies and never tasting one. And yet D. Black and D. Thorndike never read any literature with their classes. They lectured on the writers and their works. And both were deemed wise scholars and inspiring teachers.

May 26, 1949, Thursday

Everybody is excited about the coming commencement exercises. I don't particularly like the idea of marching down those hundred steps leading from the California Building to the gym. JBU is really a funny place to work in, celebrate in, or have a good time in. It is really unique. The summer schedule is out. I'll teach one course at 10:45, another at 1 o'clock, and another at 3:30. That makes good work in the heat of the day. D. Woodland, the head of the chemistry department, will teach freshman English. Last year D. Meadows taught freshman English. Everybody is welcome to try his hand at teaching the poor freshmen! In the end, it does not really matter. The present generation is not teachable; they don't care about anything except money, machines, and a good time. They are not exactly dull; they are indifferent, and instruction is wasted upon them.

May 30, 1949, Memorial Day

It rained hard in the morning but cleared, however, about 10 o'clock to allow me to go up the Hill and participate in the Commencement exercises, which were held in the gym in the valley by the swimming pool. The most unpleasant things were that first I had to wear cap, gown, and hood, and second, march down the hundred steps between the California Building and the gym. The cap gave me trouble all the time. It would not stick to my head; I perspired immensely, and since I forgot to take my handkerchief (it was left in the pocket of my coat), I suffered in silence and patience. The speaker was Mr. Cedric Foster, the famous news commentator. He talked about Christianity and communism. Since both are abstract terms and mean different things to different people, his address was rather an ordinary exhortation to the men of God to stand united against godless communism.

June 1, 1949, Wednesday

By this time all the excitement over Commencement, the turning in of grades, etc., is over. I'm enjoying a few days vacation. My impulses powerfully urge me to take the train to Kansas City for a two-day vacation in the great metropolis of the mid-west. But prudence says that it is not worthwhile. I'm likely to return not rested and refreshed but tired and exhausted. Besides, I don't really know how to kill time in a big city where I don't know a single person.

June 2, 1949, Thursday

The great idea I acquired today comes from Aldous Huxley. He thinks the modern man must live on two levels: the metaphysical-scientific and the physical-spontaneous-instinctive. That amounts to the kind of life that Moliere lived, according to van Loon, a combination of epicureanism and stoicism, i.e. intelligent living and high thinking. It is clear what we mean by high thinking; it means reading, teaching, and writing. But what on Earth do they mean by physical-instinctive living? Outside my work, which comprises teaching, reading, and writing, I indulge only in eating, walking, and sleeping. The ability to eat well-balanced, cheerful meals is not available in Siloam Springs. One can't get them for love or money. As for walking, one can walk up and down the hills and develop good muscles. As for sleeping, I sleep long hours, sometimes from 9 o'clock to 6 o'clock. I occasionally travel. I'm either too busy or too lazy to take longer trips. I also spend a vast amount of time in conversation, i.e. gossip.

June 10, 1949, Friday

I received a letter from the vice president of the Baptist college, Shawnee, Oklahoma, asking me to apply for the position of Head of the English Department. He offers 4,800 dollars for 11 months. He mentions that the English department consists of seven members and that the position involves considerable administrative responsibilities. I've not yet answered the letter, but I've made up my mind to answer in the negative. The salary is very attractive, but I hate to accept the responsibilities of the head of the department in a university with an enrollment of 1,500. Besides that, the Baptists are church people and narrow-minded, and we don't agree on many points. They probably think I'm a Baptist. They would not offer an important position to one who, to say the least, is agnostic and logical and not devout nor theological. Anyhow, I mailed the letter to Sh. She will get excited over it, and above all, it will prove that my way of doing things is much more remunerative than the way she often advocates. I believe that the building of my reputation at JBU will help me to secure a better job; she believes that one gets somewhere by constant changes. A rolling stone gathers no moss.

June 13, 1949, Monday

Yesterday I went by bus to Fayetteville. I dined at Sh.'s. It was cool and cloudy. Today it poured for two or three hours in the afternoon. It has been raining for a month, and everybody is longing for sunshine. I have finished Chekhov's *Sea Gull,* and started reading *The Three Sisters.* Nothing memorable has happened. I've not yet answered the letter from the Oklahoma Baptist University, neither have I answered the letter from Cyprus. I'm one of the worst correspondents in existence. I don't write more than half a dozen letters every year. It is not because I don't care about people. It is simply an unpolluted laziness and indolence!

June 17, 1949, Friday

I decided not to answer the letter from the Oklahoma Baptist college. I don't contemplate a change and don't see why I shall indulge in correspondence that will rouse the suspicions of my employers and upset my peace of mind. I'm not yet quite ready for change.

June 18, 1949, Saturday

I remember that exactly 10 years ago today, I received my Ph.D. at the Commencement Exercises held in the corner of the stadium of the University of Minnesota. Since that time I've had many experiences, including 32 months in the Army and seven years of university teaching as head of the English department at JBU. I've also earned about 10,000 dollars. In 1939, I was worth about 500 dollars. I still have the Elgin watch that Theo Kelly gave me as a graduation present. I really wonder what became of her. I've not seen her in the last eight or nine years. It is, however, no use looking back. There is no past. There is only this hour; let us make the most of it while it lasts. It is strange that after 10 years, the only episode at the graduation that I vividly recall is the hand-clapping from the faculty row while I was being invested with the hood and given the sheepskin.

July 15, 1949, Friday

Yesterday Mrs. Baker visited the Campus; she brought Sh. and her sister Geor. and the boy Donnie. Mrs. Baker looked white and dry like an old lady of 65. Back in the year 1939 she looked very desirable, and for a time I entertained the idea of "going steady" with her. That was 10 years ago, and she and I were comparatively young.

July 31, 1949, Sunday

My classes in World Classics, Advanced Grammar, and Juvenile Lit. are larger than ever. Last Sunday D. Brown was on the Hill, and he called a staff and faculty meeting at 3 o'clock. He announced that JBU financial troubles are about over. Mr. Jackson has left yesterday for Kansas City, Missouri. Mr. Cox has been promoted to executive vice-president and registrar, D. Wills was appointed dean, and D. Woodland is now associate dean. The library committee has interviewed a new librarian, and a new instructor of home economics has been appointed. I kept on reading, walking, teaching, and sleeping. It is a life of pleasant routine. Others may pity me, but I, who in years past spent anxious summers looking for jobs or being unemployed, now enjoy the kind of life that consists in serving others and improving myself. Sh. left for Minneapolis, Minnesota, last week. She will study Methods and Techniques of Reading at the University of Minnesota. She will return by the first of September. I'm writing this at 6 p.m., sitting on the swing on the west porch of 203 S. Wright Street, where I have been staying since 1942. The sky is clear, the trees and the streets washed clean by the recent rains. A few birds are chirping, and a few cars go by. It seems to be an Eden, but an old people's home, where the aged ones lie in bed helpless like babies, is across the street. On the side street, a man is in danger of losing his sight, and my landlord is in a hospital in Memphis, recuperating from an operation. Sickness and misery abound even in this earthly paradise.

August 7, 1949, Sunday

It has been a cool week. I taught three hours a day as usual and read, slept, walked, and loafed the rest of the day. Jane Meleskay, the red-haired daughter of the dean of women, has been taken ill with polio in Florida while visiting at the Whitmores'. This morning Rev. Schimpff mentioned three children on the Campus who are suffering from rheumatic fever. It seems that Miss Mary Shaw will not teach freshman English this year. Today, at noon, Mrs. Wills asked my advice about accepting the responsibility of teaching freshman English. I tried to dissuade her by exaggerating the amount of work involved. She is the mother of three children, the wife of the dean, and a teacher of music by profession; therefore, in my opinion, she is not the right person to undertake the important and vital job of teaching freshman English. Since Sh. left, no one has taken her place. We have had three or four teachers of freshman English, all of them novices.

About 1 o'clock I returned home and spent the afternoon reading *The History of Herodotus*, which I finished about 3 o'clock. I particularly liked his last remark, put in the mouth of Cyrus, "that soft countries give birth to soft men" and the conclusion that the preeminence of the Persians in Asia and the Greeks in Europe is due to the tough countries they inhabit. He believes that place counts more than race in developing a nation. He is probably right. As for myself, I prefer to live in a "soft" country with plenty of sunshine, cool breezes, and abundant food so I can live outdoors as much as possible. Religion, science, law, etc., originated in "soft" countries like Palestine, Greece, and Italy. The "rough" countries—Germany, England, the northern and western United States—have given us industry, factories, slums, commercial comfort, and ugliness.

August 19, 1949, Friday

It has been a rather cool day, owing to a 15-minute windstorm that occurred about 3:30 last night. I corrected the examination papers and turned the grades in. I gave Mr. Olney a check for 20 dollars to build or buy a bench for the Sunday school children. I taught three hours and kept busy the rest of the day. D. Wills will show a picture lasting one hour and thirty minutes at the Old Chapel at 8 o'clock. It is a kind of religious picture about reaching Heaven. It is a rather late performance, and I need sleep and rest if I'm going to survive the summer school mood that usually descends on students and teachers about this time!

Sh. is still in Minneapolis attending the University of Minnesota. She will be back in 15 days. Dr. Brown has left for California, and everybody feels rested and relaxed. Well, I'll dress and go out for my evening walk.

August 22, 1949, Monday

I spent the day teaching and reading. I finished Swift's *Gulliver's Travels*. Swift is really a great satirist. The contrast between men governed by passion and horses governed by reason is masterful. He shows men at a great disadvantage since they don't act like rational beings. I started reading *The Art of Writing Fiction* by Mrs. Orvis, a book that was sent to me for examination by the Prentice-Hall Company. Like all books written by women, it excels in good details but fails to grasp the whole aspect of the subject; women are good researchers but poor generalizers.

They lose themselves in small details. They seldom distinguish the forest for the trees!

August 26, 1949, Friday

Last night while I was in the Administration Building performing the duties of the Officer of the Day, a retired old man dropped in. He wanted to see the buyer for our store in order to induce him to introduce butternut squash. He then began to talk about remedies for cancer (he was sure he had the recipe and would gladly give it to Mr. LeTourneau), and other cures. He simply showed that he was slightly unbalanced or, rather, obsessed with certain ideas. This morning he turned up on the Hill and brought me a bag of grapes and peaches as a present for listening to him. I thanked him and gave the fruit to Miss Shaw and Snider at the office. I received a letter from Sh. She will be in Siloam Springs on Tuesday afternoon on her way to Fayetteville from Minneapolis. I also received a copy of the *Ethnos*, in which a column is given to the translation of the article written about me in *The Threefold Advocate*. I sounded good in modern Greek, and perhaps it has created in the minds of my fellow countrymen the picture of a highly successful man who rose from immigrant to head of the English department of an American University. A little prestige among my fellow countrymen will do me no harm. Well, it is only eight days before the end of the summer session. The plans about my vacation are nebulous. I guess I'll go once or twice to Fayetteville and also visit Kansas City.

August 18, 1949, Sunday

Exactly 10 years ago today I took the Rock Island Rocket for Kansas City and Siloam Springs. I was dressed in my best

Oxford gray suit. I wore a straw hat and carried my small suitcase, in which I carried a clean shirt, a collar, my Greek-American Bible and Mark Twain's *Huckleberry Finn*. I also remembered the plump Jewish girl who had dyed her hair blond and was going, like me, to interview with somebody for a job. It was my good luck to meet that Jewish girl more than once later in Minneapolis, and I was surprised to discover that her hair was raven black. I also remember how I asked the taxi driver for a good hotel, and he recommended to me The Plaza Hotel, which I've been patronizing these last 10 years. I also remember how warm it was in contrast to the present coolness. Well, let the dead past bury its dead.

September 4, 1949, Labor Day

I spent the day reading *Point of No Return* and correcting papers. I dined at the school. Mr. Springfield and Mr. Snider had a box of cigars, and since Mr. Seal and I made some wisecracks, they wanted us to smoke a cigar. We got a cigar, unwrapped it, and took two puffs to the satisfaction of everybody in the dining room. It was a silly thing, but the main thing is that I did it with out any feeling of bashfulness, embarrassment, or exhibitionism. It seemed natural and proper that I would puff at a cigar since I promised to do it if they got sons.

September 14, 1949, Wednesday

I took a trip to Tulsa on September 5 with the Sweets. During my stay in Tulsa, I took two bus rides and saw *Come to the Stable*. Last Thursday, September 8, I took the 2.50 p.m. train for Kansas City. I stayed at the Plaza Hotel (Room 604). I took all possible bus rides, saw all the worthwhile pictures, bought a suit of clothes and also a much-needed Knickerborke Shampoo Bath sprinkler.

I enjoyed my stay in the great metropolis of the mid-west, but to quote a trite verse, "it much grieved my soul to see what man made of man." One could see very clearly the power of Mammon. Great stores, large cafeterias, luxurious hotels, palatial motion picture houses, vast auditoriums, and interminable roads lined with imposing buildings, buses, trolley cars, trains, and stations give proof of the might of Mammon. The spirit of man is careful about toys, the latest of which are television sets. Man is not man anymore. He is either a producer, a seller, or a consumer of goods. The few of us teachers, preachers, and artists who mind the things of the spirit seem, sound, and smell superfluous.

September 16, 1949, Friday

It has rained or, rather, drizzled all day long. The retreat that was scheduled for 1:30 today has been postponed 'till tomorrow afternoon. I ate at the University dining hall. The food was chili con carne and beans. Chili, hot dogs, and popcorn are the items of American diet that do not agree with me. At my table sat the three new teachers, all of them in their late fifties or early sixties. The professor of history is well preserved; she must have been beautiful in her youth. Even now she is not ugly. There is great excitement in town on account of the first football game between the Siloam Springs High School Panthers and the Fayetteville Bull Dogs. I'm afraid the football fans will catch cold since it is drizzling, wet, and chilly. Let us hope that the excitement will drive away the cold.

September 26, 1949, Monday

I attended a special assembly at 11 o'clock. D. Brown spoke about "going the second mile." I taught two hours, from 1 to 3 o'clock, and then I returned home and spent the afternoon reading on the porch. It is glorious weather with the sun shining bright and warm and the leaves of the trees tinged with gold and red. This kind of weather reminds me of the New England falls. The papers are full of atomic items. Since President Truman stated that the Russians have exploded an A-bomb, everyone is talking about radar, defense, offense, bases, rockets, B-36's, and B-50's. It is a mad world. We are either engaged in war or preparing for or fearing war. It would be better to think and talk of peace. But peace seems to be on the defensive and war on the aggressive. Money for weapons is easily voted for, but money for education is hard to find.

October 6, 1949, Thursday

I walked down Mount Olive Street and passed by Mrs. Rapp's house, where Sh. used to room three years ago. I noticed that there were two new grocery stores on the street and a flower shop. Otherwise, the road looked as quiet and indifferent as ever. The moon shone in all the splendor of its fullness. D. Cook told me that a total eclipse of the moon will take place tonight at 10 o'clock, but I'm going to bed at my usual time. Eclipses of the moon are not as interesting as eclipses of the sun. The last time I saw an eclipse of the sun was about 20 years ago in New York. It was a cold, icy January morning, and I almost froze to death. I quite remember the pain in my back as I was riding down town in the subway train. That happened before the time I knew New Brunswick, Atlanta, Minneapolis, or Siloam Springs. It seems so long ago!

October 7, 1949, Friday

I taught two hours from 1 to 3 o'clock and then returned home, where, sitting on the porch swing, I read *Intruder in the Dust*. The story was good, but the way it was told through the perspective of a 16-year-old boy was rather tedious and wearisome. Clarity of thought and expression must not be sacrificed for technical devices that simply happen to be fashionable. I guess the story could be more clear and effective if it were told from the author's point of view instead of trying to gauge the feelings and reactions of a 16-year-old boy who, astonishingly, knows more about the race than most mature people.

October 8, 1949, Saturday

I deposited 50 dollars into my savings account (No. 478). My intention is to strengthen my savings account at the expense of the JBU Exchange. I've accumulated 2,500 at the Exchange, and that is neither wise nor proper. I might never collect such a sum, or else I'll collect it as slowly as I have accumulated it. I left that sum with the school because I wanted to help it in meeting its current obligations. I lectured today on Tennyson and Dreiser and on the contributions of the Normans to England. The Contemporary Class still suffers from the lack of books. Those ordered from Dallas, Texas, have failed to reach our store yet. I decided tonight to walk to the Kay-June for supper. I have cause to regret such a decision. I walked 20 blocks, waited half an hour, and ate a fried chicken that gave me only four mouthfuls of meat. It was not worth the trouble or the expense. I'll stick to my usual supper of apple pie and pint of ice cream. It is not only cheaper but also more nourishing and much cleaner. It is a strange thing how, in a country abounding with provisions, one fails to get a good meal.

October 10, 1949, Monday

Yesterday I went by bus to Fayetteville. It was cloudy, warm, and sticky. Sh. met me at the station, and we ate lunch at the new Ferguson's Cafeteria. At 2:15 we stood in line outside the U-Ark. Theater to buy tickets to see *Hamlet*. We managed to buy tickets and get to our seats as the play began. It was a good version of Shakespeare's play although one could spend time and energy finding fault with the prominence given to mother-complex, the drunken king, and the weakness of Ophelia. At 6 o'clock I took the bus for Westville and Siloam Springs. My landlady told me that somebody was trying to reach me by telephone from Atlanta, Georgia. I don't really know who it might be. I've not seen nor talked to most of my acquaintances there these last 20 years. Of course, the message disturbed my slumbers. To add to this nervous tension, the wind was howling all night. I woke up at 5:30 feeling the same way I used to feel while I was in the Army: restless and nervous. Somehow I finished the day's work without losing my temper and saying anything silly. I also received a letter from my brother-in-law. He wants me to pay 50 dollars to an American company for things they sent to him in Cyprus. He also stated that I've accumulated 529 English pounds in Cyprus.

October 11, 1949, Tuesday

Last night about 9 o'clock I was called to the telephone. It was Roxane calling from Atlanta. I have not seen her nor heard her voice since Christmas 1932 or 1933 when I visited Atlanta for the holidays. It was a very bad Christmas vacation. Something had happened to my spine, and I felt excruciating pain. Besides that, I was most unhappy teaching in the now-defunct Saint Stephanos College in Gastonia, North Carolina. At that time, Roxane was a freshman at Brenau. She didn't graduate 'till 1938, when I was teaching in Minneapolis. Later on she went to New York in an effort to win fame and fortune by writing. She did not break into print, but she married in 1940. During the war she was in Jacksonville and wrote me one or two letters. She was happily married and the mother of one or two children. Her phone call last night was meant to be a surprise, and it was a surprise. She sounded like a well-poised, clearly articulate woman. She asked how I was and what I was doing. I told her that I was better than ever and that I was teaching English.

October 13, 1949, Thursday

Today I received a letter from Roxane; it was, in part, an apology for the surprise telephone call of last Monday evening. She said that she has moved to Atlanta after 17 years of ill-fated travels and that she has sold some things she wrote. Well, I should not worry very much about a woman I've not seen since 1933. She must have changed in more than one way.

October 14, 1949, Friday

I made up my mind to drink at least three pints of half-and-half every week. Since I do not eat meat as often as I ought, I must increase my energy and stamina by consuming a larger amount of dairy products. The Circus is in town; even Rev. Schimpff went to see it. At class today we discussed Faith versus Reason, the problem of Religion versus Science, and of both versus Art. The last is a very complicated one. It seems that all three are needed by mankind to satisfy his intelligence (science + philosophy, truth), his esthetic sense (beautiful) and his religious sense (his dependence on powers beyond himself). One thing is sure: Art and Religion will never destroy mankind; they may lead him astray, but Science can destroy mankind. Its inventions culminated in the A-bomb, and now atomic weapons threaten to wipe out vast numbers of the human race and reduce the survivors to a life of misery and suffering. Therefore, Religion and Art must be stressed just now. They may defeat the destructive forces released by Science. I don't mean that Science itself is evil. I mean that the use of its practical discoveries ought to be restricted and regulated by men and women who believe in goodness, beauty, and good will. It is about time for Science to become the servant and not the tyrant of mankind. As a servant, she will be a blessing; as a tyrant, she will be a menace—if not a curse.

October 16, 1949, Sunday

At 4:30 while I was reading sitting in the porch swing, an elderly lady passed by, still robust and attractive to the eye, who told me that once she was a dancer and cabaret entertainer and used to make big money. Later on she married a man much older than herself. He was stricken with paralysis, and she returned with him to Siloam and took care of him 'till he died. She is left now with a house that gives her 35 dollars a month income. To make both ends meet, she keeps house for a man whose father is sick in the hospital. She earns another 60 dollars a month. She remembers the old time. She wishes she had the money she squandered when she was young, popular, and attractive. It is certainly an anomaly to meet such a person on S. Wright Street in Siloam Springs. I did caution her not to talk to everyone about her past. It might reduce her chances of being employed. Very few people in Siloam would care to employ an ex-dancer and ex-cabaret entertainer.

October 23, 1949, Sunday

On Friday I rode in Mrs. Jaquerdist's car with Miss Alton and D. Wilson to Petit Jean State Park, where I attended a College Higher Education Professors' Meeting. We started about 6 o'clock in the morning amid lightning and thunder. We ate breakfast at the Ferguson's Cafeteria in Fayetteville and then continued our ride toward Morrilton and Petit Jean Park. It rained almost all the way. We reached our destination about 12 o'clock, and after being assigned to a bunk and paying 7.50 for registration and food, we patiently waited for the lunch. The meals were extraordinarily good. The meetings were nothing to brag about. We discussed humanities in relation to general education. On Friday we were forced by the rain to stay within Hardison Hall. The evening speaker, a professor of history from the University of Oklahoma, was very stimulating, entertaining, and instructive. He stressed the fact that we are still provincial in our outlook and that, if we are to avoid World War III, we have to make an effort to understand other nations, cultures, and ideologies. What he said was not news to me, but the way he presented his point of view, with humorous anecdotes and insinuating words, was a revelation to me. It gave me the key to what one means by saying that you can inform them while entertaining them.

I slept on Friday evening in a bunk like I used to do in the barracks of Camp Robinson. I slept by fits and starts; I only slowed in the morning. Everybody was wanting to take possession of my washing bowl. I didn't even brush my teeth. On Saturday before breakfast, Mr. Ferm drove me to Cedar Falls and the lodge. It seems that Arkansas has more natural beauty than I was aware of. The speaker was D. Russel of the Higher Education Division of U. S. He developed the difference between liberal education and technical and general education. He insisted that any subject can be taught in a liberal way if we teach not only "how" but also "why." The mere knowing "how" is not enough. It turns men into helpers, dangerous specialists, and vocationalists; it's only by teaching them the "why" that you may make them liberal minded by giving them an understanding of the economical, social, and political forces of our civilization.

October 25, 1949, Tuesday

I spent the day teaching, walking, and reading. I don't know why a man of my age and rank would be greatly disturbed because a silly coed whispered something to her neighbor. I called attention to the fact that talking in the classroom makes me mad, and the very statement of that fact seemed silly to me. Well, next time I'll not say anything in public; I'll simply ask the offender to stay after the class is over. Such episodes happen once or twice a year, and they are very painful to me. After 32 years of teaching, I ought to have got used to everything!

October 31, 1949, Monday

Yesterday I went by bus to Fayetteville. It was cloudy and raining. Sh. looked thin and weak. She has not been very well lately. She had some kind of infection that made it necessary for her to take penicillin and be on a diet. She cooked a nice meal for me, and we went to the U-Ark. Theater, where we saw an uncommonly good picture called *That Midnight Kiss*. The singing and the piano playing were superb. By the time we left the theater, it had rained and it turned cold. Today it was really cold; the thermometer went down to 27 degrees this morning. I found in my letterbox two letters from home: one from my sister and one from my brother-in-law. They wanted me to send an invitation so that my nephew might come to America for study. He has not finished any school and has no diploma, and at the rate of 2.80 a pound, his family will go broke to support him in school. They wrote that the "boy" has made up his mind and that there is no way out of it. I sometimes think that children are not blessings to their parents' lives. This is Halloween evening. In the year 1923, when I was teaching in Cambridge, Massachusetts, the Greek fruit sellers on Massachusetts Avenue told me that it was a celebration welcoming winter. It was already colder than the coldest winter in Cyprus!

November 1, 1949, Tuesday

I put on my winter underwear. I walked up the Hill about 9 o'clock in the clear, cool sunshine. I loafed most of the time, looking at the pictures in several magazines, including one published by the Soviet Union. It contained pictures of the Estonians at work, at play, and at study. It seems, if the pictures don't lie (for even pictures lie), that in the Soviet Union everyone is working, learning, and studying. Well, it might be true. In Cyprus a few decades ago everyone thirsted and hungered after learning. Schools were crowded, and teachers were worth their weight in gold. Nothing came of that moment. Lawyers, politicians, and teachers proved narrow and selfish. The respect for learning has subsided. Men asked for bread, and they were given stones. They were given grammar of ancient and modern Greek languages, unhistorical history that was doctored and distorted by national myth, and they were fed on rumor and myth. The result of such education was party strife, emotionalism, and despair. Let us hope the Soviet youth's aspirations will not be dashed to the ground.

November 5, 1949, Saturday

I have read in the November issue of *Mercury* an article, "What is Wrong with College Teaching?" The man who wrote it seems to expect miracles of college professors: they must be scholars, do research work, understand the youth, and teach creatively. Some of us who have been teaching for years know that the most serious drawback in college education is the lack of knowledge, intelligence, and ambition of the students. Neither scholars nor researchers nor new methods will materially change the situation. No teacher can teach students who do not know how to read or are averse to studying.

November 8, 1949, Tuesday

It seems JBU is going through one of its chronic financial crises. I have left about 2,800 dollars in the Exchange—that's about half of all my earthly possessions. I guess if everybody was not so anxious to draw his full pay the school could operate easily. But some members of the faculty need their money or distrust the school and, therefore, rush to draw their pay as soon as it is deposited to their account. I have perhaps done an unwise thing and may be called a sucker, but it is the right thing to do under the circumstances. It is hard in this world of ours to be both good and wise; sometimes goodness seems and sounds like foolishness, and wisdom smells like selfishness. It does not seem right to be an individualist, always looking after number one, and it appears foolish to be an altruist. This confusion of values is due to the sad condition of our society. Goodness, wisdom, and altruism are virtues; if they appear to be vices and weaknesses, it is not their fault; it is the fault of the sick world. That explains why the good and virtuous man today appears to be a charlatan, while the bad and selfish man appears to be a respectable person. That's the customary morality that celebrates what is respectable and not what is best. It is the morality of the sleepers and not of the awake ones.

November 14, 1949, Monday

Yesterday D. Mort drove me to Fayetteville; we parted at the Ferguson Cafeteria. Sh. was rather ill and could not go to the movies. She lay on the couch all afternoon. Today after great mental debate, I wrote a rather long letter to my sister and brother-in-law in Cyprus, advising them against sending their only child to America for education. The youngster, from what I can gather from such a great distance, has never finished a school; he has neither diploma nor certificate. He is spoiled to the very marrow of his bones; he is too immature and too young to be thrown into the turbulent waves of modern America. I advised them to send him to Beirut University for two years and then transfer him to an American University. That will give him a better understanding of himself and the world, and it might cure him of his monomania of coming to America.

November 16, 1949, Thursday

I attended Chapel; Mr. Miller talked; he is one of the survivors of the death march from Bataan. He told something about his experiences in that march and also of his determination to go back to the Philippines and teach the gospel. He believes that motion pictures are a better medium for teaching the gospel than preaching. It may be that he is right, but I doubt it. The picture and the radio lack the human touch and human appeal. The religious feelings are too subtle and deep to be communicated by pictures that touch only the sight. The entrance into the soul is still by hearing and especially by reading. People who have not the patience to read and hear are not worth saving or being bothered about. They will turn religion into excitement or show business.

December 2, 1949, Friday

The Christmas lights have been turned on since yesterday, and Santa Claus is expected to arrive at town at 10:30 a.m. tomorrow. Of all the traditional figures, Santa Claus has survived because he has been adopted by the enterprising businessman of the United States. He is my old friend Saint Nicolas, whose holiday is held on December 6. He is the patron saint of the sailors, but in America he has been turned into a hale, stout, rosy-cheeked old man who rides a sled dragged by reindeers; he is always dressed in red, and he is loaded with gifts. Children, as well as adults, expect him to bring them presents. He is the best friend of merchants and sellers. He is not very much loved by the buyers. His hold on America is strong, and every year it is getting stronger and stronger. His arrival in every town is celebrated as the event of the year. He brings people to the business quarter and stimulates the spending of money.

December 5, 1949, Monday

Yesterday I went to Fayetteville by bus, the weather being ideal for traveling; I dined at Sh.'s and went on a long walk by myself since she had to attend a tea. About 6 o'clock I took the bus for Siloam. The moon was full and bright, and the trees, homes, fields, and hills seemed to be steeped in silver. The road between Westville and Siloam being under repair, the trip was slow and shaky.

December 10, 1949, Saturday

A rainy day; I taught five hours. I am much pleased to have been voted for a second time as the most popular teacher on the campus.

December 16, 1949, Friday

I supped at Kay-June's. Mrs. Stanfield was wrapping presents intended as a shower for Robinson and his bride, whose marriage will be solemnized on Sunday in the California Lobby. Another school wedding will take place tomorrow. Both couples are very young and deserve both pity and admiration. They will certainly need all the good luck that they can get. I hope they did not mistake puppy love for real love. The modern coeducational school has become the greatest matrimonial bureau on the continent. A girl can at least get a husband, and a boy can at least get a wife. In addition, if they persevere, they can get a degree if not an education. Love is still the regulation of men and their institutions. He can't be kept out. He must be taken into account. Our famous JBU does emphatically proclaim that it approves of marriage. As a matter of fact, D. Brown, founder of the University and chairman of the Trustees, has publicly declared that he guarantees a husband to every young lady who attends JBU. He comes perilously near to fulfilling his promise. Most of the girls who attend JBU marry before or immediately after graduation.

December 17, 1949, Saturday

Today at noon, Christmas vacation started. Everyone was anxious to get somewhere for the vacation. Two lady professors are going to New Orleans; Mr. Gilbert and family are also going to New Orleans. About a dozen of the students left for Minnesota, and about two dozen for Chicago. Once when I was young and adventurous, I used to get excited over a vacation. At present I welcome it. It is a time for reading, rest, and walking. Above all, it liberates me from routine. Life has become monotonous. One has to meet certain classes at certain hours. One has to cover so much ground; one has to attend so many meetings, chapels, and affairs. The line between indifference, neglect, and interest is very thin. If one cuts a few chapels, he appears not to be a good Christian; if he cuts faculty meetings, he is considered indifferent; one no more dares call his soul his own. It has never been harder to hit the golden mean in work, rest, and sociability.

December 24, 1949, Saturday

It is Christmas Eve. I spent the day reading, walking, eating, and worrying whether D. Wills got the present I put in his box. I also worried a great deal what to buy for my landlady. At last I bought her some soap and perfume in a set that cost 2.50. I'm glad this worry is over and Christmas shopping is over. It is really silly and expensive. This year I spent about 15 dollars in cards and presents. I received a letter from my sister Corinna. She wants me to reconsider my decision and invite her son Byron to come to America to study and be a second father to him. The boy has finished neither the Cyprus Gymnasium nor the American Academy. He has been a problem child, and his parents are apparently trying to unload him on me. I have plenty of work to do without supervising or worrying over a youngster. By nature and by education I'm very sensitive; words, or even glances, hurt me. To take care of someone will give me anxiety and worry too deep for words.

December 26, 1949, Monday

Yesterday being Christmas Day, I rode on the bus to Fayetteville and dined with Sh. It rained almost all day long. Between Fayetteville and Prairie Grove, the bus was caught in a heavy shower that looked like a cloud burst. We reached Westville on time, but the Fayetteville bus was half an hour late, so the Siloam bus did not start on its way 'till 8 o'clock. At last, about 9 o'clock I reached home. It seems to me that every time I go to Fayetteville, the weather becomes unnecessarily disagreeable. If I were superstitious, I should attribute the bad weather to divine disapproval.

December 27, 1949, Tuesday

I took long walks in the warm sunshine and ate a good dinner (T-bone Steak at 1.25). I received many cards, the most important among them from Evangeline, who has not written me these last five or six years, the Swanns, and the Wottons. I guess I must buy some extra cards and reciprocate. All of them have been good friends to me. I turned down an invitation to attend a potluck supper given by faculty to the students at the Home Economics Building. I preferred to stay at home, eat my pint of ice cream, and do some reading. Besides that, in suppers of this sort, the food is brought from different homes in various vehicles, packed in various vessels, handled by many hands and, therefore, anything but sanitary. Of course, restaurant food is not cleaner, but one at least gets just one kind of germs.

December 29, 1949, Thursday

I spent a delightful day reading, walking, eating, and dreaming. It is clear and warm. At 3 o'clock I ventured out without overcoat; the thermometer in the sun stood at 80 degrees and in the shade at 68 degrees. I finished *Man Against Myth*. The book confirmed my belief in rational thinking and social-mindedness. Faith, emotion, and feeling point an escape from the world. They are means of perpetuating existing evils. Reason changes the world. This is the voice of the Greeks. Belief in Reason = Fine Thinking. Unfortunately, Religion and the Exploiters of the leisure class, or the coupon-clippers, encourage irrationalism. Irrationalism helps them in two ways. It prevents the people from seeing things as they are, and it prevents the people from scrutinizing their ideology. It deprives people of objective reality and logical thinking. Some of the myths he demolished were that "words cannot hurt me." One has to look after oneself (a masterly analysis of selfishness versus social-mindedness). One can't be free and safe at the same time. You can't change human nature, etc. The reading of the book has revealed to me the fact that I don't know how to think. I'll get hold of a book on logic and read it carefully. No wonder I can't express myself with clarity and force! I don't know whether it is due to illogic or grammar or late years. I'm giving a course in advanced grammar, and I'm beginning to have a faint idea what makes a good sentence. At least I know the five elements of a sentence when I see them, i.e. subject, verb, complement, modifiers, and independent parts. I did not know this simple fact until two years ago. My grammar is still shaky, my vocabulary poor, and my thinking unclear. A human being who boasts of a Ph.D. from an American University who pretends to educate the world as head of the English Department ought, at least, to know how to think, how to talk, how to write, and how to read. My only consolation is that millions of human beings are not even aware of the existence of the above arts. But I'm supposed to be a leader, and a fine leader I am! For lack of logic, i.e. clear and accurate thinking, I can't distinguish fact from fiction, appearance from reality, myth from truth. I've been feeding on myth and rhetoric, not on reality and logic.

December 31, 1949, Saturday

It has been the custom of many people to review the achievements and failures of the outgoing year and make new resolutions. I remember very distinctly that once (it must have been as far back as 1917) I made a resolution to master the English tongue by the end of the following year. It was pure ignorance of the difficulty involved in that task that prompted me to make that rash resolution. I've been repeating that resolution every year since then. The older I grow, the more I appreciate the difficulties involved in mastering a foreign language like English. Very few people have ever mastered it. Millions use it as clumsily as I play piano. Anyhow, I must never give up. The worst thing that happens to a man is to stop trying and give up the struggle. Besides that, this struggle with a difficult medium of expression gives meaning and value to my life. I can't imagine the day when I'll say "I have mastered the English tongue." Its mastery is a lifelong job. I have made some progress, but the goal is still distant. I thank God that I spent the years in health, happiness, and comparative success. I earnestly pray that the new year will be healthier, happier, and more successful, bringing joy and happiness to the peoples of the Earth, preserving me and everyone from all evils, accidents, and excess of passions and giving us our daily bread and peace of mind.

January 1, 1950, Sunday

Mr. Snider drove me with his family to Lake Frances and points beyond on the newly paved highway that leads to Fort Smith. I returned home about 2 o'clock. To my distress, I discovered that I placed the package intended for Dr. Wills' present into Mr. Willis' box, and I'm not quite sure whether D. Wills or Mr. Willis got hold of the box of chocolates. I'll ask Mrs. Wills tomorrow, and if she did not get it, I'll supply her with another. It seems that I can't avoid making mistakes. Also this morning I worried for hours whether I ought to give a tip to the waitress who waits on me at the Southern Grill. She has been very attentive, giving me extra cups of coffee, and supplying me with the morning paper. If I give her a tip, I'll break one of my established rules "never to tip." This refusal to tip is not so much a matter of economy as a matter of principle. I think the employers ought to pay their help a decent salary and prevent them from expecting tips. If I don't give a tip, my conscience bothers me, and I feel both uncomfortable and unwelcome. Well, I need not worry about things that involve insignificant decisions.

January 10, 1950, Wednesday

The news in the papers is about Formosa, British elections, and the budget. As long as the politicians succeed in keeping the world in peace, I'll not get much excited. I'm afraid, however, that their stupidity and greediness, as well as their ignorance and selfishness, will eventually lead the poor and bleeding mankind to another war. It seems that universal peace has to be earned the hard way. Suffering might teach men reasonableness, good behavior, and brotherly love.

January 13, 1950, Friday

Today I attended a faculty meeting at 11 o'clock. About half an hour was spent on discussing the grade cards. It was decided to revise them since no one understood what's meant by "comprehension," "neatness," "evidence of preparation," and "cooperation." Of course, most of us understand the terms, but we are too lazy to spend the required time and effort to ascertain them. Besides that, we teachers are grading the work and not the personality of the student. It is remarkable how even highly educated persons disagree on very small questions. It seems that abstract terms are the breeding ground of discord and disagreement. No two people agreed on the definition of comprehension, class participation, or neatness. We can't communicate with abstract words, and yet we can't do without them. Definitions of abstract words do not help to remove misunderstandings. Every person's mind reacts to and interprets abstraction differently. The best way is to avoid them as much as possible. Specific and concrete terms will contribute to clarity.

January 17, 1950, Tuesday

On Sunday I went by bus to Fayetteville; it was clear and warm. Sh. had Miss Parler and her boyfriend, Joe, as guests at dinner. We talked about books, linguistics, and writers. It seems that everybody read Kafka's novels except me. Even Sh., who is by no means a wide reader, had read two of his novels.

January 18, 1950, Wednesday

I'm reading V. Bush's *Modern Arms and Free Men*. He sounds very logical and erudite, and yet my faith in his conclusions was shaken because in early 1949 he stated that it would take years before Russia would develop an atomic bomb. It is now evident that Russia has had the bomb since 1947. It seems that great men like him can't believe that others can be as efficient as the so-called democratic nations. It may be that a socialistic nation that puts public service above private profit is more progressive, and if it is so, we might as well face the fact and mend our ways. He also has the idea that Russia is run by an iron dictatorship and that 14 men can impose their will upon 190 million human beings stretching over an area that comprises one-sixth of the Earth. Since the Americans can understand only the profit motive, they fail to understand that there are nations and persons who do things not

for profit but for service. They are also laboring under the illusion
that their system is the best because they have the highest standard
of living. The Germans also had high standards of living under the
Kaiser and the French under Napoleon. Standard of living is the
result of the richness of the soil and not the government. America
just now enjoys a proper balance among food, population, and all
the evils of poverty. It is strange how men forget that 20 years
ago the whole economic system creaked at its joints and did not
amount to much. Now, with all the other countries devastated by
the war, we boast about our strength and standard of living. Not
every American is enjoying a high standard of living. No other
country's people are more insecure than America. In no other
country do so many old people walk the streets in neglect and
oblivion. These are the fortunate ones. The unfortunate ones are in
dismal old men's homes, farms, or hospitals. That's their reward for
living in God's country.

January 22, 1950, Sunday

I finished *Modern Arms and Free Men*. I also read two
magazines: *College English*, January 1950, and *S.R.L.* of last
week. Both contained interesting but depressing articles about
literature and authors. It seems that both the critics and the
teachers who write are frustrated. They seem to live in a narrow
world of letters and books, clubs and reviews, and are unaware
of the broad, vigorous life that goes on everywhere, even in the
so-called wild Ozark hills. On the other hand, it might be that I,
living in the open in a community that is almost a frontier town
in educational and cultural faculties, am still untamed, optimistic,
and unsophisticated.

January 27, 1950, Friday

In my opinion, the University is a place of opportunity and not of compulsion; we have to give the students the four freedoms: freedom from family, freedom from administration, freedom from faculty, and freedom from themselves. If they can't use freedom, they can't develop into free men and women, i.e. they can't grow into responsible and dependable human beings.

January 30, 1950, Monday

I'm reading *Lady Chatterley's Lover* by D. H. Lawrence. It is not so scandalous or hot as it was described about 20 years ago. The book tries to prove that sexual desire is what men ought to live for. Life is incomplete without sexual conversation. That might be all right for men with iron spines and stout hearts, but most of us would live longer and happier if we were moderate in our lovemaking. As a matter of fact, lovemaking makes men weak and stupid by making them empty of the life force that alone can inspire and invigorate them. The common sense view about sex is that one can't eat his cake and have it also. One can't indulge in lovemaking without feeling its effects on his nerves, brain, and muscles. The sages and saints have always known that the secret of success is to abstain from women as well as wine. You can't beget children and masterpieces at the same time. Some have done it, but they were the men who were blessed with abundant vitality. The rank and the file would live happier lives if they knew how to use moderation in love as well as in other things.

February 7, 1950, Tuesday

I've received an invitation to talk to Koinonia Fortnights Club on the subject of poetry. It is a very deep and difficult subject to talk about to ladies at 8 p.m. in a crowded and overheated room. Once or twice when I talked in overheated rooms, I perspired abundantly and made a spectacle of myself. Besides that, I feel handicapped without a blackboard. I've not yet acquired the confidence of talking to a crowd without using either notes or a blackboard. In most cases there is not any table or desk to place one's notes on, and one feels sissy and awkward holding one's notes in one's hand. But just the same, it is great fun and a great exercise. One can't learn to address crowds except by addressing crowds.

February 8, 1950, Wednesday

Today there was no Chapel. I did not know it, went to school at 10 o'clock, and had a hard time killing the two hours 'till 1 o'clock, when my American Lit. class meets. I lectured on Poe. My students, being self-righteous, were probably shocked to hear that the greatest American poet was a drunk, a gambler, and a financial failure. It is good for them to visualize that art has nothing to do with success and prosperity. One can enter the company of the great writers wearing a cheap coat.

February 10, 1950, Friday

I discussed Poe's *Poetic Principle.* I am not quite sure that I got my students excited over poetry. I don't think anyone can get them excited about anything except food, sex, sports, and money. I returned home about 3:30 and read President Conant's Report for the year 1949. My name is in the *Harvard Directory,* and I have been receiving these reports since 1945. President Conant stressed the three new general courses to be given to all students in their freshman and sophomore years as part of the general education program. It certainly makes me envious to think that

President Conant is only four years my senior and is by this time known both as an educator and a scientist throughout the world while I'm a poor, ignorant, and unknown teacher of literature in an unaccredited freshwater college.

February 17, 1950, Friday

Since Monday, I've been invited to Miss Williams' wedding on Tuesday, a potluck supper at the Home Economics House on Wednesday, and a faculty meeting today at 11 o'clock. Mr. Olney, Mr. Seal, and Mr. Ben Ward told the faculty about the training they give to the students at their laboratories. D. Woodland, who seemed feverish and ill, got up and inquired why the other departments— for example, the music and chemistry (her own)—had not been permitted to tell about their efforts in training students. It was voted that the other departments would also describe the training they give to the students. My English department is like the Marine Corps, always ready. I can present a very convincing picture. We train students for five general purposes: (1) for culture, (2) for communication, (3) for social and emotional adjustment, and (4) for world citizenship. The fifth specific purpose is we teach them how to think, read, write, and observe. The day was very beautiful; the sunshine and the breezes made one think of spring and love.

February 19, 1950, Sunday

My conscience has been bothering me on account of two decisions I made. First, I received an invitation to Miss Irene Williams' wedding. I entirely ignored it. I did not send the customary gift, and I attended neither the service at the Methodist Church nor the reception at the Ozark Hotel. Second, I received a letter from Mr. Patsalos from New York, asking me to lend him 65 dollars to pay his tuition fee at the New York University. Since the boy, or rather, the man has been suspended from Tulsa University and since his father wrote me that his son ran into debt in spite of his sending 150 dollars a month, I thought it neither wise nor expedient to wire the 65 dollars. My decision may be prudent, but it gave me great discomfort. I hate to refuse aid, but at the same time it may be a mistake to encourage his propensity for borrowing. I'll write him a nice letter tomorrow, but I'll not send the money. After all, I've never seen him, and although he was in Tulsa for over a year, he did not even write a note.

February 23, 1950, Thursday

Today it is Election Day in England. My interest in the elections is academic. I should like the Labor Party to win; it will strengthen our Democratic party's policies and demonstrate once and for all whether Socialism is a success or failure. Five years—especially five years after a devastating war—cannot demonstrate the capacity of Socialism to bring peace and prosperity to a country. Since the polls were closed by 1 o'clock Central Standard Time, tomorrow the papers will have definite news about who won the elections. Meantime, I'll brush my teeth, say my prayers, and go to bed. I'm still reading Jean-Paul Sartre's *The Age of Reason*. That boy from Cyprus sent a wire asking for 65 dollars. I did not even bother to answer him. Every time I tried to get in touch with one of my fellow islanders, whether relative or not, I have found them asking favors that would be to their harm for me to grant. For example, this boy had been working in New York since last summer. He ought to have been able by this time to save 65 dollars to pay the tuition for two courses at N.Y.U. Besides that, if he was good and reliable, his father, who is wealthy, would have supported him through school. As for my sister's family, they don't even write to me because I advised them against sending their 17-year-old son to America. He has neither a diploma nor education, he never finished the gymnasium, he quit the American Academy, and he is spoiled to the very marrow of his bones. What can such a boy do in America? Besides that, both the parents of both the boys are well to do, and America is the country for the poor and the oppressed and not for the spoiled children of the rich and the arrogant. The sons of the poor and the oppressed build this country, and somehow it is only the poor and the oppressed who become good Americans. The rich are the arrogant who fail to understand the temper of America; they usually go to the dogs.

February 24, 1950, Friday

Until now, at 8 o'clock, it is not quite sure whether the Labor Party has won a clear majority in yesterday's election in England. I received two letters today: One from the Socony-Vacuum Co., asking how I'll reimburse them 25 pounds they paid me by mistake. There was also another airmail from that boy from Cyprus who is demanding the 65 dollars to pay his tuition fee. I hope it will be the last I hear from him. He must have received my letter yesterday morning or afternoon. It was mailed Monday afternoon, and since it happened to be Washington Day on Wednesday and there was no mail delivery, he did not get it 'till yesterday. His letter was dated Tuesday afternoon. I advised him to go and see the International Tribute of Education. This will perhaps help him to get into a college, and then he will begin to receive his allowance from his father.

February 25, 1950, Saturday

The British elections disappointed me. The Labor Party won the elections by a very narrow margin; some call it an unworkable majority and predict another general election in three months. It seems curious that everybody to whom I've talked seems to be Tory or conservative. Everybody longs for the good old times and thinks that old ways and old slogans will serve society, as if individuals are afraid of innovation. They are afraid of the adaptation necessary to develop a new society. They prefer the established error to novel truth; they are afraid to get out of their rut. But societies and individuals fulfill their destinies by constantly changing, not by remaining still. Motion is progress; stagnation is death.

February 27, 1950, Monday

Yesterday I went to Fayetteville. Sh. met me at the station, and we dined at the Blue Mill. I returned home by the usual way, via Westville and Watts. It was a pleasant day for traveling and walking. Today I went to the bank and asked the banker to send 25 pounds to the Socony-Vacuum Oil Company of Nicosia, Cyprus. They have to send the money through the Kansas Bank. The letter I sent to that boy from Cyprus was returned to me. He left the place without leaving a forwarding address.

March 4, 1950, Saturday

It has been a rather busy week. On Tuesday evening I talked to a ladies club on Poetry; on Thursday I was officer of the day and did not return home 'till late in the evening. Today I taught four hours and read and loafed the rest of the day. I borrowed *Harper's* and the *Atlantic* from the library and started reading them. Magazines and newspapers are the vehicle by which one who is lost in the heart of the Ozarks can keep in touch with the outside world. I settled all my affairs except buying a new hat. From now on, to avoid worry, I'll meet all problems with speedy decision. I'll answer letters promptly, pay my bills when they are due, and generally face every situation with energetic volition. Out of sheer laziness, I let things drift and then worry and fuss about my weak and vacillating will.

March 5, 1950, Sunday

I made a fool of myself twice today, once by telling Mr. Cook that some women have not the knack of catching men; he was scandalized, answering, "So you think that women chase men." Of course they do, if Spenser and Shakespeare and Shaw know what they are talking about. But one must be careful of speaking like that to elderly men who are married, who are the sons of ministers, and who have been and in part are still missionaries. The second time I made an egregious fool of myself in such a way that the less that is said about it, the better. Let it be buried in oblivion, and let the world never know how foolish a man can be in spite of his erudition, education, and philosophy of life. There are moments when passion or emotion or pity routs one's reason, and a man, no matter how well disciplined he is, can't escape behaving like a fool more often than he cares to acknowledge or admit. Since no harm was done and the motive was pure and noble, only remotely touched with selfishness or earthliness, I'll forget it and solemnly promise not to repeat such an error again. It is good for one to be reminded how insignificant it will appear six months hence. Like Milton, I'll say tomorrow "to fresh woods and pastures new."

March 6, 1950, Monday

I deposited 40 dollars into my bank account. I received a letter from my brother-in-law, in which I read that my nephew is already in England visiting factories and shops. He intends to visit

Switzerland on his way back to Cyprus. I bought apples, cake, and ice cream and made a feast of them. It is good, sometimes, to get away from the restaurant and school food.

March 12, 1950, Sunday

Except for two or three trips to town, I stayed in my room and read two or three tales by Chaucer. I also thought and daydreamed. It is curious how one, once forced to inaction by either weather or disease, becomes introverted and thinks of his past mistakes and successes and dreams of a glorious or dismal future. The wise man should live and work in the present. The present is the result of the past, and the future will be the result of the present. What one does, thinks, and dreams now will decide what his future will be. It is good for one's soul, body, and nerves to spend one day by oneself once in a while. As it is, we wallow in gregariousness; we avoid solitude; we are afraid to be alone; and yet solitude and silence give birth to strong and sincere souls. It is still true that the strongest man is the man who can be most alone. I'll go to bed early, hoping that no storms will disturb my slumber.

March 20, 1950, Monday

Yesterday I went by bus to Fayetteville. It was cold and snowy. Sh. met me at the station, and we dined at the Washington Hotel. Mr. Poindexter was our guest. He plans, or rather, planned to go to Athens and wanted to discuss the matter with me. The meal cost me 3.20. I returned home by way of Westville and Watts. The road is still under construction, and the trip is rough and slow.

Miss Sweet phoned me, but I told her that I was slightly indisposed and had better stay home and nurse my cold. The truth is that the supper and the program will last about two hours. Yesterday

I wasted the day in traveling and visiting. Today I simply had to stay home and do some reading. I have already wasted time, and time now does waste me. I'm neither rich nor famous nor wise.

March 25, 1950, Saturday

A rather hectic day; it is rather warm and windy. I taught five hours. I must be tired because I noticed and was irritated by trifles. I must take it easy and relax over the weekend. I'm glad that I don't have to travel anywhere tomorrow. Going to Fayetteville is not as pleasant as it used to be. It is a tiresome trip, taking me over two states and at least four counties. Sh. is either ill or unreasonable, not to mention fantastic in her demand for attention or devotion. A man of fifty ought to concentrate on winning fame, pursuing truth, getting knowledge, and practicing virtue.

March 27, 1950, Monday

I read in the papers about dust storms in Oklahoma and Kansas and tornadoes in Little Rock. Last night the wind blew with great velocity. I got up in the middle of the night and closed the windows. I also read in the *Tulsa World* that at least five persons saw "flying saucers" circling the town. The talk about flying saucers has been going on now for two or three years. It seems that the minds and souls of the people are so inflamed by talk of the commentators, pictures in magazines, and prophecies of religion that, in their excited condition, they imagine to see things. Perhaps they see something, for the atmosphere is not free of flying objects. Planes, birds, meteors, and their imaginations lend themselves to the imagination in different aspects. Some who see them are merely people with poetic minds who like to make pseudo statements.

March 31, 1950, Friday

Today I got mad at a student for laughing in the American class and ordered him to move up to the front seat. I might have been unnecessarily loud and excited, but he has been imitating my voice for some time to the merriment of three or four young ladies who sit before and beside him. From now on he will sit in the front seat. I don't like to have episodes like this in my classrooms.

I got a haircut and bought a pint of strawberry ice cream and two cakes of Dial soap. With the coming of the hot weather, I'll begin to bathe in Dial soap to keep myself free from any body odor. The key to healthy living is cleanliness, cheerfulness, and proper diet.

April 4, 1950, Tuesday

I received two newspapers from home. The big news was the heavy snowfall of last February, the heaviest in 55 years. The women wore slacks on the occasion, and there were snowball fights and accidents from slippery roads and sidewalks. The poor Cypriots are very little equipped to stand the siege of real winter. They must have thought the world was coming to an end with one foot of snow on the ground.

April 5, 1950, Wednesday

At the meeting Mr. Gilbert talked about tests and test measurements; he divided the tests into subjective and objective and discussed the advantages and disadvantages of each kind. His system of grading rested on an elaborate statistical procedure that I failed to grasp. I always grade according to my own sweet will or make my own tests on the spur of the moment because I don't really believe in tests, quizzes, and examinations. If a college student does not like to study, it is no use compelling him. The university is a place of opportunity and not compulsion. Many professors give tests almost every week. It is the only way by which they can force their students to study their assignments. I know that my students do not study the assignments with either concentration or attention, but it is their own affair. My duty is to teach, not to test.

April 8, 1950, Saturday

I left yesterday at 4:30 for Cowskin Lodge on Grand Lake. We stopped at Southwest City, Oklahoma, to buy fishing licenses. Only Mr. Whaley and Mr. Winters were brave enough to buy the licenses at 2.25 each. Mr. Cook and Rev. Schimpff thought the price exorbitant and did not buy licenses, although they carried their fishing equipment with them. We reached the lodge at about 6:10, and supper was served immediately to the 28 guests who made the party. After the meal we walked to the boathouse, where, under cover, sitting on couches under electric lights, Mr. Snyder, Mr. Seal, Pres. Brown and others were fishing. It was a revelation to me; I always associated fishing with sailing boats, sun, and winds! I turned in about 10 o'clock but slept in a bed between Mr. Joe Smith, who snored moderately, and Mr. Springfield, who snored violently. It was about 2 o'clock before everybody was in and one could sleep. About 5 o'clock Mr. Harold Ward and other ambitious souls got up, turned on the lights, dressed, and went out to fish. It was useless to stay in bed, for which I paid at least four dollars. I got up at 6 o'clock, shaved, and dressed and went out for a walk with my friend Mr. Cook. At 7:30 we had breakfast and then made fun of the fishermen who caught no fish. We ate a heavy chicken dinner and loafed on the porch 'till 4 o'clock, when we started for home, which we reached at 6:10. It was a good day; it cost seven dollars, but since the trip was free and the meals were excellent, the expense was not prohibitive. It cost the party, including minimum, boats and services, over 225 dollars. The owner of the lodge must have realized at least a hundred dollars profit. The view from the lodge reminded me of the blue Mediterranean Sea.

April 11, 1950, Tuesday

A cool, clear day; I went back to work after a three-day vacation. I felt very well except for the misery of wearing a new hat. Every time I put on a new suit of clothes or a new hat or even a new tie, I feel embarrassed; it takes a few days before I feel normal. Last night I stayed in the Administration Building from 4:30 to 8:30 p.m. as substitute for Fred Olney, who had to teach our evening class of war veterans. I ate a free meal and listened to the radio programs of Firestone Co., A Railroads, and Bell Telephone. I returned home about 8:45. On the way, as I approached the house of Mr. Pickle, I heard a continuous whistling and croaking and, for a moment, thought I was to face a rattlesnake crawling in the night. It proved to be the croaking of the frogs that made their home in the water left in the ditch. I went to D. Sugg and gave him the prescription for lenses sent to me by my brother-in-law, who, I guess, takes delight in pestering me with small commissions that one can't perform in a small village like Siloam Springs.

April 18, 1950, Tuesday

Since last Sunday I've been in a great emotional upset. It cost me a good night's rest, and the result was a kind of nervous headache. Last night I slept better, and today I availed myself of the sunshiny morning and stayed outdoors as long as possible. By tonight I'm perfectly cool and calm. To control his emotions one must analyze and understand them. One does not like to face facts squarely, and this cowardice or weakness results in one's never gaining freedom from emotional upheavals; work and walking are good help also. But the problem is rather intangible, and one can't solve it unless one faces it squarely and frankly and fearlessly.

April 19, 1950, Wednesday

A cool, clear day. Last night it rained but, for a change, it did not lightning or thunder. I had about half an hour's talk with Mrs. Thornton in her car in front of the University store. She told me that she is planning to go back to school to get a Ph.D.; she is sure that she can get a 6,500-dollar-a-year job. She has a large family and will leave her family to the care of a woman. She is presently making 200 dollars a month. She had an offer from a Methodist School in Texas to become head of the art department. Besides business affairs, we discussed the younger generation's lack of appreciation for art. Mrs. Thornton is the teacher of art at the University.

April 21, 1950, Friday

My emotional upheaval has subsided; it is terrible to fall prey to excess of passion. Now I feel like a vessel sailing smooth seas. What I need is coolness and calmness even in passion. If one is going to be upset for two or three days and lose sleep for an emotion, that emotion is not worth the candle. It is a pity that I'm neither as calm nor as collected as I seem. Better inner control will increase my power for concentrated attention.

April 24, 1950, Monday

Yesterday I went to Fayetteville. Sh. entertained the Carters. D. Carter took us for a ride to see the mountain that moves; we never reached our destination since on the way up the car developed high temperature, and we had to stop and fill the radiator with water. We borrowed unceremoniously from a farm whose occupants were away. I'm afraid I made a fool of myself. I always do by not being able to keep silent and let the other fellow do the talking and the questioning. I returned home about 8 o'clock feeling rather tired after a long day's ride. I must have ridden at least 150 miles.

April 25, 1950, Tuesday

In today's *Joplin News* I read an article about Cyprus. The writer thinks that the communists are gaining ground in the island, which he calls the stronghold of the Mediterranean. He is afraid that the communists will attach the island to the Soviet Union. The islanders were always in sympathy with the Russians because they were of the same religion and because they hate England. The islanders will someday suffer annihilation because the British and the Americans have turned the island into an air base. The Russians, who are only five hundred miles away, may bomb the island mercilessly to drive the Americans away, and in doing so they may entirely ruin the cities and the ports of the island. The island is so small that one or two A-bombs would wipe out its population and render it uninhabitable for generations. The British and the Americans, of course, will evacuate the island, and that will be merely a chapter or a page in the history of World War III. It is a pity that poor, innocent, ignorant people would be sacrificed to power politics. It has always been the fate of the poor island since the days of the Babylonian Empire. Egyptians, Phoenicians, Persians, Greeks, Romans, Arabians, Crusaders, Venetians, Turks, and British have ravaged and ruled the island. The Cypriots must be a tough race to survive so many conquests. I'm proud to be the child of such a hardy and tenacious race.

May 4, 1950, Thursday

Tomorrow Sh. and two other members of the U. of A. faculty are supposed to visit JBU, and, of course, they will be my guests. Unless Providence sends a car and a driver, I don't know how I'll entertain them from 4 o'clock to 6:45, when their bus will leave for Fayetteville. I'm sure that Sh. is at the bottom of the visit. She likes to find an excuse to visit Siloam.

May 11, 1950, Thursday

Between rains and meetings, Sh. visited Siloam Springs twice since last Thursday. On Friday she came by bus with two professors of English. I showed them the Campus and took them to the Southern Grill for supper. On Sunday she visited the town with Miss Graham. They attended services, and then I took them to dinner. They left at 3 o'clock for Fayetteville. Today I received another letter from her, asking me to arrange a interview between D. Brown and a teacher of Mathematics. Well, I'll visit Fayetteville this coming Sunday, and before I arrange the interview I'll have to know what the interview is for. If it is for a job, it is better to see Mr. Cox. Dr. Brown does not care to see applicants for jobs.

May 13, 1950, Saturday

I received a letter from Sh.; she expects me to visit Fayetteville tomorrow. She will probably meet me at the bus station. There are rumors that the road between Siloam Springs and Westville is closed on account of floods, but the little bus had left yesterday on time, so I guess there must be some detour by which one can reach Westville. Besides that, by tomorrow if no torrential rains fall tonight, everything will be dry. It will not take long for the Arkansas sun to dry fields, roads, and streams.

May 16, 1950, Tuesday

Last Sunday I went to Fayetteville. Sh. and I dined at the Ferguson's Cafeteria; two dinners cost $2.37. Last night Mr. Sweet drove Mr. Chine and me to the home of the couple who employs the two displaced persons whom I helped a few months ago to get in touch with the Ukrainian student who attends JBU. After the torrential rains of last week the country looks green and fresh and clear.

June 20, 1950, Tuesday

Sunday Mrs. Thornton drove me to Springdale, and then her 14-year-old son drove me to Fayetteville. I lunched at Sh.'s, and at about 3 o'clock the Stouts came for a visit. While the women were engaged in conversation, Mr. Stout, his grandson, and I drove to the Agri. Experimental Station of the U. of A. and saw the bulls, the cows, and the chickens. I returned home about 6 o'clock. After a meal at the Southern Grill, Mrs. Sweet and her son Willie D. drove me five miles east of Siloam Springs to see a wreck. Two cars, both from Tulsa, Oklahoma, collided, and two of three persons were killed. Everybody was there. What must have been a staggering misfortune for the sufferers was to the idle Sunday crowd a spectacle and subject for gossip and speculation. The victims were carried to Siloam Springs Hospital, and people were standing outside while the doctors in the fluorescent-lighted operating room made valiant efforts to save or patch lives. According to the papers, the 12-year-old daughter died yesterday.

June 30, 1950, Friday

Since last Sunday we are involved in the Korean affair. The Northern Koreans have invaded South Korea, and, therefore, our military and political leaders have ordered our powerful Navy and Air Force to bomb the Reds. It seems to me that we are abusing our force. May God protect us from what the Greeks call Nemesis. In our strength we forgot reason and moderation. We soon came to the conclusion that Russia is behind the Northern Koreans and, therefore, that we ought to show the world we do not intend to tolerate more Red expansions. We behave like children. Let us hope that the Russians, out of prudence, will take it lying down. Otherwise, we are in danger of being involved in another war; and some of us who have lived through two wars already are sick of the whole affair. I'm still using the comb and still have the uniform the Army gave me during the last war. Since prudence has deserted us, let us hope that the enemy proves wiser and more temperate and averts from mankind the misery and the sufferings that a World War III would visit on a weary world.

July 8, 1950, Saturday

Yesterday I was officer of the day and spent the evening listening to the news over the radio. The Koreans are still advancing, and President Truman has ordered the Draft Boards to begin functioning and draft about 500,000 men between the ages of 19 and 25. I hope that the war will be localized; it would be sad for my generation to go through three world wars. No other generation has gone to so many great wars. We are entitled to a few years of peace so that we can think and create and construct. Ideologies are good, but they take one's time and energy and prevent him from the main concerns of life, i.e. self-development, service, and creation.

July 9, 1950, Sunday

The young son of Mr. White, the coach, drove me to Chapel. I sat by the door; soon D. Woodland came in and sat beside me. This is the second time we have sat side by side in Chapel. It will give the idlers something to gossip about.

July 10, 1950, Monday

The news from the Korean front was cheerful. The Americans have stopped the advance of the Northern Korean Army by the use of bombers and fighting planes. We are engaged in a real war; let us hope that it will be localized. Let us hope that vindictiveness will not carry us beyond the 38th parallel and involve us in a longer war. We trust too much in our might and very little in our right. We have been so accustomed to bombings that we are not bothered by them anymore. We rather take pride in our capacity to deliver staggering blows. That we destroy homes and kill women and children do not seem to affect us in the least. Our leaders entered the Korean war with the assurance that Russia and China were bluffing. We behave like children carrying chips on their shoulders.

July 13, 1950, Thursday

Everybody is talking about and discussing our presence in Korea. We are surprised to find that the Koreans love their country and are ready to defend it against us, who have no business to poke our noses in their affairs. To them, it is a war for unification of their country; it is like our civil war. We would not welcome any third power entering the conflict on the side of the South, but we are now siding ourselves with one party against the other. Our justification is that we are stopping communistic expansion. Some of our congressmen are clamoring for the A-bomb to be used against the Koreans. That would be a crime. It would cost the lives of children and women, and it would brand us as barbarians who abuse their power. It would be a confession of defeat. If all our powerful fleets, Air Force, Marines, and soldiers can't defeat 150,000 Koreans and we have to use the Bomb against them, there must be something wrong about us. The use of a bomb might spread war and calamity over the entire globe. Our legislators ought to be saner and cooler. But it is no secret that they are petty, vindictive, narrow politicians who talk without thinking and act out of vanity and self-interest. The A-bomb ought not to be given to children, but let us hope that prudence and patience will prevail. Let us hope that even at the eleventh hour, calamity can be averted and mankind may proceed toward greater unity, peace, and prosperity.

July 15, 1950, Saturday

The news from Korea is far from heartening; the Americans are still retreating, and reinforcements are on the way, but everybody is impatient and mad. It is amazing how Christians who teach love and tolerance can in the twinkling of an eye turn into bellicosity and forsake Christ. Human nature has not changed; violence and war and danger appeal to men's instincts, and no amount of teaching will ever change them. Americans are undoubtedly the most pious and the most educated nation on the face of the Earth, but let somebody disagree with them, and they are ready to kill him and skin him.

July 19, 1950, Wednesday

President Truman asked for 10 billion dollars to get the country ready to combat communism on all fronts; he demanded partial mobilization. On the Korean front, the Americans are holding their own and effected a landing on the coast of Korea. Some of the boys have received the classification cards. The one I saw classified the owner as V-A, which may mean 5-A or Veteran-A.

July 21, 1950, Friday

I gave two tests, one in Juvenile Lit. and another in American Lit. I spent the rest of the day reading *A Writer's Notebook* by W. S. Maugham. It is a great book full of observations and reflections on men, manners, art, and life. Like Ulysses, he has seen many cities, manners, and councils; he lived in England, the United States, France, India, and the Pacific Islands. He even lived in a boardinghouse in my native town of Nicosia. He mentioned that the boardinghouse was kept by a short, stout Greek who charged 10 shillings a day for room and board. Unfortunately, he writes nothing about Cypriots and their customs. The few persons he describes are those he met in the boardinghouse. It would have been interesting to hear the opinions of a great writer on Cyprus. He could probably have made the same remark about the Cypriots that he made about the Hindus: He was impressed by the patience of the overworking, undernourished peasantry. This is true about the peasantry of Cyprus. They are a hardworking, half-starving class of people who deserve better of God and man. They are kept poor, ignorant, and unknown by the combined influence of the English authorities; the Greek Orthodox Church, which preaches patience, fatalism, and blessedness to the poor; and the Cypriot usurers, who fatten on their blood. Undernourishment brings disease, lassitude, indifference, and stagnation. The few dance, eat, drink, and make merry; but the many work, weep, go hungry and thirsty, and suffer.

July 25, 1950, Tuesday

Today is Election Day, but I did not vote since I forgot to pay my poll tax. The news from Korea is worse than ever. The Koreans are still advancing on the West Shore, threatening the communication of the U.S. Army.

July 30, 1950, Sunday

The Americans are holding the line in Korea. Everyone is talking or discussing drafting, universal military service, the A-bomb, and whatnot. It is really a mad world to live in. Instead of talking of schools, hospitals, roads, factories, and shops, we talk bombs, planes, warships, and tanks. It is considered unpatriotic to talk of the unity of mankind and the brotherhood of man. Mankind is divided in East and West, in Reds and Non-Reds. They are keen on exterminating each other. Throughout the whole world, there is not a strong voice of poet, prophet, or philosopher, of sage or saint, to bid them to stop being immature and act like mature human beings. All of us are death-bonded. Let us at least march toward our graves accomplishing something mighty and sublime to conquer time. Let us create, improve, and build. Let us stop fighting; let us begin working.

August 4, 1950, Friday

The Korean War is going on as usual. The Marines have landed, and everyone in America thinks that the war will be over in a few weeks. Meantime, by our backing the Nationalists on the island of Formosa, we are likely to get involved in a long and costly war with Communist China. It seems that our politicians can't understand that there is a limit to our resources and that the other nations have a right to be either monarchies, dictatorships, or democracies, according to their own sweet will. It seems to me that the United States is embarking on a long war with Asia. Although we are the strongest nation on Earth, we don't feel secure.

August 10, 1950, Thursday

The Americans, according to the papers, advanced 13 miles today in Korea. I really don't see how things will end. We are at the edge of a peninsula and have a whole continent against us. We might be lucky if the Asians plus the Russians quit fighting either out of prudence or out of fear, but if they prove stubborn and keep on fighting, it will be a long and costly war. It might in the end prove to be another Sicilian expedition. We will either have to pull out or be driven out. It was quite Don Quixotic to rush to the support of the South Koreans and wage an offensive war about 10,000 miles away from home. Planes, radios, and fast boats have eliminated space, but just the same, it will be proved awfully costly and hazardous to keep an Army so far from home. Let us hope for the best but be prepared for the worst.

August 11, 1950, Friday

I got a haircut and, of course, we talked of war and draft and politics. I guess I must be more careful of my words. Just now, everyone is suspected of being communist or radical or whatnot, especially if he is an alien. I'm the only alien in this small Arkansas town. I'll simply stop talking either politics or economics. I'll bother no one, and I hope nobody will bother me. This attitude is not exactly patriotic, but it is hard nowadays to be both honest and patriotic.

August 15, 1950, Tuesday

Today being Assumption Day, I recall the days I used to

spend in Cythrea, the village nine miles east of Nicosia, where my godfather lived. On that day, we used to feast after the 15-day fast. It was a happy time for me as I was young and adventurous, thirsty for knowledge and experience. I wonder what became of the persons with whom I used to associate in those days. That was about 36 years ago. I guess most of them must be dead because they were much older than I. A few must be living and, in a scientific world, still carrying on some of the customs bequeathed to us by the past, both classical and Christian.

August 18, 1950, Friday

I drew from the Exchange 40 dollars and plan to save a few dollars for my vacation. I want to go to Dallas, Texas, by train. It is about time to visit mighty Texas, about which I hear and speak so much. Besides that, I've been visiting Kansas City, Missouri, every September. Change is sweet. I must not grow timid and repetitive. I must not fear to venture into the unknown. My plan to visit Europe must be postponed. We are in war, and only God knows when or how it will end. Meantime, let us keep calm and cool and try to realize our aspirations. It is really unfortunate that I have spent the first fifty years of my life in times of war. When I was born in 1899, wars were raging. Then came the Italy-Turkish War, then the Balkan Wars, then World War I, the Greco-Turkish War, then World War II, and now we are entering World War III. Some of our leaders clamor for direct attack against Russia. They are not going to waste ammunition on Koreans or Chinese or Indo-Chinese or Bulgarians or other satellites. Well, it will mean a war of catastrophic magnitude. Those who will survive will not be better off than the dead. Bankruptcy, starvation and revolution will stalk the globe. Sometimes, I admire Thucydides. He predicted accurately what will happen: History will repeat itself because men will act the same way under the same circumstances. Since everybody feels insecure, everybody will take refuge either in flight or in attack.

August 24, 1950, Thursday

I had a long talk with Mrs. Thornton in the Coffee Shop. She told me that her oldest boy was called back to the Navy and that she herself was offered a job as art-supervisor in the Siloam Springs School System. I advised her to accept the position. JBU will probably not need her services if the enrollment drops on account of the draft. She also told me that it is the kind of work she most likes and that the salary is bigger than what she gets at JBU. She will also have the summer free for travel and study, and she will have the weekends for relaxation. She was also worrying about her daughter Marjorie, who is engaged to a boy called Bruce Smith, who is also likely to be called to service.

September 1, 1950, Friday

The summer session will be over tomorrow. Some professors have already given their final tests, turned in their grades, and left for their 15-day vacation. I'm still undecided on what to do about my vacation. I hate to travel, I hate hotels, and I hate to stay at home. I have some kind of pain about and around the neck, and I was scared lest I caught the mumps from Snider, with whom I dined and talked yesterday at the dining hall. I always fear catching a disease about which I hear. It is part of my anxiety complex. Sometimes when I see a motion picture or read in a book about some character's disease, I fear that I'm getting that disease. That's, of course, sheer imagination. It must be a trauma from my early childhood. After all, I grew up among ignorant though highly superstitious and pious people and probably got more than my share of fear, anxiety, inferiority, and other complexes.

September 2, 1950, Saturday

I gave my last test today at 1 o'clock, thus bringing the long summer sessions to an end. I'll correct all the papers tomorrow morning and turn the grades in Monday and begin to get ready for my annual vacation trip. Sh. is still somewhere in Ohio and will not be back to Fayetteville 'till the 10th of September. Last night President Truman spoke to the nation. The Korean War must have sobered him. He said that we believe in a strong United Nations, that we want neither Formosa nor Korea and that we are planning neither defensive nor preventive wars. And yet he asked for a three-million-man Army by the middle of next year. It is unfortunate that our deeds do not square with our words. We talk of peace, and yet we bomb the Koreans out of house and home; we say we hate war, and yet we vote 16 additional billion dollars to arm ourselves and our so-called allies in Europe and Asia. No wonder the Russians do not believe us. I guess they must be afraid of us, and we are afraid of them. Meantime, we poor mortals must manage to live a creative, productive, and useful life in the din of planes, bombs, shells, and propaganda. It seems that the end is everywhere. Materialism, commercialism, superstition under the guise of religion, and war have taken possession of mankind. Art still has truth; we must take refuge there!

September 4, 1950, Labor Day

At 9 o'clock I went up the Hill and turned in my grades. I met D. Wills, who told me that Sh. had been ill while visiting

Miss Hunter at Wheaton, Illinois. Since she wrote from Ohio, she must be well by this time.

September 12, 1950, Tuesday

I left for Kansas City, Missouri, last Thursday afternoon. I stayed at the Plaza Hotel (Room 606). I saw four shows, rode the buses and streetcars, and ate breakfast at the Thompson Cafeteria out of sentimentality. I ate my first breakfast in Kansas City in 1939 at the Thompson Cafeteria. This time I saw about 30 recruits who came under the command of a corporal for breakfast. They were receiving their physical examinations. How well I remember the first meal the Army paid for me in Little Rock! Every time I visit a great city, I return home with a feeling of futility. There is a great city—full of cars, buses, and streetcars; shops, factories, stores, restaurants, movies, theaters, and whatnot—and I'm not able to perform any of the jobs required for the maintenance of the city. I could, of course, sell, wash dishes, clear streets, and mop floors, but jobs with big salaries would be impossible for me. Therefore, I thank Chaucer, Shakespeare, Milton, Spenser, and the American writers and poets for their readings and discussions that give me a living. It seems that some remnants of Renaissance or culture still survive in a modern city. A Negro restaurant had the sign "Apollo Restaurant." (It may be that a Greek was running it). On the truck of a store, there was written in Latin "Veritas Vincit." Here and there one could see impressive churches and cathedrals. One thing is evident in a big city: the slums where the Negros rot and the mansions where the rich live. From the slums to the palaces, the line runs deep. The slaves are still with us; the masters are still with us; somewhere between them are the wage-slaves—the so-called employees. The city is also full of old men, pitiful wrecks of a senseless struggle for existence. It is a great city but not laughing, not smiling. People who are well dressed and well fed go about looking worried, nervous, and unhappy. During my three-day stay, I don't recall to have heard human laughter. I saw only one smile; a waitress smiled at me; it was a professional smile; it lacked sincerity, warmth, humanity.

September 14, 1950, Thursday

I spent the day reading, walking and resting. About 2 o'clock I started walking up the Hill. Mr. Olney picked me up and drove me to the Hill. There was no mail for me except for a card from Sh., telling that she has already returned to Fayetteville. On the way back I rode with the Olneys. Mrs. Olney is taking care of the Hallowells' baby while Mrs. Hallowell is teaching. The car contained four children. I guess children are a blessing to their parents, but to a confirmed bachelor like me, they are a nuisance. I like to look at them, play with them, educate them, but I don't like to own any of them. The psychologists probably have a name for a man like me, but I don't know it nor care to know it. I really want to leave behind two or three brainchildren, one or two books that will be read by future generations. Sometimes when I read the works of writers like Christopher Morley and Philip Wylie who are unquestionably more intelligent and more artistic than I and yet write for the moment and not for eternity, I despair of the whole affair. It seems impossible that I'll survive by my brainchildren. And yet one must work and study, observe, and write. The future lies in the lap of the gods. For example, 15 years ago it seemed impossible that I should ever become a professor of English and teach in an American university. I was at that time teaching in small afternoon schools maintained by immigrants; therefore, I must not despair but keep on working and writing with head, heart, and hope.

September 16, 1950, Saturday

D. Cook collected a dollar from me for a subscription to *Literary Digest* and 50 cents for a dozen eggs I'll carry tomorrow to Sh. when I visit Fayetteville. I met a few former students in town. I also visited my new classroom, Cathedral 108. It has neither doors, nor floor, nor plaster on the walls, nor blackboards, nor lights. I guess by next week this time that the new, powerful 25-man crew will put everything in order.

September 28, 1950, Thursday

The Korean War is drawing to a close. According to the reports from the front, resistance dwindles. Seoul is in the hands of the UN forces, or rather, the American forces. Again, it is a case where might makes right. The 150,000 North Koreans, or Ko-Reds as the papers call them, faced the fleets and the Air Force of the so-called English-speaking peoples, and, of course, the odds were against them without the help of either China or Russia. The world will perish not so much from the aggression of the Reds as from the stupidity and conservatism of the English-speaking nations. The United States of America used to be progressive, liberal, and not afraid of ideas. Unfortunately for mankind, during the last 40 years the United States has grown fabulously prosperous and, hence, conservative. Any new ideology or philosophy is regarded as undermining the Constitution, democracy, or the American way of living; therefore, it must be crushed. For crushing it, the United States uses the muscles and the blood of the people. The workers produce the machinery and weapons that kill their fellow workers, and then their sons use them. In this democratic country, we don't have universal military service. We have Selective Service. It means that the prosperous, who can attend colleges, medical or engineering schools, are deferred while the poor are sent like cattle to the slaughter. Even if the prosperous are drafted, they serve as officers either in the Air Force, the Army, or Navy.

September 30, 1950, Saturday

The Northern Koreans have been driven to the 38th parallel, and now the question of whether or not to cross this parallel and invade North Korea faces the United Nations. The most bloodthirsty are the South Koreans, who only six weeks ago were complaining of aggression. Now they want to invade the North Koreans to establish a united, free Korea. Meantime, our military leaders continue to draft men in an effort to build a mighty Army. Seventeen billion dollars have been voted for so-called defense, and that sum must be spent. I personally think that no one is threatening the United States. We suffer from fear, or rather, we pretend to be afraid in order to indulge in operations that benefit not a few individuals. War makes good business. Everything is booming. There are more men employed today than ever before. People get excited about war and forget the unsolved problems at home. Class strife and the cry for social justice are labeled unpatriotic, un-American, and even communistic.

October 10, 1950, Tuesday

I sent a letter home, authorizing my sister to draw from my Cyprus account 400 pounds to build a two-room apartment with a bath and then return the money gradually. I'm sure lending money to one's people will cause friction, but it is the only thing my sister has asked me to do for her these 10 years. Besides that, an apartment may come in handy someday if I ever visit Cyprus.

October 13, 1950, Friday

I decided to attend the Higher Education Meeting at Petit Jean Park on October 20 and 21. I needed a change, and I'll probably derive some benefit as well as pleasure by attending meetings in which educational questions are discussed. I have not traveled much lately and must sometimes get out of my rut. Tonight I met Mr. Durham in front of the Sisco Store. He looks prosperous and healthy. He is superintendent of a school system in a Missouri town at 4,000 dollars a year. He told me that he already has five grandchildren. I said that he looked too young to be a grandfather. I bought a pint of ice cream and ate it. I'll got to bed early. Sh. wrote me that she got me a jar of Rise shaving cream.

October 15, 1950, Sunday

A very fine, warm day. I read in the morning on the porch and then went to Chapel, where I heard Rev. Ferm preach a sermon, "We should be like Him." In the dining hall D. Wills invited me to ride with his family to Fayetteville. He was going to bring home his eldest daughter, Ruth, who was visiting the Weathers. Sh. was in bed resting. We visited the Weathers' home in Terry Village, ate fruit salad and cookies and started for Siloam about 6 o'clock. We reached home about 7 o'clock. It was a delightful trip. I brought with me the jar of Rise shaving cream. It promises speed, comfort, and thorough cleanness. I'll try it tomorrow. I hope it will not prove a disappointment. I hate brushes; they get wet and dirty.

October 22, 1950, Sunday

It has been a very interesting week. On Thursday afternoon I rode with D. Wills to Petit Jean Park for the Higher Education Meeting. We reached our destination about 7:30. I slept in the dormitory on an Army bunk. The first night I slept well since it was quiet, but the second night I slept by fits and starts on account of the noise, lights and "traffic." I attended all the meetings, including the business meeting. I didn't get any vast amount of information, but I met some of my old friends, including Mr. and Mrs. Haley, Miss Masie, and others whom I know by sight but not by name. D. Carter was there too with his wife and two children. Rev. Ferm drove me back to Siloam yesterday afternoon. We drove under rain 'till we reached Alma, and then we emerged into cloudy, but dry, weather. My landlady gave me a book to read called *Look Younger, Live Longer*. It stressed diet as the source of health, wit, longevity, and all the other blessings of mankind. Food is essential to one man's existence; we are what we eat; and good food brings good mood. One must pay attention to what one eats, but to make a religion of diet is just as bad as to make a religion of exercise, sports, fresh air, water, and whatnot. Each has its place in the scheme of things. Intelligence must coordinate all these agents for a good and full life, without neglecting thinking, reading, traveling, and conversation. If we are merely the result of our digestion and our sex relations, then we are still slaves to carnality and animality. We have not attained spirituality and humanity. What we put in our minds is perhaps more important than what we shove into our stomachs.

October 26, 1950, Thursday

Last night I attended a faculty and prayer meeting. Dr. Brown was present; it was hot; and I fell very ill at ease during the long prayers. After the prayer meeting, which was, by the way, a service by itself with its three songs, sermon, and prayers, the faculty meeting took place. Various members of the faculty were called upon to give reports on the Petit Jean meeting of last week.

When I was called upon, I excused myself on the grounds that I was not ready and could not locate my notes. I was not willing to speak in front of the president, vice presidents, deans, etc., without the help of a blackboard. Besides that, people who do not hear me often are likely to notice more acutely my foreign accent.

October 30, 1950, Monday

Yesterday I rode the bus to Fayetteville. I dined with Sh., and we availed ourselves of the beautiful weather to take a long walk. D. Brown and his barnstorming party were also in Fayetteville, but I did not see any member of it. They must have left before 5:30. Today I received a letter from my sister. I'll send her a power of attorney to draw from my account 400 pounds to build a two-room apartment and bath. I hope that my generosity will not involve me in unnecessary squabbles. I still believe in Shakespeare's "neither a borrower nor lender be."

October 31, 1950, Tuesday

I'm still reading *Stalin*. I can't decide whether he is a villain or a hero. The only undeniable is that he has been successful. He has made communism work. He built in 30 years the mightiest empire the world has ever seen. He has outlived rivals, enemies, critics, and whatnot. He is indeed a man of steel.

November 2, 1950, Thursday

It has turned cold this morning. The crews were busy installing steam pipes in the Cathedral of the Ozarks. In spite of the cold, some boys appeared in shirtsleeves; it must be either habit or aversion to change. I lighted my stove both morning and evening. Everybody is excited by many events: the attempt of the Puerto

Ricans to assassinate President Truman, the counter offensive of the North Koreans that trapped about 5,000 Americans, the death of G.B. Shaw, and the Pope's declaration that the Virgin Mary ascended to heaven not only in spirit but also in body. At school everything is quiet.

November 5, 1950, Sunday

Yesterday it was really cold; the thermometer went down to 30 degrees. I put on my winter underwear, and I'm glad I did because there was no heat in my new classroom (108 Cathedral Building). Today I stayed at home, reading, resting, and dreaming. Sometimes I wish I could go to a show or visit a friend. I'm really living like a monk; I know only my room at 203 S. Wright Street, the Southern Grill Restaurant on Broadway, and my classroom on the Hill. Only the books, the magazines, and newspapers and one or two trips a year put me in touch with the wide world. Just now, everybody is wondering what the United States will do in Asia with the entrance of the Church into the Korean conflict. The Chinese armies have already inflicted defeats and casualties on the so-called UN troops. We are in danger of finding ourselves engaged in a long and costly war with China. We are really tactless. We expect the Asians to believe that we entered the Korean conflict for the ideal of freedom and justice. Nations judge us by our deeds, not by our words.

November 6, 1950, Monday

Everybody is excited about tomorrow's elections and McArthur's branding the alien intervention in the Korean War. It now appears that the whole United Nations' Army barely escaped being annihilated by the Red Chinese. I personally don't approve of a war with China. It will exhaust both our material and human resources, and in the end we will have to finance its reconstruction. War never settled anything; it simply leads to other wars.

November 9, 1950, Thursday

The elections are over; the Republicans made gains; the Democrats still control the Senate by a slim majority of two. The war in Korea is still going on; it might be that the Chinese will refuse and then that United States planes will bomb them, and the war will follow. It seems that once a war is started, it will not die out; it will generate other wars.

November 11, 1950, Saturday

I guess I'll have to buy a new overcoat. The one I have I've been wearing since 1942 or 1941. It has become unspeakably shabby. All the ladies of my acquaintance had hinted to me last year that I needed a new overcoat. The news from the Korean front is that the allies have resumed their advance, but they are feeling their way cautiously since the last week's reverses. The UN forces are fearful of the presence of the Chinese. Some sources think that the Chinese are merely volunteers; others say that they are regular Army Red Chinese divisions. Well, it is a pity that human beings have to kill each other in sub-zero weather on mountains, in valleys, and on the seas.

November 16, 1950, Thursday

Last night I attended a faculty prayer meeting. Rev. Ferm preached on Job and his woes, and then D. Wills introduced Mr. Blackburn of the Arkansas State Department of Education. After preliminary remarks we saw a motion picture on how to improve our teaching. The stress was on communication. The teacher's aim is to communicate knowledge, and all means must be used to achieve this purpose. Talk, pictures, blackboard, movies, and demonstrations are permissible if they help one to get his message across. Although I approve of visual education, I still believe that the best way of communicating thought is by clear, crisp, witty talk. Ice cream was served at the end. I reached home about 9:30. Mrs. Brown told me that there was a long distance telephone call for me from Fayetteville. I called immediately. Sh. wanted to tell me that she was leaving for Topeka to attend the funeral of her Uncle Thomas and that she would let me know when she returns to Fayetteville.

November 19, 1950, Sunday

I took a brief walk about 4 o'clock. Last night while lying slumber-less on account of the heat—it was 72 degrees, and I wore winter pajamas and slept under two blankets—I conceived the idea of writing a utopia in which the perfect system of education thrives, combining the best elements of communism, socialism, and democracy. There would, of course, be no diseases, no crimes, no hospitals, no courts, no jails. Preventive medicine and psychotherapy would eliminate all these ills that the flesh and the spirit are heirs to. Marriage would be based on love, although some philosophers say that love is not the best engineer. The life of reason would take the place of the religions of today. Worship would be service to mankind. Men would live not for profit and power but for service and self-improvement. In this book I'll pour all the ideas about education, society, life, and religion, which I have gathered from my readings and observations. It will be an arduous task, but it will at least be creative. It is no use teaching subjects that I know and writing events in a diary that nobody will care to read. A man is to be judged by his fruits.

November 23, 1950, Thanksgiving Day

I corrected papers 'till 11 o'clock and then dressed and walked up the Hill for Thanksgiving dinner. We had turkey, mashed potatoes, celery, cranberry sauce, etc., all for 75 cents. The Browns Jr. were there, and the Coxes, the Winters, both of the Sniders, and a few others. It was a very quiet affair. The ladies at my table were discussing plans for a trip to Tulsa tomorrow. There are rumors about peace in Korea. It is reported that the Chinese, somehow, are not willing to fight the Americans. I hope the rumors prove true. On this day, I thank God for my health, happiness, prosperity, and opportunities for service.

November 24, 1950, Friday

A very cold day; the temperature went down to eight or nine degrees. I put on my heavy overcoat. It is old and shabby; I bought it from Frances in 1941 for 15 dollars. It belonged to her son, who did not like to wear it. The boy was later killed in Germany. The overcoat has one good property: it is really heavy and warm. I'll try to buy a new one either at Pyeatte's or Penney's. Both my landlady and Sh. have already hinted more than once that I need a new overcoat. Since it was a day of vacation, I spent it reading in my room. I walked up the Hill about noon and turned in the grades. There were very few students left on the Campus, and those few were complaining of the cold prevailing in their heat-less rooms. I sent a letter to my brother-in-law in London. I invested about 1,000 dollars on them. I'll refuse from now on to pay any bills, even when they deposit money into my account in Cyprus.

November 30, 1950, Thursday

Everybody is worrying once more about the war news. The Chinese have pushed us back, and everybody is clamoring for the use of the atomic bomb. It seems that everybody believes that the atomic bomb will bring the war to an end in the twinkling of an eye. It might, but the consequences might be dreadful. The French and the British statesmen want to build a buffer state between Manchuria and Korea so as to avoid trouble with China, but it seems that our own strategists believe that we are honor bound to reach the Yalu River and establish a unified, democratic Korea. We are simply wasting good men and throwing away good money on illusionary projects. The Koreans are neither able nor willing to practice democracy. Of course, our real fear is that Russia might extend its sphere of influence over the Korean peninsula. Even if it does, I don't see what difference it makes to our defense. We still rule the seas and the air, and we have long-ranging bombers and great productive capacity. But a perverse spirit has entered the American mind since the end of the war. We transferred all of our hatred from the Japanese and Germans to the Russians. As far as I can see, vast oceans separate us from them. But we got close to their borders, and they, of course, try to retaliate in kind. The whole affair shows how immature both the leaders and the public are. God only can have mercy on poor mankind, especially on the middle and low classes.

December 3, 1950, Sunday

The news from the war front is still bad; the Chinese are threatening to engulf the whole UN Army in Korea. I hope that the French and the English will bring pressure on the United States to settle the Korean War and avoid war with China. The whole affair is ridiculous and makes no sense. To save Korea for democracy, we have turned it into desert with our bombings, landings, advances, retreats, and whatnot. The whole peninsula, the home of 23,000,000 people, is in ruins, and the inhabitants—instead of democracy—got famine, cold, sickness, and intense suffering. The fact that 52 nations did not contribute more than 40,000 soldiers shows that their hearts are not in the war. If the 53 UN nations believed in the war and had supplied about 10,000 soldiers each, there would have been by now over half a million soldiers in Korea, and the war would have been over long ago. As it is now, it is a United States war against the whole of Asia.

December 10, 1950, Sunday

For supper I ate a pint of ice cream with peanuts. I sent *Man Against Myth* to Sh. by Willie, who is going to Fayetteville tonight. Everybody is talking about war and the chances of peace. Of course, peace is possible if common sense and not magical thinking prevails. Every nation wants to save face, or not to lose prestige. It is better to save men and be in peace than to save face and prestige.

December 13, 1950, Wednesday

On the war front, the allies are evacuating troops from Korea. The Chinese are either regrouping or waiting for the cease-fire command from the UN. Everybody thinks that we ought to get out of Asia as fast as we can since we don't have the manpower to fight the Asians on the ground. We might molest them and bother them with our Air Force and Navy, but by this warfare we can gain only their ill will and enmity. The time may come when they will also develop an air force, and then they may pay us the same compliment by bombing our bases, ships, and cities.

December 15, 1950, Friday

There is a kind of railroad strike: President Truman will speak tonight at 9:30. He is expected to declare a state of emergency, freeze salaries and prices, and urge expansion of the armed forces. We are just now evacuating northeast Korea. We are constantly told that we have inflicted staggering casualties on the Chinese, but still we have to retreat. It seems that even the least-equipped armies can win a war without numerical superiority. Alexander the Great with four divisions defeated vast numbers of Persians and other Asians. It seems that the modern weapons have made equals of white and yellow, European and Asian, fighters.

December 16, 1950, Saturday

I returned home about 1 o'clock and spent a delightful afternoon reading the *Journal of Higher Education*. It is for deans and administrators, but it is of great interest to the professors also. For example, the North Central Coordinator spoke to us three weeks ago about "a student-centered college." I did not know at that time that he belonged to the Progressives and not to the Classicists and Liberals. I also read about what kind of teachers the colleges are looking for. A good college teacher must have at least four qualifications. He must be a scholar, he must be able to teach, he must see his subject in relation to the other subjects in the curriculum, and he must have health and be an exciting human being. With emergency declared, mobilization upon us, it will be difficult to get good or bad teachers for the next 10 or 20 years. Besides that, the A-bomb haunts mankind. A few atomic bombs may change atmospheric conditions and make the Earth uninhabitable or turn us all into beggars who are glad to get enough food to keep body and soul together. Scholarship, art, literature, music, and whatnot may be forgotten and neglected for many generations. The Athenians once plunged into a war that lasted for 27 years. At the end, life became so hard that stoicism, cynicism, epicureanism and agnosticism undermined their mental, moral, and physical stamina. Let us hope that the scourge of war may be avoided and that mankind may be allowed to work out his destiny in an atmosphere free from fear and want.

December 19, 1950, Tuesday

Yesterday I did nothing except read, walk, and dream. I want to go to New Orleans, and yet the length of the trip, the expense, the trouble, and whatnot prevent me from taking the trip. Anyhow, I can't go until Christmas, and by that time I'll probably be able to make up my mind. I also want to buy a new overcoat, and I'm perturbed and disturbed at the idea that I have to put on my new suit of clothes. There is no greater horror to me than putting on new clothes. It must be a holdover from childhood. It is unreasonable; everybody seems to rejoice in wearing bright ties of all colors, and I change them three or four times a year. I mailed cards to 25 friends and acquaintances of mine. Once I used to delight in sending cards, but by now it has become a sad necessity. I'll have to buy some presents for the children of some of my friends. Sh. gave me a nice hairbrush, and I gave her a wristwatch band.

December 21, 1950, Thursday

At 6 o'clock Ms. Sweet drove Martha, Willie, Mr. Cline, and me around the town to see the Christmas trees and decorations. Most of the houses did not exhibit any decoration at all. Only a few houses had Christmas trees standing in the yard. The town is poor, and the people are too busy making a living to worry over Christmas decorations. I bought my last Christmas presents—five boxes of chocolates—not of the finest or the best. They cost me six dollars. This year I gave about 18 dollars worth of presents and cards.

December 22, 1950, Friday

The Johnsons gave me a nice box of cakes of soap; I'll take it easy and relax over the weekend. Everybody, including my landlady, is leaving tomorrow noon for somewhere. I was planning to go to New Orleans, but somehow I can gather neither the courage nor the enthusiasm to start on a trip.

December 24, 1950, Sunday

It is Christmas Eve. I spent the day very quietly reading *Building the British Empire* by J. T. Adams. The weather is clear and warm. I didn't go to church, and I'm glad I didn't have to go anywhere. It is a real relief not to have to attend anything. I spend my life attending meetings, chapels, assemblies, classes, and whatnot. At noon I met the Friscoes; they looked prosperous and sleek; they are still at Stillwater. I gave one dollar as a Christmas present to each of the waitresses at the Southern Grill and bought a package of candy at 75 cents for the Sweets, who invited me tomorrow for dinner. Mrs. Wills phoned that Sh. will be at her home tomorrow and asked me to drop in for a visit. Everybody—the Johnsons, Mrs. Brown, and Landlady Cline—have left Siloam for Little Rock or Tulsa. The town was crowded with soldiers and Marines on furlough. They look abominably young; they are like grown-up scout boys. I hope they don't feel the same hostility toward the Army that I used to feel. Of course, they are young, and military life may be an adventure and a challenge to them. All the same, on this Christmas Eve, let us pray that the scourge of war may speedily pass away. There is nothing more unreal than war. For all the other evils—famine, accidents, droughts, etc.—men can blame luck or fate, but for war, they can blame only themselves. It is a man-made evil. It is the legacy from his animal ancestry. He will never become human until he ceases killing his fellow men.

December 26, 1950, Tuesday

I got up as usual yesterday at about 7 o'clock, and after bathing and shaving I returned out in the warm, sunshiny morning in search of breakfast. All the restaurants and drug stores were closed. I returned home, ate a few biscuits and a slice of cheese in foil, and drank a glass of water. I was invited to the Sweets' for dinner. I was hungry by 11 o'clock, and at about 10 minutes to twelve I phoned, asking when I was expected. About 1:30 p.m., came the answer, and dinner would be served at 2 o'clock. I took another trip to town. The only open restaurant was Nora's, famous for its messiness and filth. I drank a cup of coffee. I didn't even finish the cup; it was dirty. At about 1:30, dressed in my new suit of clothes I bought last September in Kansas City and carrying a small Christmas gift, I walked to my hosts' home. I waited 'till 3:15 before we sat at the table. It seemed that the mistress of the house could not get the turkey browned. After the meal, I left immediately for the Wills', where Sh. was spending Christmas. I reached the place about 5 o'clock. The Cooks were there, and after staying 'till 6 o'clock I returned home, glad that such a great holiday so disturbing to men without a home was over. Today I ate at the Youree, the Southern Grill being closed from Christmas to New Year's Day. At noon I ate at the University; the meal was good and cost me nothing. I saw Sh. off at the bus station; Mrs. Hodges was there to see her elder son off to Fayetteville. The UN forces have retreated below the 38th parallel; the Chinese are prepared for a new attack.

December 27, 1950, Wednesday

I bought an evening paper and read the news. The Chinese are massing their armies; if we bomb their communications, we are going to tax ourselves to extinction, and the draft boards are calling men to the armed forces. It is a mad world; the less one thinks of it the better. Someday reason and love will rule the world; now we are ruled by emotion and hatred.

December 28, 1950, Thursday

It is hard to find anything to record when life is so quiet and uneventful. Of course, I can write down my thoughts and feelings, but this is not the aim of this diary. I must be as objective as I can and keep a record only of happenings rather than observations and thoughts.

December 29, 1950, Friday

I saw Mrs. Sweet today. She was going to Tulsa to take a plane for California. I also saw D. Wilson; she spent ten days in Tulsa; these adventurous elderly ladies, considerably older than I, put me to shame. I dare not travel; I dare not fly; I dare not stay in hotels; I am really a coward afraid to call my soul my own. It must be due to my early environment of fear, superstition, and poverty. But the holdover from childhood must be routed.

January 1, 1951, Monday

I saw Sh. off at the bus station; she had been visiting the Cooks. This being the first day of a new year, I pray that I may spend the coming year in health, happiness, success, and service to God and man. I'll keep on improving myself and improving others; I'll scatter, or rather, peddle ideas. The Chinese in Korea are pressing hard on the UN troops, i.e. American troops.

January 4, 1951, Thursday

The Chinese occupied Seoul, the capitol of South Korea, this afternoon; they also developed another encircling movement. It seems that the UN Army, which is really the United States Army, has to evacuate Korea, and that would be much better. We are going to lose face and prestige, but it is better losing those intangible values or essences than losing men in a useless and fruitless war. Nobody believes any longer that we are fighting for a great ideal; we simply blundered into Korea; we defeated the North Koreans; and instead of treating them generously, we asked them to surrender and bombed their cities, destroyed their factories, and pushed up to the Manchurian border. Then out of the blue, the Chinese struck us hard, and we reeled back, losing men and ground. We are out numbered, and, it seems to me, outsmarted also. It is about time all the Europeans get out of Asia. The Asians have learned how to fight.

January 8, 1951, Monday

I listened for 10 minutes to President Truman's speech today at noon. He blamed all the evils of the world on the rulers of the Soviet Union. He charged them with imperialism and aggression. I guess the Russians think the same thing about us. It depends on which side of the fence you stand. We take it for granted that every revolution is instigated by the Russians and that we are honor bound to safeguard democracy and freedom all over the wide world.

January 15, 1951, Monday

I read in the *Tulsa World* that a survey made in 55 colleges and universities has disclosed that the morale of the students is exceedingly low. Most of them don't care about their studies since the only prospect in wait for them is soldiering. In the University of Oklahoma, 60 percent of the students failed in their midterm exams. Even we, who are not immediately concerned about "draft," are disturbed.

January 17, 1951, Wednesday

It seems that men thrive on wars, and this may be an explanation for the war scares, rearmament programs, and whatnot that at present pester the bewildered sons of Adam. The Church ought to condemn the men who amass fortunes by manufacturing weapons of war. The Church, of course, does and will never do anything of the sort. The so-called religious leaders get excited if a poor man gets drunk or kisses or sleeps with somebody else's wife, but they do nothing to curb war, social injustice, or class exploitation. On the contrary, they seem to sanction and bless them. Once war and social injustice are banished from the face of the Earth, the ordinary man will find something better to do than indulging in wine and women. It is misery and frustration that drive men to drinking and wenching. A free, full life will express itself in art, play, and creative activities.

January 18, 1951, Thursday

I bought a pint of ice cream and noticed that its price is at present 30 cents. Only yesterday it was 25, and a few years ago, 18 cents. According to the statistics, prices are the highest in the history of this non-too-cheap country. There is a possibility that prices will be frozen this week. Meantime, our president bears pressure on the UN to declare China an aggressor for interfering in the Korean conflict. I guess we can defeat China since it has neither bombers nor

A-bombs, but it will be a great shame to bomb populous cities and kill millions of innocent women, children, and old men. Our offense might stink to high heaven, and God might raise an avenger.

January 20, 1951, Saturday

The great issue nowadays is whether to draft or not to draft the 18-year-old. Some people argue that at 18 most boys are still children; others say that one is mature by 18. The truth is that nobody wants to do the actual fighting. Everybody, if left alone, prefers his own comfort and ease. It is the politicians and the allies and the manufacturers who are the most belligerent. They have already got into uniform millions of men and painted such fine pictures of invasion and attack that appropriations are easily made. As far as unprejudiced observers can discern, the Russians never threatened the safety, the independence, or the security of the United States. But although they did not bother this country, they are supposed to have threatened Europe and Asia and Africa. Therefore, we feel honor bound to protect these continents. Although I'm not an isolationist, I disapprove of such immense solicitude for the rest of the world. It does not show unselfishness; it shows desire to exploit others for our benefit. We are really fighting for oil, tin, and rubber, and not for ideals.

January 24, 1951, Wednesday

I gave a test and loafed and doubted and dreamed the rest of the day. I consulted Snider and Springfield about my Pension Fund Insurance. Both were of the opinion that I ought not to surrender it since I could afford to pay the 38.85 monthly premium. They assured me that the Social Security monthly is very low, about 5 dollars a month. The United States wants to brand China as aggressor so our mighty planes might bomb Chinese cities and kill innocent women and children. Nehru, who seems to be the sanest leader alive today, blames the United States for the continuation of the Korean War. The question about what the peace of the world hangs on is this: The Chinese say that they will give the order "cease-fire" after a meeting of the UN delegates takes place. The United States says this: No meeting unless the order "cease-fire" comes first. It is really asinine to have countless millions of people suffer and die simply because we or the Chinese want to save face. It seems to me that a powerful group in the United States, for reasons of their own, either conquest, fear of the communist ideology, desire for profit, or simply for sheer wantonness, ardently desires war. After all, they will escape all the hardships; they will make money; they will eliminate undesirable elements; the sons and daughters of the people can be conditioned to fight a war against the Russians and the Chinese. The first are Reds, the second are yellow, and both are atheists, communists, and enemies of God.

January 25, 1951, Thursday

I gave two tests and turned in my Pension Trust Insurance Policy to be changed. I decided to carry it on at my own expense. I rode to town with Mr. Ross, who was carrying an innocent lamb to be slaughtered, dressed, and put in the "locker." The poor animal looked fat and sad as if aware of his impending fate. In pity I stroked its head, but it tried to butt me.

January 27, 1951, Saturday

At last the long expected freezing of prices and wages came upon us. But, somehow, for the chief item, i.e. food, the prices are to remain fluid and are expected to rise. As it is, food prices are the highest in the history of the country. It takes 70 cents to eat a steak sandwich with French fries and a glass of milk. Milk is 23 cents a quart, and some kinds of ice cream are 30 cents a pint.

February 3, 1951, Saturday

I'm still debating in my mind whether to put on or not to put on my new suit of clothes! I'm like Hamlet, a victim of indecision; I can't make up my mind either about small or great things! Of the four mental processes, weighing of decisions is the hardest with me. Sometimes a day is spoiled because I can't make up my mind whether to eat breakfast before I go to school or eat breakfast and return home and then go to school. To do or not do, to go or not go, are the problems that perennially plague me and pester me. It is distressing, to say the least.

February 19, 1951, Monday

The newspapers' headlines announced that the Americans pushed the Chinese back; yesterday it was the Chinese who pushed the Americans back; I'm sorry for the poor boys, both Chinese and American, who are sacrificed for causes that perhaps tomorrow will appear foolish. It is only five years since Germany and Japan surrendered unconditionally. But by today the Nazis are being freed from the jails, the Germans are urged to rearm, and we are training a new Japanese Army. So all the sacrifices, the tears, the agony, the corpses that were spent for the defeat of Nazism, Fascism, and Japanese imperialism were for nothing. We are rearming Japan, Germany, and Italy in order to avert or invite war with the Soviet Union. Let us hope that our former enemies have short memories. We are very naïve in believing that the Japanese, the Germans, or Italians, the countries of whom we destroyed and the children of whom we killed, will fight by our side. I'm afraid they will turn the weapons against us. After all, they can fight Russia at their leisure after they help it to drive us from either Asia or Europe.

March 2, 1951, Friday

I spent the day teaching and reading. At 11:30 I attended Chapel. D. Thompson preached a long sermon (it lasted 'till 12:15) on the qualifications he expected of those who would go to the lands beyond as missionaries. Men and women of high intelligence and energy will not become missionaries. Last night a certain Greek called D. Nicholas Thomas showed a film on Greece. He said that he had returned from Greece, where everybody thirsted and hungered for the gospel, and that he intended to return to Greece in the near future. He left last night. He acquired all the mannerisms of the evangelist. He might be earnest and sincere, but Greece is not a field open for missionaries. The Greeks are proud of their own brand of Christianity, and nothing is more obnoxious to them than the introduction of new sects and beliefs. They are, of course, behind the times, but that does not bother them at all. What they need is sanitation, agriculture, science, and industry. They have too much religion already.

March 15, 1951, Thursday

Mr. Springfield asked me to loan him 2,000 dollars to buy Seal's house. I told him to see if he can get it from the University Exchange. I hope that he can't do it because I hate to lend money on any pretext. Loans always breed discords and hard feelings. The United States sent me a note to the effect that I owe about 13.50 more in income taxes. I already paid 431 dollars. I'm afraid if the war with Korea lasts longer, the expenses will be bigger and, therefore, the taxes higher. We might dislocate our economic system by trying to beat communism. We might ourselves turn into socialists, if not communists. According to yesterday's dispatch, UN forces reentered Seoul, and they are approaching the 38th parallel. Let us hope that this time, being chastened by former experiences and losses, the UN will stop and build a strong defensive line so that at least the war will be localized.

March 26, 1951, Monday

Yesterday being Easter, I traveled to Fayetteville, where I dined and walked with Sh. I saw two great forest fires blazing unchecked. On my return I bought a pint of ice cream, which I shared with my landlady in exchange for a piece of cake.

April 15, 1951, Sunday

On Friday morning at 6 o'clock I left for Little Rock. D. and Mrs. Wills drove me first to Fayetteville, where we picked up Sh., and then drove to Mount Gaylor for breakfast. It was cold and windy. We reached Little Rock about 1 o'clock. I stayed at the Marion Hotel, Room 665. It was a nice room with a shower bath and private toilet all for 3 dollars. We had a hard time finding the junior college because it was moved outside of town two years ago. I reached it just in time for my address on Fitzgerald's *This Side of Paradise*. I shortened my address to eight or 10 minutes, to the relief of everybody. I managed to give my address without the slightest stage fright, and everybody, of course, said that they enjoyed my speech tremendously. Let us hope they were not merely being polite. After the banquet we drove Sh. to 610 Oak Street; it took us quite a time to find the street; it was about midnight before I lay on my comfortable bed. On Saturday I was a member of the panel but talked only for two minutes. There were too many people anxious to monopolize conversation. We had a coffee hour in the beautiful library of the junior college and a brief business session, and by 12 o'clock the meeting was adjourned. An elderly man drove Mrs. Wills, Sh., and me to 610 Oak to wait for D. Wills to pick us up and take us to the hotel and lunch. We checked out about 2 o'clock and drove on highways 10, 64 and 59 through Fort Smith, Sallisaw, Watts and Siloam. Fort Smith's streets were crowded with young soldiers from Camp Chaffee.

April 18, 1951, Wednesday

I drew from my school account 750 dollars and gave them to Mr. Marion Snider to pay for his car; it is a loan to be paid by installments in two years. Mrs. Stanfield told me this evening that she heard a rumor that Mr. Springfield resigned his position in the University. It might be since I've not seen him at his desk these two days. I'll be sorry if he goes away. He was a great friend of mine. I'll ask Mr. Snider tomorrow and get the inside story, or probably D. Brown will tell us tomorrow. Also, Buddy Brown has been away from the campus for some time.

April 19, 1951, Thursday

I taught one hour and then attended Chapel. D. Brown preached the first half of the hour, and then from 11:30 to 12 o'clock we listened to MacArthur's speech to the Congress. It was a good speech, but it was full of half-truths. He thinks that we ought to blockade China, help Chiang Kai-shek, and bomb Manchuria and the coastal cities of China in order to finish the war in Korea. That means spreading the war rather than finishing it. Besides that, we don't want to imitate the Germans who, 10 years ago in their confidence in air power, began to bomb cities and factories and whatnot. In the end, of course, their own cities were destroyed and their own children and wives were killed or maimed. Since the Chinese, or even the Russians, have never used what we call "strategic bombing," I don't see why we should start something that later on might recoil on us. Of course, we are sure that we are supreme in air; so the Germans believed; so the British believed when they ruled the seas and shelled the ports of the world. It would be wrong to ally ourselves with the reactionary regimes of Chiang against a government that does something for the people even if that government is distasteful to us. Of course, those who shout the loudest for war are those who do the least fighting or sacrificing. They are the Republicans, the commentators, the newspapermen, the so-called Christians (rather the fanatic type of Christians) and, in brief, those who never saw nor hope to see a battlefield. It would be a real tragedy to involve ourselves in a war with China simply because we were too obstinate and too stubborn to acknowledge that we backed the wrong house in the Chinese civil war. We ought to help the Chinese people to attain higher standards of living instead of thinking how to bomb the cities and unleash on the coasts the Nationalistic Army of Chiang, if such armies really exist!

April 24, 1951, Tuesday

The Chinese have started a new offensive and advanced 12 miles. We are still debating whether MacArthur or Truman is right! The English government is split; the dissenting Minister is accusing A. of subordinating British policy to the U.S. policy and undermining the existence of their country. Being spring, the youngsters' minds are turned to thoughts of love; Venus is still powerful in spite of Christ, Mars, and Mammon. She reigns supreme in the hearts of men and neither religion, nor war, nor inflation, nor depression interfere or hinder her activities!

April 27, 1951, Friday

A hot day; I taught and loafed and worked. I got two books on communism for the man who runs the Dixie Store. He wants some material for his speech to the Rotary Club. The Chinese are still advancing, although our commanders maintain that they have killed 30,000 of them in three days. At this moment the Chinese are only 13 miles from Seoul, the capital that has been captured and lost four times already in 10 months. It seems the UN must send more troops to the Korean peninsula, but everybody wants to send planes, warships, and whatnot except for exactly what is needed to overcome the Chinese armies.

April 30, 1951, Monday

Yesterday Mrs. Thornton drove me to Fayetteville. We picked up Sh. and went to the University Theater, where we saw *Born Yesterday*. Government business is getting more and more complicated as the years go by, and even the extraordinary people don't know how our national government is run. Everybody is aware that corruption, inefficiency, and politics rule supreme. But it is an old story. Democracy and efficiency rarely go hand in hand. After the show we drove to the Chicken Little and ate fried chicken. Then we drove Sh. back to Fayetteville, and after visiting for a few minutes we drove back to Siloam, which we reached about 8:30 p.m. It was a good day, although it cost me about 5 dollars. The Americans still hold Seoul, but the Chinese are only five miles away from it.

May 5, 1951, Sunday

The war in Korea goes on; our politicians staged an investigation about MacArthur's dismissal; it is certainly a pitiable joke to be killed in wars you don't know why you are fighting while the politicians discuss the cons and pros of a conflict. My sympathy goes out to the poor boys who are fighting in Korea and dying for their native land. I guess only one kind of war is sacred and holy: to fight and die in defense of one's country. But to fight 12,000 miles away from home—it seems to be imperialism no matter how you phrase it. Each nation ought to stay at home and mind its own business. God knows each nation has social, economic, and political problems to keep it busy for centuries. It may be that unwillingness to tackle the problems at home is the chief cause of wars. It is like the individual's inability to "know himself" that drives him to daydreaming or action and very rarely to thinking, which is his proper business.

May 12, 1951, Saturday

Last night I had the Ferms as my guests at the Chicken Little. We ate salad, fried chicken, strawberry short cake, all for 4.81. After the supper we drove to Fayetteville and saw the exhibition at the Art Building. We returned home about 9:30. Today I taught and read as usual. The students were in "bad humor" either on account of yesterday's "sneak day" or tonight's junior-senior banquet or Emily Dickinson's poetry. It was with great difficulty that I refrained from scolding their very obvious indifference. A sense of humor can prevent a teacher from making a fool of himself. I drank a pint of half-and-half, and I ate about a dozen cookies my landlady presented me with. I got a letter from D. Neudling, chairmen of the Department of Classics at the University of Arkansas: he wants me to pinch hit for him during his year of absence. He promises only one year's employment. Of course, I will not consider it. I'm well established in Siloam Springs, and I'm teaching what I most like to teach, English and

American Lit. It seems that either Sh. or D. Carter must have given him my address.

June 3, 1951, Sunday

About 1 o'clock D. Wills picked me up and drove me to Eureka Springs. It was raining most of the time. We reached the church on time to see Susan Pinkley married to Don Ferguson or Anderson. Both were JBU graduates. D. Smith performed the ceremony. The groomsmen and the bridesmaids were also students of JBU. After the ceremony we went to the bride's grandmother's house for the reception. We received a piece of cake and a cup of punch. About 4:30 we started for Siloam, which we reached at 7 o'clock. I bought a pint of Ward's ice cream, and, having eaten it, I'm going to bed early.

June 4, 1951, Monday

Well, I should not worry about it. I received an announcement for a job from Oregon College of Education, Monmouth, Oregon. They will pay over 5,000 dollars to get a man who does not speak "accentless" English. It is a great pity to not even dare apply for such a good job, but I guess one must accept what the philosophers called necessity and learn to cooperate with the inevitable. I just met and dismissed my classes today. I read and loafed and rested. I supped on a quart of milk and bananas. My favorite restaurant is closed, and there is no use spending good money on food I can't eat.

June 8, 1951, Friday

Rumors about truce with the Chinese are flying around. Marshall is in Korea; two top officials of the English government have disappeared; the general opinion is that they went to Russia.

One of them was the top man in British-American relations, and the other in Far Eastern questions. Another question that bothers me is the meat scarcity that has been threatened by the administration's determination to control meat prices. We in Benton County are more concerned about the Chicken of Tomorrow Festival, which will start in Fayetteville at the University of Arkansas on Monday, June 11, and will last 'till the 16th. As for myself, I'm neither studying hard, nor writing clearly, and speaking forcefully. I'm simply vegetating.

June 15, 1951, Friday

The war news is the same; the UN forces are still advancing; MacArthur and Co. are still agitating for war against China; the president urged the Congress to vote strict control to keep inflation down. That inflation is here I'll prove by mentioning two items: yesterday I bought a quart of homogenized milk and three bananas at 51 cents; today I bought a quart of milk and a package of crackers at 53 cents. These items used to cost only 30 cents at the most.

July 2, 1951, Monday

I went to Fayetteville today with Mr. Kennedy. It was raining. We dined at Sh.'s on tuna fish salad, coffee, and cherry pie. I wanted to see a show, but Kennedy was anxious to return home to help his wife can beans, so we returned home at about 3:30 p.m. Last night I supped at the Springfields. Buddy Brown and his wife, Mr. Hodges and his wife, Mr. Griffin and I were the guests. They served fried chicken with salad, tomatoes, and coconut pie. After the meal we inspected the foundation of the house Buddy Brown is building on a lot behind the Home Economics Building. I returned home about 8:30 and went to bed. The Koreans, or rather, the Red Chinese accepted Ridgeway's offer for meeting in order to discuss terms of Armistice. The fighting is still going on.

August 10, 1951, Friday

Last Sunday I went to Fayetteville; it was hot, but I enjoyed both the trip and the meal. Everything just now is very quiet. D. Brown is away; and the summer work is easy and pleasant. I usually leave for the Hill at 8:30, I read under the tree 'till noon with two or three recesses and visits in the meantime, I eat at the dining hall with the young couple whose name just now escapes me, I teach grammar from 1 to 2:10 and world classes from 2:10 to 3:25, and I then return home. I spend the rest of the day reading on the porch, walking, or visiting with the people who live at 203 S. Wright Street. It is not a heroic life; it is rather prosaic and quiet, but it is pleasant to me. I remember many dreary, dark, and weary summers, during which I was either employed at menial tasks in order to keep body and soul together, or I was looking for a teaching job. I feel that God planted me where I can best grow. He will remove me to better positions and employments when the fullness of time comes. My task just now is to learn all I can, to improve all I can, and serve mankind to the best of my ability.

August 18, 1951, Saturday

Today my students were listless and apathetic; it might be that the heat got them down, or because it was Saturday afternoon, or because *Hamlet,* which we are presently reading, is above their comprehension. Anyhow, the present day students are in many ways inferior to those of the past years. I'll keep my eye on the great goal of my life: to become another Plato, a wise scholar, and a great teacher to educate the world and live in the memory of posterity. To use an expression of Thoreau, I must cease to be a provider for the poor and immature and become one of the "worthies of the world."

August 27, 1951, Monday

Yesterday I went to Fayetteville. Sh. met me at the station. We ate at Ferguson's. She intended to show me her new apartment, but since she had a bilious attack on Saturday, she was unable to do it. I returned to Siloam in a terrific rainstorm. D. Brown is expected to be on the Campus tomorrow afternoon; he will tackle many problems dealing with the providing of housing and classrooms for the Military Academy that is moving from Sulphur Springs to Siloam Springs.

September 12, 1951, Wednesday

Last Monday I left by the morning train at 5:40 for Kansas City, Missouri. The trip was delightful, but difficulties started when I began looking for a room. The Plaza Hotel was full, so I went to the Union Station and phoned the President, but it was full. Then I placed my suitcase in one of the lockers and took the bus for up-town. I visited half a dozen hotels asking for a reservation for the night. Such hotels as Phillips, State, Dixon, Continental, Commonwealth, Lee, Aladdin, Howard—all of them were chock-full; a convention was going on. By 11:30 I gave it up. I decided to go and see *David and Bathsheba,* eat a good meal, and take the 4 o'clock train and return to Siloam. After the show I walked across Main Street to McGee and asked the same question at the desk of Andrew Jackson Hotel. The clerk told me that there was only one empty room, number 410, without bath or closet. I could have it for 1.53 if I wanted. I paid it right away and then took that street car and visited the Swope Park and looked at my friends like the hippo, the elephant, the monkeys, and the sea lions in their new pond; and I also saw the golden eagle fed. I returned to the Union Station, picked up my suitcase, and then took a taxi for the hotel. I undressed and lay in bed and slept by fits and starts. I got up at 7:30, shaved and washed, and checked out. I deposited my suitcase in the same locker, No. 86, and after a breakfast at Harvey's I took the bus and traveled all the way to El Paseo, and then back to 59 and Parallel. I saw the flooded area with the dirt and the ruined factories and homes. At 10:55 I went to the show, where I saw Bing Crosby in *Here Comes the Groom*. At 4 o'clock I took the train and returned home. It was a short but invigorating vacation. Today I visited the Hill, the first time since Labor Day; there was a letter from Roxie; she wrote me that her book was to be published in the spring of 1952 and that she wanted to tell me about it, and that she was working at Davidson's Publishing offices and that she has two children, one 10 and one 6 and a half, and that she wants to hear from me. I really ought to write her; but God knows to what it may lead. I don't know whether she is still living with her husband or with her parents. I have not seen her these 19 years, i.e. since 1932 when I left Atlanta for Gastonia and then for New Brunswick and Arkansas. Once she thought she was in love with me and kept a very furious and fast correspondence 'till she met somebody in New York and married him. Well, I'll sleep over it; there is no need to hurry.

September 17, 1951, Monday

Yesterday I went to Fayetteville. Sh. met me at the bus station. We ate at Ferguson's and then took the bus for her new apartment at 637 Whitham St. (Building 3, Apt.4), into which she moved two weeks ago. Everything about it is brand new. It is a very nice

place to live in, although it is about five blocks away from Old
Main, where she holds classes.

September 18, 1951, Tuesday

I spent the day in the Cathedral of the Ozarks giving
English placement tests and attending the registration of the
transfers and the freshmen. It was a very tedious, long day. About
4 o'clock we called it a day, and I started for home. I bought some
apples and ice cream as a dessert to a hamburger deluxe I ate at
the Southern Grill. I must watch my diet; my stomach does not
function properly. It seems that there is a limit to the bad food one
can eat with impunity. Restaurants and schools do not serve fresh,
clean food. It is a great pity that in a rich country like America,
food is neglected while clothes, shelter, sports, and machinery are
cherished and worshipped. But man is what he eats, not what he
wears or drives or rides.

November 22, 1951, Thanksgiving Day

I've not written in this diary since September 22. I've been
trying to write a novel. I almost finished it, but I think it is
worthless. Since September 22 I've done nothing memorable. I
traveled more than once to Fayetteville; I saw two plays, *Medea*
and *You Can't Take It with You;* I attended a concert; I took a long
trip to Baton Rouge to attend a Modern Language Association
meeting. I read half a dozen books and attended faculty and prayer
meetings. Today I went with the Cooks to Fayetteville; we ate
Thanksgiving dinner at the new apartment of Sh. The weather was
cloudy and warm, and I enjoyed the meal, the trip, and also a visit
to the Veterans Hospital, where we called on Mr. Stanfield and
Mr. Darling. On my return home, my landlady offered Miss Linty

who lives downstairs and me a nice dessert, a piece of pumpkin pie. I'm reading *Louis XIV in Love and War*. It is about 8 o'clock, and I'm going to bed.

November 26, 1951, Monday

I read nothing except *The Reader's Digest*. The articles are of popular interest, and they are certainly colored by the prejudices and beliefs of the prosperous upper-middle class: They show hatred between the Americans and the Russians; they praise the deeds of our so-called allies and condone the sins of colonialism and imperialism. The French are lauded for keeping an Army of 200,000 men in Indo-China at the expense of a billion dollars a year, and we are praised for our work in the Pacific Islands and especially in turning Japan into a democratic country. All these statements are brazen lies; no one can turn 83,000,000 men and women into democrats in six years. We are not ruling the Islanders for their own good but for our own. The French are not combating communism; they are trying to reestablish their rule over a colony that revolted. The Malayans, Iranians, and Egyptians are our enemies simply because they want to free their countries from the dominion of Europeans who have no business to be there. The fault of the countries is that they possess rubber, oil, and a canal. These blessings to those countries attract the exploiters of the west, who invoke ideology to defend their iniquities. People are afraid to say we want rubber, oil, and tin. They say we defend Western Civilization.

December 3, 1951, Monday

A summer day, warm and clear; yesterday I went to Fayetteville; I dined at Sh's on steak and vegetables, and then we went to the U-

Ark. Theater, where we saw Jose Ferrer in *Cyrano de Bergerac*. It was a great show. It reminded me of the first time I saw the play in New York with Hamden as Cyrano; at that time I was going with Lucille, who later on got married to someone whose name I don't anymore remember. It must have been 25 years ago, at least. How time does fly! Mr. Haley drove me to town. He told me that he has already sent home 10 Academy boys and girls. One of the girls he suspects to be pregnant; she confessed she indulged in carnal conversation with a man before she came to school last fall.

December 11, 1951, Tuesday

I mailed my first Christmas card to Wallis Olsen in India. I sent it by regular mail; it will reach him probably by the end of January. I guess it is about time to sit down and write a letter to my folks in Cyprus. I simply don't know what to write them about. I've not seen them these 30 years. As a matter of fact, I've not seen my brother-in-law and my nephew and niece at all; I've only some pictures of them to go by. I like to write to them, but they usually manage to get me into trouble. They are either clamoring for a visit to Cyprus or for money; I guess someday when the wars and the rumors of wars subside, I'll take a trip to Cyprus and visit the places where I spent the not-very-cheerful and careless years of my childhood. But meantime, I must work hard, look forward, and try to become one of the "worthies" of the world. I'll probably help my poor islanders more if I become famous; my example might set ambitious souls on fire and give the island inspired leaders in political, social, and spiritual activities. As for myself, I shrink from plunging into any activity in the turbulent and muddy waves of Cypriots or Greek affairs. I'll simply wear myself out and be of no use to anybody. It is simply by becoming a great artist-philosopher, another Plato, that I can be of any use to my fellowmen everywhere and to my fellow countrymen at home.

December 13, 1951, Thursday

Mrs. Thornton and her son Dickey drove me last night to Fayetteville. We called first at Sh's, and all of us drove to Chicken Little for a chicken dinner. After the dinner we returned to Sh.'s apartment, and at about 7:30 we left for the U-Ark. Theater, where we saw *The Innocents,* a play based on Henry James' *The Turn of the Screw.* It was good entertainment. We drove back in beautiful moonlight. I'm rereading Henry James' *The Lesson of the Master.* It is a great story on a great theme. An artist can't afford to have a family and children; they will prevent him from reaching perfection; he will think in terms of providing clothes, home, education, and comfort for them; he will turn mercenary; he will write not for posterity but for prosperity. His eyes will be on the financial returns. He will sacrifice quality to quantity. An artist should be able to be poor.

December 16, 1951, Sunday

About 2:15 D. Wills and Mrs. Wills picked me up and drove me to Fayetteville. We called at Sh. She was in bed, recovering from a bad headache she had had the day before. She dressed and went with us to the ballroom of the Student Union, where we heard The *Messiah* rendered by a large chorus of the University of Arkansas. I got glimpses of D. Carter and his family; also of Mr. Weathers and his daughter; and there was, of course, the inevitable Willie Sweet. We drove back immediately because the Wills children had to appear in a program at the Presbyterian Church at 7 o'clock. It was cold in the car, but conversation made the trip short and pleasant. I bought a pint of ice cream at Chandler's and returned home. The stove has been already lighted, and the room was comfortably warm. I'll "fix" my laundry and go to bed early; I have to get up early tomorrow since I have to attend a meeting of the Educational Policy Committee at 8 o'clock.

December 21, 1951, Friday

This is the first day of Christmas vacation. I spent it reading at home and walking. This morning it was intensely cold; it went down to five degrees. There was a sprinkling of snow on the ground; one at least could walk. About 2:39 p.m. I took a walk to the station and then stopped at Millsap's and bought four boxes of chocolates at 3:60 for presents for the children of certain friends. Tonight I was invited to attend D. Wills' birthday party, but I did not go. It is rather cold; his home is outside the Campus on University Row, and I don't enjoy parties. I'll give him a present tomorrow. He has been very nice to me. He drove more than once to Fayetteville, and he is my boss.

December 23, 1951, Sunday

I spent the day at home reading. At intervals I took walks; it is clear and mild. I didn't go either to church or to Chapel. I talked to nobody except my landlady. My conscience is bothering me for not giving a Christmas present to the little waitress at the Southern Grill. She antagonized me by being too courteous these last few days. I got a notion that she is trying her best to win from me a present. That's enough to burn me up. It is a wrong attitude, but I cannot help it. Anyhow, such small affairs must not disturb me. The truce has not yet been signed. The exchange of the lists of prisoners has been completed; there remains the problem of policing the parties engaged in war so as to prevent the building up of forces from further fighting. Our losses amount to over 100,000 dead and wounded. It has been quite an expensive war. We are near losing even the air supremacy. I guess it is time for us to call it a day and get out of Korea as decently as we can.

December 25, 1951, Christmas Day

I got up about 6:30, and about 7:30 I ventured out in the misty, moist air for breakfast. All the restaurants were closed. I returned to my room and feasted on crackers, cheese, apples, and Baby Ruth nuggets. About 12 o'clock I walked to the Cook's house, where Sh. was also a guest. The meal consisted of chicken, mashed potatoes, pumpkin, peas, and preserves. It was rich but not well served; it was messy; the coffee was black and cold. Anyhow, I did justice to the meal, being hungry. While the Cooks retired for their usual "nap," Sh. and I took a walk in the keen, cool air. We returned to the Cook's home about 2 o'clock. The women wanted to see Betty Stout's, or rather, Mrs. Tiffany's new baby. We drove to the Stout's place at the edge of the JBU Campus and, for that matter, the edge of the state of Arkansas. Mr. Tiffany was still striving to get a Doctor's Degree, and he is writing his thesis about Theogony. We entered into a vivid discussion about the Greek and Jewish theogony. He regarded the Greek thoegony to be the result of philosophy or at least projection of man to the infinite, but he regarded the Jewish theogony to be revelation. I pointed out to him that it might be the difference between Semitic and Aryan races; between Greece and Palestine; between reason and faith; between man and woman. This argument went on while I suffered from a splitting headache, which I contracted either from my not drinking my two or three customary cups of coffee or from the hot atmosphere in the room of the Cook's and the Stout's. Mr. Cook drove me home; I was really sick; I got two aspirins and lay down for a while before I recovered from my headache. Sh. gave me a present, a pair of slippers. I tried them on; they fitted, if not perfectly, at least satisfactorily. Well, this Christmas Day I thank God for the health, leisure, freedom, position, friends, and love that I enjoy. I wish these blessings to all the people on the face of the globe. May God give us peace, health, and prosperity.

December 27, 1951, Thursday

I finished *The Closing Ring* by Winston Churchill: He certainly knows how to boost himself and the British. To read his books is to get a glimpse of a great man who is ethnocentric, anti-communist, and aristocratic. In his whole book no mention is made of the common man. No buck private appears; his heroes are the Big Three, marshals, admirals, and generals; one gets the impression that these exalted personages exist and have their being without the toil, the sweat, and the tears of the common man. When the list of casualties is transmitted to him, his comment is that they did not die in vain. Of course, they died in vain; we don't have peace on Earth; we still have colonialism and exploitation of the so-called inferior races by the white races and especially those called Anglo-Saxons. We are still spending billions on armaments, and at present wars are going on in Korea, Egypt, Malaya, and Indo-China. We knocked down the Italian and German states, and now we set them up; it simply does not make sense to me. Those who were killed are buried and forgotten. Those who survived live in fear and insecurity. The four freedoms have been betrayed, and poor mankind is getting ready for a greater and bigger slaughter.

December 29, 1951, Saturday

A very beautiful day. I spent it reading, walking, and resting. I received a Christmas card from home with the general view of Nicosia, my native town. I can't make either head or tail of it. I can recognize the lofty minarets of Santa Sophia, but the other features are unrecognizable. The city must have changed immensely during the last 30 years. It looks pretty but must be smelly and dirty with its inadequate supply of water both for drinking and cleaning purposes. While walking along Jefferson I met Miss Spivey, who once used to teach Home Economics at JBU. She looked well groomed and prosperous. She said that she had finished her education and gotten her master's degree and is now working with the University Extension. I dropped into the Cathedral of the Ozarks this morning. Two workers were busy installing the new screens or shades in the classrooms. I also noticed that somebody had swept the floor and cleaned the blackboards, or rather, the greenboards. Well, I'm going to bed early tonight. Last night I did not sleep very well. I ate a rather heavy meal, a round steak with French fries and cherry pie and two large glasses of milk.

December 31, 1951, Monday

Yesterday I went to Fayetteville. I dined with Sh. and enjoyed a good day, the weather being unusually warm; today the thermometer showed 75 or 80 degrees, and I'm writing now in my room with the door and window open, wearing my pajamas with no heat in the room. I walked and read and dreamed. This being New Year's Eve, I must thank God for the health, happiness, and success I enjoyed during the whole year. I pray that all the years of my life be as happy, healthy, and wise as this past year. My regret is that I've not yet created anything.

January 8, 1952, Tuesday

Since the beginning of my college career, Shakespeare has been my most unsatisfactory course. The students don't respond; they can't understand his gorgeous and vital expressions or his subtle motivations. They are too immature to read with profit and pleasure the works of the greatest writer of modern times. As he himself says somewhere, he is caviar to most students. I tried to make his words actual, but even modern instances cannot be grasped by students who have never seen a play or fallen in love or lost their parents or suffered any privation or grief. Well, I'll follow Thoreau's advice. I'll become one of the worthies of the world instead of an instructor to children.

January 17, 1952, Thursday

Yesterday D. McCartney, the North Central Coordinator, paid JBU a visit. I attended three committee meetings and a faculty meeting. I attended enough meetings to last me the rest of the year. Today we had Chapel; it was yesterday's Chapel postponed. D. Brown was elated by the coordinator's prophecy that we are going into the North Central! He promised to do five things: to increase the professor's salaries, to finish the cathedral building, to remodel the mechanical building, to enrich the library, and to build a new library. That's quite an ambitious program. Everybody was, of course, elated, especially D. Woodland, who seemed to walk on air. To me it seems immaterial whether we belong to an accrediting agency or not. I might get a few dollars a month more, but I'll probably have to fill in more blanks and attend more meetings than I like to. Anyhow, now that the excitement is passed, I'll get down to work and catch up with my reading and sleeping.

January 22, 1952, Tuesday

Last Sunday D. Wills drove me to Fayetteville; he dropped me at Sh.'s apartment while he and his family visited the Weathers. We attended an orchestra concert dedicated to Mozart music, and then we ate scrambled eggs and stewed apricots, and by the time we set the kitchen in order, the Wills returned and picked me up and drove me to Siloam Springs. I started writing a new novel. This time I made an outline, and I know how it is going to end. The trouble with my other literary efforts was that I started without knowing how to end the story.

January 28, 1952, Monday

For the first time since I came to this part of the country, school closed for an epidemic. The town schools closed for a week on account of flu. Thank God, the University is still untouched, although a few of the students were sick for a few days. The cause of the epidemic must be the unusually mild weather we have had since Christmas. It must have encouraged everybody to go out in shirtsleeves or lightly dressed, and this is an invitation to colds and flu. Being the kind of creature who imagines he has every disease he reads or hears about, I had to persuade myself that nothing was wrong with me. Just the same, I'll sleep long hours, take long walks, eat well, avoid crowds, and keep myself in prime physical condition.

February 1, 1952, Friday

I've already met my spring semester classes. All of them, except for the Victorian that replaced the Contemporary course, have shown an increase in numbers. The English Lit. class doubled itself. This noon I did not eat at the dining hall; they served a kind of Mexican dish, chili con carne, which I don't particularly like. I, therefore, walked to the coffee shop for a bowl of Campbell's Soup and crackers. I sat next to Mr. Stephenson, who was eating a savory dish of boiled potatoes, onions, and meat loaf. Mrs. Stephenson filled another plate for me, gave me four slices of bread, plenty of butter, and a cup of coffee, so I had a good meal. She refused payment; she told me that I was guest of "Pop."

February 5, 1952, Tuesday

Last Sunday I went by Fayetteville. An old man, the only bearded man in town, rode the bus also, returning to Booneville to the T.B. Hospital. I dined at Sh.'s on steak, beets, apple salad, coffee, and Fig Newtons. About 4 o'clock an old lady who teaches at the U. of A. paid us a visit. Mrs. Weathers told her that she could secure a job at JBU by seeing me. Of course, I told her to see D. Wills, who does all the hiring. The lady must be over 68 or 70; her hair was white, but she was well preserved for her age. She told me that retirement meant almost death to her. She was, or is going to be, pensioned off for the U. of A on account of her reaching the age limit. She drove me to the bus station. One of the passengers was Mr. White's (the superintendent of schools) sister-in-law returning to her job after a week's compulsory vacation on account of the closing of the schools for the flu epidemic. She is a rather attractive woman, reminding one of Mrs. Pickle and Mrs. Crain. At Watts the car developed mechanical trouble, and the driver parked it in front of the hotel and told us to take it easy. He was going to phone to Stillwell for a bus to come and pick us up and carry us to Siloam. So she and I sat in the car and talked shop for one hour 'till the carryall came and took us to Siloam. It was wet and dark, and the drugstores were closed, so I could not get my usual pint of ice cream. On my return trip, the wife of the Patterson factory manager picked me up. She wore slacks, and she seemed conscious of them.

February 8, 1952, Friday

I received from Roxane the jacket of her book that will be published next month. She promised to send me a review copy. I guess she must be all excited to get her book published at last. She had already revised it about 14 times. The great news of the week is the death of King George of England. I was born under Queen Victoria, and I remember King Edward and the two Georges. The lives of the kings of England, being decorative rather than useful, do not affect the destiny of the world.

February 11, 1952, Monday

A very fine day, I spent it walking, teaching, and reading. Yesterday I went with the Sweets to Tulsa, Oklahoma. We started at 8:30 and reached Tulsa in time for the service at the Boston Avenue Methodist Church. The building is a magnificent structure of stone and steel in semi-gothic and modernistic style. The auditorium was vast, airy, and well lighted, the seats comfortably upholstered, the choir garbed in light pink gowns, the music not overly loud, and the sermon given by D. Galloway only 18 minutes long. It is a rich man's church, and everything provides luxury, comfort, brightness and, let us hope, worship, and meditation. We also visited the so-called Rose Chapel, a church by itself, the museum, the library, and the waiting parlor. After the service we drove along the Tulsa streets, roads, and boulevards; and I was not the least impressed by its residential section. Atlanta, Minneapolis, and New York boast of vaster, richer, and more elegant residential sections.

February 17, 1952, Sunday

Many events took place last week. On Thursday the Faculty Women's Club gave a party for raising money. I went with Mrs. Thornton and the Haleys. We played games and paid 10 cents for each game. I was chosen King of Hearts and had to sit on an armchair with D. Wilson as my queen.

February 29, 1952, Friday

It has been a rather pleasant and profitable week. Last Monday I was invited to supper at the guesthouse by the Home Economics girls. The other guests were the "big shots," President and Mrs. Brown, the Springfields, the Sniders, the Coxes, and the Wills. I was the only bachelor in the group. Yesterday the 19th Annual Missionary Conference started with Mr. Douglas and Rev. Thomas (a Hindu) as speakers. I attended today's service at 11 o'clock. Both speakers sounded like foreigners to the ears of us westerners. The Hindu man at times was hard to follow. His vowels, and sometimes his consonant sounds, were not clear and distinct. I deposited 40 dollars into my savings account (478). I now have 5,300 dollars in my account besides 4,000 in the University Exchange. I gave D. Cook a 50-dollar bond as my contribution to the University church since last month I got a raise. My salary at present is 325 a month. I collect about 265, the rest being withheld either for income tax or for the Social Security Fund.

March 2, 1952, Sunday

Last night Mrs. Thornton drove me to Fayetteville. We picked up Sh. at her apartment (at 637 Whitham St., Building 3, Apt. 4), and then we dined on chicken at the Chicken Little and then went to the U-Ark. Theater, where we saw a very good presentation of Shakespeare's *Merchant of Venice*. Although the play bristled with many anachronisms in hairdos and dresses and lighting and staging, it was a very good performance. Portia was played by a young lady whose hair was black and made in today's style called "pony tail." We returned to Siloam about midnight.

March 18, 1952, Tuesday

I finished Roxane's book a few days ago. I rather liked it and wrote her about it. I'm also reading the Koran, the Bible of Islam. It is a book that repeats with emphasis the obvious truths that one must have faith, do good works, pray, and give to the poor and thus please God and escape eternal punishment. It is a taboo religion fit for immature rather than mature people. In some passages the prophet's animosity equals that of Hitler's in *Mein Kampf*. Neither is classical; they don't follow the path of the middle; they don't know that the good is "a mixed process." No wonder their followers are bigots and storm troopers. They judge everything by certainties; they are intellectual robots; the future belongs to the follower of the Greek tradition of Reason, Order, and Beauty.

March 27, 1952, Thursday

It has been long since I wrote in this book. I've not been busy; I've simply been lazy. The weather has been sometimes chilly and sometimes hot, and I got the spring fever. Last Friday Mrs. Thornton, her son Jimmie, Coach Parker, and I went to Fayetteville, and after picking up Sh. and dining at the AQ Chicken House in Springdale, we saw Tennessee Williams' *Summer and Smoke*. The play is psychological. Alma, the daughter of a minister, is too spiritual to even allow her lover, the son of a doctor, to kiss her; she hates anything that reminds her of the beast; she minds only the things of the spirit. Her lover, in desperation, falls victim to the blandishments of a Mexican girl; he finally finds himself becoming a fine doctor and marries a girl who is not ashamed to say that she wants to be kissed. Alma, at the end of the play, is represented as a streetwalker making advances to a salesman, who calls a taxi and takes her to his hotel.

April 6, 1952, Palm Sunday

About noon I returned from a long trip that took me to Conway, Searcy, Little Rock, Arkadelphia, Hot Springs, Fort Smith, Westville, and Siloam Springs. D. Wills, Mr. Olney, Miss Carlson, and I started on Friday at 5 o'clock on a tour of inspection of libraries. The first day it rained, I had a sore throat, and I developed a headache, so I felt very miserable. The only sunshiny spot was the visit to Harding College, where the young, pretty librarian Miss Allston enlivened the whole routine by taking us to the Coffee Shop for cups of coffee and showed us all the new buildings on the campus. After the inspection of the Harding library, we drove to Judsonia, the small town that was demolished by a tornado last month. It was a sight to inspire fear and pity. Houses, trees, cars, churches, and schools became piles of wood, stones, and sticks. People lived in tents while their homes were being rebuilt. The first night we stayed at Magnolia Courts in Little Rock and ate a good meal at the new Franke's Cafeteria. Henderson College in Arkadelphia has a good library, but the librarian was cold and anxious to get rid of us as soon as possible. We reached Hot Springs about 6 o'clock and drove up to the tower and visited the springs and drank a cup of the hot water from the public fountain. Although the water is medicinal, it tasted like any other hot water. We drove as far as Mount Ida and spent the last night in Mount Ida Cabins. It was cold, and I coughed almost all night. Today after eating breakfast at Mount Ida Café, we drove first to Fort Smith and then home. This is the first trip that I ever took with all expenses paid. It was delightful. Tomorrow I have to get up at five and go to the annual fishing trip on Grand Lake. I still have some throat irritation, but I'll overcome it by a light meal, two aspirin, and a good sleep on my own bed. To tell the truth I hate to go on trips. I prefer to stay at home and read and study. But it is no good for me to be cut off from the ordinary life of traveling and playing.

April 11, 1952, Good Friday

Last Monday I started at 5 o'clock for Cowskin Lodge on Grand Lake. I rode in the school bus with about 20 other members of the JBU staff and faculty. We had breakfast at Grove, Oklahoma, and we reached our destination about 9 o'clock, and while the others were fishing I sat in the sun trying to shake off a cold that gave me a sore throat and made me cough. I still have traces of it. The weather was ideal, and I enjoyed very much the meals and the sight of the curling, laughing waves. We returned home Tuesday evening. On Wednesday evening I rode with the Sweets and Mrs. Cline to Tulsa, Oklahoma, to see a rather sophisticated comedy of manners, *The Moon Is Blue*. The tickets cost 3.65 each. Since I paid for the meals (6.25) and had to pay for two tickets, it cost me about 15 dollars to see a three-act comedy. The fishing trip cost 9 dollars, so in one week I spent about 25 dollars in what we call recreation. Today I taught two hours and attended a faculty meeting. At noon I dined with Mrs. Thornton, her daughter Margie, and Miss Alton. We had beans, onions, cornbread and coffee, a very satisfactory meal. I've been reading

Voltaire's tales; they are simple and wise. I received a letter from Roxane; she expects me to write a review for the Arkansas papers to promote the sale of her book. I've never yet written a review for publication, and I'm too busy to write something for a girl I've not seen for exactly 20 years. My conscience also bothers me for not sending a birthday present to Mrs. Doolittle, D. Cook's mother-in-law, on her 90th birthday. Well, I shall not let such affairs worry me. I've work enough to do in perfecting my command of English, teaching my subjects, and behaving.

April 21, 1952, Monday

It has been a memorable week. On Friday at a quarter to seven, D. Woodland picked me up and drove me to Fayetteville, where we picked up Sh. and Miss Parker and drove to Searcy, Arkansas, to attend the annual College Teachers of English meeting at Harding College. We reached Searcy about 2 o'clock; we stayed at the Mayfair Hotel (my room was 195 and cost me 1.75). The meeting was of not unusual importance; the banquet cost 1.40, and the speaker, Mrs. Gould Fletcher, who read some extracts from her husband's diaries while at Harvard, was very interesting and inspiring. It was a weird thing to have your diaries, to which you trusted your most secret thoughts, fears, and hopes, read to strangers by your own wife only three years after your death. At the same time it is great to be enshrined in the memories of future generations.

April 23, 1952, Wednesday

The news of the day is as follows: floods, strikes, truce talks, politics, and rumors of wars. This being an election year, the politicians try to raise issues to besmirch personalities, discredit policies, win votes, and to be elected. Democracy is the best government; its machinery, however, is vulgar and undignified. Issues become so complex and involved that one knows not what to vote for. One, however, need not bother very much. Most people are born either Democrats or Republicans, and no arguments can shake their loyalties to party. The independents are intelligent enough to vote democratic candidates to the offices. Although they are not Democrats, they loath the smugness, conservatism, and coldness of the Republicans. But although people have already made up their minds, they want to see a vigorous campaign and want the candidates to spend money, time, and effort before voting for them. The people want to be entertained. They then take revenge upon their future rulers.

April 25, 1952, Friday

It might be "age," or it might be the spring, but it is a fact that I've been daydreaming of late. I imagine myself heir to a splendid fortune of 50,000 dollars and building a modern home on a hill in Arkansas and enjoying leisure to write, travel, and read. Another of my dreams is returning to the island of Cyprus and becoming principal of the Cyprus Gymnasium and reorganizing it and making it a progressive school stressing classical, commercial, and vocational education. All these dreams of fame, fortune, and usefulness are pleasant, but I need concentration, study, and work.

April 28, 1952, Monday

Last Saturday I went to Fayetteville and saw *The Merry Wives of Windsor.* Since Mrs. Thornton drove with her brother and sister-in-law, Mr. Parker, Miss B. Wilson, another young couple and I followed in Mrs. Thornton's car, driven by her son Dickey. We all met at the Chicken Little, and after a chicken dinner, we drove to the Little Theater of U of A and saw the play. The play was well staged, but the actors murdered Shakespeare's English. It seems that the clear enunciation of Shakespearean lines is the supreme test of clear and correct pronunciation. Some of the characters talked and acted not in character. But, on the whole, it was a notable production. I dimly remember seeing the play once, perhaps 20 or 25 years ago, in New York City with Otis Skinner as Falstaff. We returned home about midnight. Yesterday I went to church. D. Schimpff preached a sermon about being one in Christ. It is a great idea; it is the idea of one flock and one shepherd. The trouble is that we Christians overemphasize Christ, the Mohammedans stress Mohammed, and the Jews stress Moses, so it would be better if everybody stressed unity in God. The God of the Christians is the God of the Jews and the Muslims; by such a stroke perhaps the whole of mankind might be brought together as children of one Father in Heaven.

May 5, 1952, Monday

I finished the Koran and started reading Haskell's *Cicero*. I hope I don't get into trouble by quoting the Koran now and then. People might think I've turned into a Moslem. This month's *National Geographic* had an article and pictures about the island of Cyprus. The writer asserted that although life in the cities has undergone tremendous changes, country life stood still these 40 or 50 years. The pictures showed castles, churches, sheep, goats—all unusual characteristics of the island's life. They did not show any modern city or any modern hotels or schools or even a modern street. Nicosia contributed only the medieval cathedral turned into a Mosque; there was no mention of its suburban homes, coffee houses, moats, parks, and gardens. It is funny how a visitor to another country will observe only objects different from those of his own country. Anyhow, the article praised the islander's hospitality, industry, frugality, and good cooking.

May 6, 1952, Tuesday

I attended three meetings—one at seven o'clock, another at 11 and another at 4. I taught only two hours. All the meetings were not worth the time invested in them. The weather is warm, and I'm teaching and walking in shirtsleeves. I got rides to the Hill both ways. About 8 o'clock I took a short evening walk. It will help me to sleep better, and it will keep me fit. Since I get up very early, I'll go to bed early although I can scarcely hope to sleep; there is a concert going on in the Community Building across the creek, and the music permeates my room. It is Music Week in Siloam Springs, and tonight is JBU night. As a loyal member of the institution I ought to have attended, but it is too hot to immune one's self in a building. Besides that, I'm not musically minded. I enjoy good music but prefer comfort to the enjoyment of sound. To attend a concert after attending three meetings and teaching two hours is to invite fatigue and nervous exhaustion. I know the "natives" can take everything in their stride; that's why they are victims of hypertension, or rather, Americanitis. I'm a poor and powerless Cypriot, and I have to husband both my mental and physical resources. I'm not as strongly vitalized as they are; and I'm not young any more; I'm in the 52nd year of my age and prefer to go slow, take it easy, and relax. At least that's what I'm teaching and preaching, and I ought to put in effect my own advice and admonition.

May 8, 1952, Thursday

A warm summer day; I taught two hours and spent the rest

of the day reading on the porch of "my house" or under "my tree" on the Campus. For reasons that I can't explain, I became very communicative today. I told Miss Alton that my class in Victorian Poets is made up of preacher boys whose minds are closed and, therefore, unteachable. I told my word mechanics class about my not tipping in Siloam Springs but tipping when traveling in order to explain "extravagant." I also told them a lie—that until now I've gotten fired 19 times to illustrate the difference between one person who says I have failed three times and another person who says I'm a failure. In both cases, the statements were excusable. I was trying to get my point across; all the same it was neither wise nor decent to intrude one's self into one's teaching. I'll stop it from now on and become as objective as one can be. I can illustrate statements by attributing sayings and actions to somebody else. I also talk too much about the uncomfortably warm Chapel; that can get me into trouble. I also crack jokes about the food. It would be wiser to work in silence. My tongue might get me into trouble yet. It got me into trouble before, and there is no guarantee that the past will not repeat itself. Besides that, a man of my age ought to know better than to bear his heart upon his sleeve and confide his troubles to strangers.

May 9, 1952, Friday

Students are getting worse year by year. Poetry and literature seem to them superfluous, irrelevant, and useless. Since they cannot read, they don't understand and enjoy. Since they lack sensibility, sensitivity, and experience, great poetry leaves them bored and indifferent. They want to acquire mastery of expression without reading intelligently. Of course, a wise man knows that this condition existed since time out of mind. The old professors simply lectured on the writers and discussed the poems, but they never attempted to read them with the class. They were much wiser than we. There is a danger that our insistence on reading, comprehension, and evaluation may drive students away from English literature. The classicists with the insistence on reading and analysis killed both Greek and Latin. Anyhow, one can only do his best; the rest is in the lap of the gods.

May 12, 1952, Monday

Today I made a fool of myself twice. First, in the dining hall I protested to the hostess because of the small quantity of food I can eat, for which I pay full price. It was both unnecessary and silly. I must either stop eating at the hall or keep my mouth shut. Second, one of my students in American Lit. laid his head on the desk, and I told him that if he wanted to sleep, he had better move to the front seats so one can't see him through the open door and jump on me! This remark was idiotic and unworthy of a man who has been teaching since 1918. It seems that I'm far from being a reasonable human being. I'm still governed by my impulses, emotions, and, above all, signal reactions. This fear of criticism by superiors is the remnant of my past experience with the schools of Cyprus and the Greek-American schools in the United States. At JBU nobody watches me. I'm on my own and ought not to be so touchy because a student comes late or unprepared or is sleepy. Students are usually careless, listless, and apathetic, especially the last week of the school year. I must get rid of all petty fears, worries, vexations, and annoyances.

May 25, 1952, Sunday

I read enough today to last me for two days. It is such a relief not to have to attend either services or to visit Fayetteville. Just to sit on the porch and read a good book is pleasure for me. I pray to God to give me strong brains, strong eyes, a strong body, leisure, and peace of mind that I may always read, study, teach, and educate mankind. I guess I must sit down and write that letter to my folks in Cyprus. I'm not a good correspondent: I postpone writing to my folks in Cyprus because I have to write in Greek, and it seems to me so hard to express my thoughts and feelings in Greek. I am one of those unfortunate ones who has not a mother or native language. All the languages are surface languages to me. But all the same I can express myself better in English than in any other language.

May 30, 1952, Memorial Day Friday

Mr. Cook was supposed to drive me to Fayetteville for a Chicken Little party at 4 o'clock. Since he sent his car to the garage to have its motor changed, he was not ready to start 'till 7:40. We did not reach Fayetteville 'till 8:45. We ate fried chicken at Sh.'s and visited awhile 'till about 10:30, when we started on our way home. It was exactly 11:35 when I reached my room. Since Mr. Cook is old and his car is old and the traffic heavy, I was a little nervous all the way. The weather, however, was ideal, so we neither perspired nor froze. Sh. was proud of the air conditioning unit she installed in her apartment. It cost about 400 dollars, but I guess it pays in the end to be comfortable. Today, by the way, is the 7th anniversary of my discharge from the Army. How time flies! At that time I thought that once out of the clutches of the Army, I was going to get down to work and become a famous man. Insensibly, routine, indolence, and indifference settled like frost on my life, and I'm not better, nobler, nor wiser than I was then; I'm a little wealthier and fleshier. All the same, I'll keep on working; only those who endure to the end succeed.

June 5, 1952, Thursday

Last Sunday I went to Fayetteville. I visited Sh., who was greatly disturbed and troubled by some students who kept phoning her and threatening to come to her apartment and get the examination questions. The Sweets dropped in about 5:30, and after driving Sh. to Miss Parler's apartment, we drove to Siloam Springs. It was quite a relief not to have to take the bus that goes through Westville and then change for Siloam.

We started summer school last Monday. All my classes materialized, but the number of students enrolled is rather small. In Advanced Grammar I've only nine, about seven in Amer. Lit., and four in composition. Just the same, I've never worked harder in my life. I have to start at one and keep on teaching 'till 4:45. It thundered and rained today, and it was wet all day. I kept indoors and this does not contribute to raising my spirits.

September 1, 1952, Labor Day

I've not written in this book since June. It has been dry and hot all summer. It did not rain at all in June and only a few times in July and August. The first session I taught three straight periods from 1 o'clock to 4:45; the weather and the long hours almost put me out of commission. The second session, however, was very pleasant. I taught only one class from 2:15 to 3:30. It was my favorite one, Word Mechanics and Phonetics. Besides teaching I traveled to Fayetteville more than once, and I read many books sitting either on my swing on the porch at 203 S. Wright street or on the bench under "my tree" on the Campus of JBU. Thank God, I enjoyed perfect health all summer long. Only once I was troubled with a headache and had to take two tablets of St. Joseph aspirin. I ate my meals at the Southern Grill and at the University Cafeteria.

Tomorrow I'll be officer of the Day, and sometime this week I plan to take a trip to Kansas City for pleasure and business. I need a new suit of clothes and an overcoat. Out of inveterate habit I buy my clothes at Richman's. I've been doing it since 1936, that is to say, since I left New York. I'm sorry I neglected putting down my thoughts and observations daily, but it could not be helped. It was stiflingly hot in my room. It would have taken a heroic soul to sit in it and write, and God knows I'm not a hero.

September 2, 1952, Tuesday

I spent the day loafing. I walked up the Hill twice, about 11 o'clock to draw 50 dollars from the bank and eat dinner, and at 4 o'clock to report for duty as Officer of the Day. I sent a card to the Commonwealth Hotel, asking them to reserve a room for Thursday evening. It is the first time I have had a room reserved. I don't know how it is going to work out. About 2:30 I went to D. Sugg's and had my eyes checked and new glasses ordered. About 7 o'clock after I locked the office door, a car dropped by the door. The owner introduced himself as a professor of English at McMurry University, Abilene, Texas, and wanted to visit the Campus. I gave him directions and asked him whether he ever heard of Mr. Lord. He said he had never heard of him. I started walking to town when one of our boys driving a truck picked me up and drove me to my very door. I'm glad he did since I was in shirtsleeves and felt cold. Since yesterday afternoon the temperature has fallen considerably. It must be the result of the terrific windstorm that hit Fort Worth, Texas, yesterday. According to the papers, 85 percent of the planes on the airfield were damaged.

September 15, 1952, Monday

Since September 2, I traveled to Kansas City, Missouri, on September 4 and returned on Saturday, September 6. I went primarily to buy a new suit of clothes and see some shows. It was clear and hot. Yesterday I went to Fayetteville. Sh. had invited Mrs. Bell to call at 4:30. She brought her little baby boy and installed him in a movable pen, and we watched him perform. I returned by way of Westville; the road between Watts and Siloam is in a messy condition on account of repairs. I inhaled an infinite quantity of dust. Today I gave the famous English Placement Test to about 100 freshmen and transfer students. I was really surprised at the great number of new students. All of them are young, ranging from 17 to 21 or 22. The stream of war veterans has dried up.

September 25, 1952, Thursday

My schedule is very pleasant and easy. Three times a week I teach two hours a day; two times, one hour; and one time, three hours. I'll lie low, and perhaps Dr. Wills will forget to find ways and means to complicate it. I paid my membership fee to SCMLA and hope to be able to attend its annual meeting in Denton, Texas, on October 31 and November 1. I've never really been in Texas, and I've heard so much about the state that I'll do my best not to miss this opportunity. Pre-election activities are in full swing. Nixon was accused of bribery, and he accuses the others of other "vicious" practices: The campaign is of a smearing kind, platforms are forgotten, and every candidate does his best to prove himself an angel and his opponent a devil. Meantime, boys are killed in Korea, prices are rising, and everybody seems to be swimming in money. It is really a mad world, but it is a good world, and only a fool would not enjoy the spectacle that is daily unrolled before him.

September 26, 1952, Friday

I received an announcement for next season's plays to be given by the U-Ark. Theater. I'll phone Mrs. Thornton, and if she is willing to drive me to see the shows, I'll buy a season ticket. It is a little tiresome driving 60 miles to see a show, but one needs a little excitement and entertainment once in a while. In a small town one gets into a rut or a routine. I'm glad Sh. lives in Fayetteville. It has given me opportunities to travel, see shows, and meet some interesting persons, including professors and artists. As for politics, it seems that the Republicans will not disown Nixon. They have their own definition of corruption. If one accepts deep freezers and minks, one is corrupt, but if he accepts money, one is patriotic; he uses the money to ferret out communists. He is particularly incorruptible if the money is donated by businessmen. In this country the businessmen are above reproach. They can do everything and get away with it, and why not? They are neither communists, nor "pinks," nor radicals, nor even thinking beings. They are merely lovers of gain, greed, and money and, consequently, conservative, safe, and stupid. They really stand in the way of social and moral progress. They might some day for lack of ideas find themselves broke. It is the despised New-Dealers and so-called radicals who pulled them out of the great depression and won the last war. It happened that both of these activities increased the wealth and the power of the businessmen, and so they are now afraid of new ideas, new adventurers, and new experiments. But people without vision perish, and inflation might turn out to be as disastrous as depression. Their house of cards might crash upon their heads!

October 3, 1952, Friday

I taught two hours and attended the first faculty meeting of the academic year; it was held at 11 o'clock in C108. I did at least two silly things. I'll attend the Petit Jean Conference on Higher Education on October 17 and 18. The accommodations are not good; one sleeps in bunks, and there is no place for one's clothes. We usually start up early in the morning and reach the park by noon; I usually get nothing out of the meetings. The other silly thing is that I signed for my membership to AEA and NEA; it will cost me 12 dollars. I'll get two magazines a month; I'll scarcely glance through them.

October 6, 1952, Monday:

Yesterday I drove by taxi to Fayetteville. It happened that Harry, the taxi driver, was going to Fayetteville to check the battery of his "talkathon" telephone and took me along with him. We had a flat tire between Tontitown and Springdale; he changed the tire in the rain and then drove to Fayetteville and drove me to 637 Whitham.

October 7, 1952, Tuesday

A man driving a truck with a load of two pigs for the slaughterhouse drove me to town. The two unfortunate animals were eating in the truck, quite unconscious of the fate that awaited them. I bought a pair of winter pajamas, and I took a walk in the cool, crisp breeze. I'm still reading Tolstoy's *Childhood, Boyhood, and Youth*. He underwent the influence of the Greek Eastern Church with its lents, confessions, communions, and the other religious practices. It seems that I imbibed my anticlerical feeling from either my reading of Voltaire or from the teacher Argyropoulos, who taught me Religious History in my sixth grade. He was sarcastic and sly about everything. He taught the subject, but he despised priests, masses, fasts, ceremonies, and whatnot in his heart of hearts. As a highly sensitive boy, I caught my religion from him; after all, religion is not taught, it is caught. I'll say the same about my love for erudition. I caught it from Mr. Michaelides, the man who taught me Greek Lit in my last year in gymnasium back in 1917, and also from D. Black of Boston University and Kittredge of Harvard. I will not call these men my inspirers; I always liked to read books, but they were what I aspire to be, and in this respect they were the embodiments of my dreams. It is only lately that I've dared to visualize myself as an artist-philosopher, a wise scholar and a great teacher bold enough to educate mankind, to make men wiser, better, more humane, more mature. I'm still inarticulate, but I'll keep working, and God will not let me taste failure and frustration.

October 11, 1952, Saturday

The war in Korea has started with a new ferocity; the Chinese are attacking in great strength, and the UN forces are trying to stop them and counterattack. The campaign for presidential election is going on with Stevenson, Eisenhower, Truman, Taft, Sparkman, Nixon, and many others too numerous to mention talking and trying to confuse the poor voters as much as they can. Well, more power to them. I have always been voting the Democratic ticket, and I don't see any reason for changing my old habit. The Republicans don't have anything to offer except generalities, and they will probably plunge us into depression and stagnation. They are looking backward instead of forward; they are afraid to face situations created by the planetary consciousness. They put property rights above human rights.

October 12, 1952, Sunday

It is Columbus Day; we don't celebrate it in Arkansas, but it is celebrated in Boston and New York and wherever many Italians live. I remember a particular Columbus Day; it must have been in 1921 or 1922. It was a sunny day; I was teaching and living in Cambridge, Massachusetts, at that time and attending Boston University. I spent the afternoon walking along the banks of the Charles River: Next day I had to take a test in English history. I felt excruciating pains in my back; I hastily finished the paper, turned it in, and rode on the subway home. I was almost sick unto death. It was simply a cold, which I caught by walking too long in the open on the previous day. Miss Sh. happened to be in town today, and she phoned from the Cook's house.

October 13, 1952, Monday

Since last week, everybody seems to give me more than my money's worth. The laundry bill was only 40; it is always about 90 cents; somebody made a mistake. The waitress at the Southern Grill charged me only 30 cents instead of 40 cents for breakfast. Tonight the clerk at the Allen store charged 25 instead of 55 for a package of ever-sharp blades. Well, I didn't correct them because I don't correct them when they overcharge me, and they overcharge me oftener than they undercharge me.

October 19, 1952, Sunday

Last night about 8 o'clock I returned from Petit Jean Park, where I attended the fourth annual meeting of Arkansas Higher Education. We left at 6 o'clock Friday morning, October 17, in Mrs. Thornton's car; Mr. Haley, Mr. Cook, and Miss Porter were the other members of the party. We were blessed with perfect weather; we reached our destination about 11:10, and after registering we attended the first meeting, during which D. Horn spoke on something like the present needs of education. The meals, for which we paid 1.50, were disappointing. They were not better than the meals served at JBU's cafeteria, which cost only 45 cents. I attended all the meetings, visited Stout's Point and the falls, and the house of D. Hardison, who's lived on the mountain since 1911. He has been instrumental in developing the park with its lake, halls, and boathouse. He talks of nothing but the trees and the rocks of his beloved mountain. We returned home last night healthy, happy, and wise although I narrowly escaped an accident that would have cost our lives. We narrowly escaped a head-on collision with a speeding car. Mrs. Thornton must have been shaken because she allowed Mr. Haley to drive her beloved Packard for one or two hours. Accidents on the highway seem to be unavoidable. We saw a wrecked car and a lady hurt and limping being led out of it.

October 24, 1952, Friday

I'm awfully sleepy. On Wednesday night I attended a faculty meeting; which lasted 'till 9:30 p.m. I did not reach home 'till 10 o'clock. Last night I drove with Mrs. Thornton and her boy Dick to Fayetteville. We picked up Sh., and after dinner at the Banks' we went to the Arts Theater of the U of A, where we saw *Dreamgirl* by Elmer Rice. This being the UN Day, and incidentally my "official" birthday, I enjoyed the meal immensely. The election campaign is entering its last week. It has degenerated into pure "mud throwing." I don't blame the candidates; I blame the system. If Plato had his way, the candidates for high offices would pass rigid tests and examinations to find out their mental capacity, ability, and breadth or narrowness of view. It would have been much cheaper and more profitable. I guess the candidates themselves would like such a procedure. As it is now they make fools of themselves over the radio, before the television, at whistle stops, and whatnot. It is a pure waste of time, effort, and money.

February 2, 1953, Monday

I heard Eisenhower's talk over the radio. He is recalling the Seventh Fleet, which guarded Formosa. The Republicans have been talking of unleashing Chiang-Kai-shek's armies. Let us hope that this step will not involve us in a real war with China, necessitating the presence of large forces to invade Manchuria, China, and Indo-China. The measure may be wise, but it is certainly vicious; it will perpetrate civil war in China; it will cost the death of many Chinese, either Nationalists or Reds, and it might lead to a Third World War. As for the domestic affairs, he sounded like Truman with his concern for the farmers and labor; about taxation, he said that there will be no reduction of taxes for the time being. Except for lifting the ban on Formosa, there was nothing new. I doubt whether the Chinese Nationalists have the sea and air force necessary to support a landing on the mainland.

February 7, 1953, Saturday

On Thursday evening I saw *My Wife's Family* played by members of the Senior Class. Both the acting and the play were funny in more than one way. Last night I rode with Mrs. Sweet and Mrs. Cline to Fayetteville. Mrs. Sweet visited her son, Willie, and we ate at the Banks'; the prices were exorbitant, and the food abominable. I bought a pair of shoes. They were supposed to give a silver dollar for every pair one bought. They ran out of silver dollars, so they deducted one dollar out of the price. In spite of that, I paid 8.15 for the shoes. The price controls have been removed by the

Republican administration; they still believe in demand and supply. I hope the nation will not regret the unrestrained competition. Cooperation is the thing we most need. All of us need leisure to study, to think, to invent, or simply to live. We don't want to spend our time making or worrying about a living. Modern science has given us abundance of goods and cheap services. Why should we create the unnatural situation of restricting production when no profit is derived and pay exorbitant prices for services? We are supposed to be the freest nation on Earth. We are the slaves of the big corporations and companies who run factories, railroads, mines, telephones, telegraphs, radios and television, gas, water, and electricity. We pay no tribute to kings and lords. We pay big prices to manufacturers and producers. Oh, for a deliverer from the economic injustice; O, for freedom for mankind to study, to invent, to live! Such freedom and deliverance are not likely to occur in my days. But the fact that I and others have gotten a glimpse of such marvelous opportunities is encouraging. Thoughts and dreams have a way of becoming reality.

February 12, 1953, Lincoln Day

I received a letter from Silas, whom I've not seen since that memorable September afternoon in 1936 when I took the train at the Grand Central for Minneapolis, Minnesota. He didn't say much about his health or his affairs, but since he mentioned that he is still working the same job and that he expects soon to be pensioned off, he must be all right. Both he and Corta seemed very remote and strange. Time and distance destroy everything. Well, I'm going to bed early since I've to get up early to meet my 8 o'clock class. Since the Republican administration "unshackled the Nationalists" (to use their pet expression), nothing has happened or is likely to happen. The Nationalists don't have either the Air Force or the Navy to invade China. I doubt if they ever had the men. Anyhow, they were bound to do something, and I hope they didn't commit any errors. It would be downright stupidity to find ourselves involved in a war with China supported by Russia—it might prove the Sicilian expedition of the American democracy.

February 14, 1953, Saturday

It is St. Valentine's Day, but since its celebration took place two or three nights ago, everything was quiet on Campus. We had "a special Chapel" at 11 o'clock. D. Brown announced that a Texas oilman gave the school about 1 million dollars. The money is enough to finish all our buildings. The announcement that caused a genuine applause was that the Military Academy would be moved to California.

February 24, 1953, Tuesday

On Sunday I went to Fayetteville; Sh. served two nice steaks with spinach and tomatoes on the side. Yesterday at 11 o'clock I attended a meeting of the Missionary Conference. A Negro preacher from Nigeria preached a sermon; he dealt with his own conversion and the customs of Nigerians.

February 27, 1953, Friday

I "conceived" a short story, in which the hero would be my nephew Byron who runs away from home as often as he can. This is explained by heredity; his great-grandfather was a rover, a pirate, so he is sent to America to his uncle, who, being a wise professor and knowing the boy has a tendency to roam, advises him to become a salesman. Instead of sinking boats and carrying away "booty," he collects cash. The boy is cured of his wanderlust and becomes a successful man selling agricultural machinery to distant countries.

Last Wednesday I rode with Mrs. Thornton and her youngsters to Fayetteville, where we picked up Sh. After a chicken dinner at the Chicken Little, we went to the University Theater, where we saw *The Giant from the South,* a play written by D. Morris of the U. of A. The play was based on the life and works of Thomas Wolfe. It was episodic; it lacked conflict, or rather, it had too many minor conflicts; it abounded in chances both modernistic and classical. It was interesting, but the author tried to do too much. It was a spectacle rather than a play. The staging was much more interesting than the play itself. Anyhow, one must be grateful, for it is at least an original play, although the material is taken from the life and works of Thomas Wolfe.

March 1, 1953, Sunday

There is no event either national or international that deserves notice. The war in Korea is still going on; the President is playing golf in Georgia; the politicians are quarreling like little children at the UN meetings; youngsters are drafted; and now that the price stabilization program has been revoked, one reads about prices falling and prices rising. It is too early to tell whether removing all restrictions and allowing free competition will lead us into depression or inflation or whatnot. One thing is certain: We have not yet solved our economic problems. Wars, both hot and cold, have created prosperity but also inflation.

March 14, 1953, Saturday

Since I wrote in this book, many events have happened. Stalin died and was buried last Sunday; the world is still wondering how his successor, Malenkov, will act. I prepared and delivered an address to the Faculty Women's Club on John Dewey's "Reconstruction in Philosophy." D. Brown has been on the Campus and discarded all the plans we made about the library; he intends to build it according to his own plans and ideas, which, in the end, means that the money will be spent and we will not have a library. The best news is that the long drought is broken. Last night it rained all night; the papers reported many "twisters," or tornadoes, in Texas, Oklahoma, and Arkansas around Russellville.

March 31, 1953, Tuesday

I've just returned from Cowskin Lodge, where I spent today and yesterday in a "so-called" fishing trip. I did not fish but sat in the open air, ate three good meals, and drank Cokes and coffees. I slept in the same room I slept in last year, but in the room in front of me slept Mr. Joe Smith, Cecil Smith and Mr. Whaley. It was cloudy and stormy on the lake last night, but it did not rain very much. This, by the way, is the last day of spring vacation, which started last Saturday, March 28. Since this year the commencement exercises are scheduled for May 25 and our examination week is eight days previous, we are almost in sight of the end of the academic year. Whether or not I'll teach this summer, I'll not know 'till June. I'd like to teach, or I'll be at a loss how to spend about four months' vacation starting on May 25 and ending probably on September 20.

April 6, 1953, Monday

It has been raining since Saturday evening. Yesterday being Easter, I went to Fayetteville; Sh. served, of all things, Hormel Beans and Bacon, salad, and coffee. Since it rained, I spent 85 cents on taxis alone, besides 1.50 on fare. On account of the rain, the unpaved road between Watts and Siloam Springs was muddy and full of puddles of water.

April 8, 1953, Wednesday

D. Brown announced that the plans for the library have been revised; it will be a bigger library, and it will be ready for occupation next Christmas. Let us hope so! To me the most interesting event of today is the unloading in the library of about 500 books bequeathed by a U of A teacher of English who died a few days or months ago. I don't even know her name. Some of the books are modern novels and biographies in good editions. Once they are catalogued, they will provide me with very good reading. All these events, plus the warm spring weather, filled me with a nameless joy. I even said a silly thing to Miss Steyer about Mrs. Jaderquist. Of course, I told her not to repeat it to her, but I'm sure she will. It will give Mrs. Jaderquist a vague and indefinable notion or suggestion that I'm in some mysterious or marvelous way in love with her. Such remarks judiciously made dispose women to one's favor, and although nothing happens, they feel friendly and protective; and I need as many friends and protectors as I can collect.

I received a letter from home from my sister Corinna; she writes that she visited my sister Polyxene in Lemesso and that both are happy and healthy.

April 11, 1953, Saturday

It rained last night, and it rained today, thus spoiling the activities centering on the dedication of the Arkansas Building and the new KUOA station. I saw a few of the alumni on Campus. There was Mr. W. Shelley, the first student whom I lectured to on

American Poetry. He and a girl, whose name I can't recall, were the only students in American Poetry in the fall of 1939. Mr. J. Miller, Mr. Wright, Mr. and Mrs. Black, and two or three others were also on the Campus. I visited for a while with them.

April 19, 1953, Sunday

On Friday morning D. Wills drove Mrs. Wills and me to Springdale, where we boarded the 7:22 bus for Little Rock. It was a leisurely trip with many rest stops. We traveled to Fort Smith, where we rested for 25 minutes, and at 10:15 we started for Little Rock by Highway 10. We lunched at Danville and reached Little Rock by 2:20. We took a taxi for the Arkansas Education Building on West Fourth Street. From there we phoned for reservations at the Sam Peck Hotel and then attended the meeting of the Arkansas Teachers of College English (ATCE). Mrs. Wills was on the program; I was put on the program by Mrs. Gladys Brown, but since it was about "The Proficiency of the Incoming Freshmen," a subject about which I don't know much, I put Mrs. Wills on the program. The 10-minute speeches and the discussion were illuminating. Every university is in the same boat as JBU. By 5 o'clock I developed a light headache, owing to fatigue, excitement, and the heat of the hall. When the meeting ended, Faulkner drove us to the hotel. After washing and eating a light supper made of apple pie, ice cream, and milk, I wanted to walk to Main Street and see my old hunting grounds, but it was windy, cloudy, and rainy. Since I did not want to attend the banquet and hear D. Faris' address on "Hillbillies I Knew," I went to bed in Room 312 and slept well and got rid of my headache. During the night there was a violent thunderstorm that hit hard in Tulsa, Fort Smith, Newport, and other places, killing one, injuring 64 people, and causing about 1 million dollars damage. On Saturday I got up early and walked six blocks to Main Street; it was cold, windy, and cloudy. The streets were empty; only a few Negroes were on the corners waiting for buses.

April 29, 1953, Wednesday

Last Saturday Mrs. Thornton, her son, three other youngsters and I drove to Fayetteville, and after picking up Sh. and dining at the Chicken Little, we saw at the University Theater a comedy, *For Love or Money*. It was smart, silly, slightly filthy, and amusing. This is the last play of the year. It seems that Mrs. Thornton might accept a position in Alabama, and then I'll have to hunt for another driver.

Although the Koreans have returned the sick and the disabled war prisoners, there is still no agreement about the exchange of the other prisoners since neither can agree on two points: the neutral country to which the "walking prisoners" would be transported and the duration of their stay in the neutral country. People of good will and desirous of peace, as both parties loudly proclaim to be, ought to reach an agreement on both of these rather insignificant items and put an end to a conflict that has caused untold misery to both invaders and defenders.

May 4, 1953, Monday

I ate breakfast at the Youree, which has been under a new owner since last Monday. I was dumbfounded when the waitress presented me with a bill amounting to 51 cents for two fried eggs, toast, and coffee. Eggs 25 cents, toast (one piece) 10, coffee 10 (first cup), and 5 cents on the second cup, and one cent tax. Well, I pay 35 cents for eggs and coffee. I'm afraid the new owner will have to close shop very soon. He either does not know his business, or he wants to make quick profit and get out as fast as he can. Mr.

Glidewell told me he bought *The Dixie News* business for 4,000 dollars. That's an exorbitant price; the whole stock consisting of magazines, newspapers, and 25- or 35-cent editions of books cannot amount to more than a thousand dollars, unless he bought the building with it. I don't think the poor man will make money out of the store. He will be lucky if he can break even.

May 12, 1953, Tuesday

It has been a week of tornadoes, high winds, rains, and storms. Waco and San Angelo in Texas were hit by tornadoes. Even Siloam Springs, according to the AP, was hit by a "little twister." Russellville was hit by a tornado last Sunday, and many residences were demolished. Last Sunday I visited Fayetteville. Sh. moved to another apartment near the campus of U of A at 900 Douglas. It is not as new and cheerful a place like the 637 Whitham, but it is cooler and more spacious.

July 21, 1953, Tuesday

I've not written in this book since May. I went through illness—passing a gallstone—late in May. I taught first summer session three hours a day; I started summer session II yesterday. I'm at present teaching a freshman class at 8:15, a Greek class at 9:30, and Word Mechanics and Phonetics at 3:30. The classes are the smallest since the summer of 1945. It was abnormally hot all June, but July has been wet and cool. My landlady (Mrs. Cline) went for 22 days to Billings, Montana. I availed myself of the opportunity to cook my own breakfast and supper. I visited Sh. more than once. I was in Fayetteville last Sunday; Mrs. Sweet met me by accident and drove me home, thus avoiding the roundabout return by Westville and Watts.

September 3, 1953, Thursday

Summer is over. Last Saturday I corrected the examination papers, turned in the grades, and walked home with a great sigh of relief. It had been a long, dreary summer, all work and no play. I took only two or three trips to Fayetteville, read books, slept long hours, and took it easy. Two or three important events happened. Mr. Storm Whaley, who had been associated with station KUOA for 19 years, resigned. Mrs. Thornton, the teacher of art at JBU, usually nicknamed "my driver" because she used to drive me to teachers meetings and theater shows, has also resigned and is leaving tomorrow for Troy, Alabama, where she is to teach at the State Teachers College. She drove me last night, perhaps for the last time, to Fayetteville, where we were guests of Sh. at 900 Douglas. Her two youngest sons, Jimmie and Rexy, rode with us. Their exuberant spirits and their playing with balloons little agreed with the nerves of a 54-year-old bachelor like me. Perhaps the most important event, an event that may have future consequence, was a letter from Roxie, who is presently employed by the Compton Adv. Company, Rockefeller Center, New York. I've not seen her since 1933 or 1932; she wrote that she wants to see me and talk with me and compare notes. I wrote her a letter last Monday; I don't like to begin trips to New York. New York City is associated with hard work, poor, shabby rooms, the New York Library, Riverside Drive, New Brunswick, Lucille, Mary, and whatnot.

September 4, 1953, Friday

It seems that we are living in a new age without being aware of it. We, the aged people, have lived so much in recollection and expectation that we scarcely have time to look around us and see or hear what is going on. We, of course, listen to the news commentators, we read awhile in *Harper's* and *Atlantic,* we attend teachers meetings of all kinds, but the speakers and the writers of what we hear and read do not belong to the younger generation. They are elderly people like us. For example, Secretary of State Dulles, Wilson, and others who spoke today or yesterday are older than I am. They belong to an age that still thinks in terms of political chicanery, national security, and opportunism. That Asia has changed, that the weapons—A-bombs and H-bombs, plus gasses and bacteria—are available for the extermination of mankind, these gentlemen seem to be blissfully unaware. Even the President, playing golf in Colorado and lending money to Iran, is not completely aware of the great changes that occurred during the last few decades. We preach peace and practice war, the same way we preach Jefferson and practice Hamilton.

September 6, 1953, Sunday at 11:15 a.m.

Everybody has gone to church. The house on 203 S. Wright St., usually known as "The Clines' Residence," is quiet. I'm sitting on the west porch writing this entry. It is ideal weather, clear, and slightly cool. The sky is the loveliest blue, and the trees have not yet lost their tender greenness. I'm still reading *Current Prose,* and I'm still debating whether and where to go for vacation. As a rule, I go to Kansas City, Missouri, stay at the Plaza Hotel, ride the street cars, eat at the Forum Cafeteria, visit the zoo, see one or two shows, and return home. I've been doing this since 1946, and it is both sissy and idiotic. Why don't I go to some other city? Why do I like to do the same things over and over again? Why do I hate to try new experiences? The only new experience I try is reading new books. I've even been going with the same woman for 14 years. People must laugh at me, but I don't care. Anyhow, just now, as the new school year is about to begin, I pray for strong eyes, a strong brain, and strong body that I may read, learn, teach, write, and educate the whole world. Sometimes I lose sight of my goals in life: "to become another Plato and educate the world." I waste my time and energy in doubts, fears, hopes, and regrets. Since I received a letter from Roxie, I've also begun to dream of love just as I used to do in the 1920's when I was obsessed with Lucille. That obsession brought me almost to destruction and oblivion. I have survived failure by the grace of God and favor of men. Any regression to daydreaming and laziness might be fatal at this time.

September 9, 1953, Wednesday

I read in the paper that Mrs. J.E. Brown Jr. gave birth to a baby girl on September 2. She has already left the hospital for her home. Everybody is rejoicing over the victory of Adenauer. He has already served notice to France that he wants the problem settled, and he also declared his intention to liberate the 18,000,000 Germans under the Soviet rule. How he is going to do these things simply because he won an election is beyond me. He also favors rearmament, and unfortunately, the American government supports him in this respect. It took us six years of bloody wars to wreck Germans, and now after eight years we are anxious to finance the rebuilding of a new German Army. We are so blinded with our fear and suspicion of Russia that we urge both Japan and Germany to rearm as a check to Russian expansion. Let us hope that the rearmed Germans and Japanese will forget that we bombed their cities and killed their children and women and made them eat humble pie.

September 10, 1953, Thursday

Earthquakes in my native island of Cyprus were announced

over the radio this morning. Since I was busy with the retreat in the Baptist Assembly Grounds, I did not listen to other broadcasts, and today's papers did not carry any news of the earthquakes. The news was that the coast of Paphos and the eastern coast were the worst sufferers.

September 11, 1953, Friday

I wrote a letter home asking information about my sisters, their husbands, and children. According to the AP news, 40 persons were killed, 100 wounded, and 2,000 made homeless. The hardest-hit section was the southwest coast around the little port of Paphos.

September 25, 1953, Friday

Today I received a letter from my landlady in Minneapolis, Minnesota, in which she enclosed a clipping from a newspaper containing an account about D. Aris, the dentist from Cyprus. According to the report, he closed his office and went to Tufts College in Boston and Geneva, Switzerland, to study peridontics. I also saw in the *McCall's* magazine the picture of Roxane serving a kind of cake she called Karipodita. I've not seen her since 1932 or 1933, and she looks to be a very mature and charming matron, although she is still a little plump, not to say stout.

I also received two letters from Sh. She will meet me at the bus station next Sunday, and we will eat at Ferguson's Cafeteria. She is too busy, just now, to cook for me.

September 29, 1953, Tuesday

I received a letter from my brother-in-law Socrates. He wrote that everybody is well and that the capitol had not experienced any damage on account of the earthquake that demolished villages on the west coast of the island. He also mentioned that he is sending me Cyprus papers, in which I can read details about the catastrophe, as he calls it.

October 4, 1953, Sunday

At last it started raining yesterday evening, and it has been drizzling since then. I spent the day at home reading and resting. Since it was wet I did not go to Chapel but listened to the sermon on the radio. Last Friday I went with my "new drivers," the Haleys, to Fayetteville, where we saw the first production of the U of A theater season, *The Curious Savage*. It was a comedy, but since the action took place in an asylum and all characters except the Doctor and the nurse were crazy or slightly neurotic, it was called a tragic comedy. We visited both Sh. and John, the son of Mr. Haley, who is studying law at the U. I was introduced to his "girl," who came all the way from Little Rock to visit him and see the football game between U of A and Texas Christian University. They looked to me and, of course, to the others, exceedingly young. I guess the youngest of the group, Mrs. Haley, must be in her 50's, and Sh. and I are over 50. We did not return to Siloam 'till midnight. I got a letter from home. They write that they are all right and that I should not worry.

October 10, 1953, Saturday

I received a letter from Sh., in which she accuses me of neglect for not taking her suggestion to visit Fayetteville tomorrow, Sunday.

October 11, 1953, Sunday

I spent the day at home reading *Harper's* and *Current History*. A professor described his adventures in Greece in an article in

Harper's Fulbrighting in Greece. He seemed to have had a good time, although he found it difficult to teach in English. His public lectures were well attended, although he had to read them in English paragraph by paragraph and then wait for an interpreter to read the paragraph in Greek.

October 17, 1953, Saturday

I spent Thursday and Friday traveling to and from Petit Jean Park, where I attended the annual Conference on Higher Education. I rode with D. Wills, Mrs. Wills, Mr. McCormick, and Mr. Potter. I returned with D. Ellis. The weather is clear and warm. The only attraction added to this year's conference was a trip to Mr. Winthrop Rockfeller's vast mansion or estate now in the process of building. The estate covers 800 acres, and when finished, it will contain artificial lakes for irrigation, air strips for landing planes, lodges for staff, and whatnot. The water will be pumped from the river and stored in artificial reservoirs.

October 18, 1953, Sunday

I filled in the blank form and mailed a request for a room in one of the residence halls of Oklahoma A & M at Stillwater for the coming conference of S.W.M.L.A., scheduled on November 13 and 14. I listened to "Weekend," a Sunday feature of the ABC network. The most important items were a short speech on fraternities and a list of the new plays now on Broadway. The citizens of Siloam Springs are shocked at the death of Rev. Cooley, who was preacher of the Methodist Church for years and was at present district superintendent of Fayetteville. He was killed in an automobile accident near Clarksville last Friday. He was a young and capable preacher, and his sudden and premature death caused universal grief. The last time I saw and heard him was at the funeral of Rev. Cline on December 28 or 29 of 1952. Both ministers, Rev. Stewart and Rev. Cooley, who officiated at Rev. Cline's funeral are dead now! Both looked to be in good health, and little did they dream that they would follow him in a short time.

October 24, 1953, Saturday

I received a bundle of newspapers from home in both Greek and English. What impressed me greatly was the number of colleges, commercial schools, or lyceum gymnasiums that were advertising for students. Most of the schools were of the junior high school type, and most of them were practical schools or vocational. I also noticed that the prices of potatoes, tomatoes, meats, and watermelons are very much higher than they were in 1920. The papers contained descriptions of the earthquake that shook Paphos last September. It seems that those who got up early and went out to the fields were spared; those who stayed at home, mostly women and children, were buried under the debris.

November 1, 1953, Sunday

Last Thursday evening the Haleys and I drove to Fayetteville and saw *Romeo and Juliet*. It was a good production, although the players "mouthed their lines." On Friday the Library Committee met for one hour and a half to discuss the plans for the new library. Last night being Halloween, I walked up the Hill and judged the costumes, D. Woodland and Mr. Wills being the other judges. Before judging the costumes, I tried my hand at putting a ball into a basket and hit, to the merriment of everybody, the light bulb and brought it down to pieces. The most amusing part of the celebration was the throwing of pies at the faces of two students for a fee. It seems that it is hard to hit somebody with a pie. Only once was the face of one student hit.

November 3, 1953, Tuesday

I listened over the radio for the returns of the off-year elections. The counting of the ballots had not yet been completed, so I've to wait 'till tomorrow to learn whether New Jersey, Virginia, and New York elected Democrat or Republican leaders. The Republicans have been in office scarcely one year, and they've begin to "stink" already with their Dulleses, McCarthys, Bensons, and even their Eisenhower, who seems to be afraid to assert himself for fear of losing his popularity with the people or the support of his own party. He wants to eat his cake and have it also. He may lose the confidence both of the people and of his party. He has not cut taxes, and prices are soaring.

November 17, 1953, Tuesday

The weather continues to be dry and cool. Last Sunday Sh. visited the Cooks, and I was invited to eat lunch with her. She left by the 6:41 p.m. bus. I heard over the radio the pros and cons of Truman's hiring and firing of the late T. White, a supposed Russian spy. It seems that the Republicans, instead of governing the country, aim at unearthing old documents and past history. A great nation looks forward, not backward. The impression is created both abroad and at home that our best and most intelligent citizens are either communists spies or at least communist sympathizers.

November 24, Tuesday

Thanksgiving vacation started today at 5 o'clock. I'll spend it at home reading and resting. Today I attended a faculty meeting at 11 in C108. Mr. Cox brought up the question of sociology textbooks. JBU was mentioned in the *Arkansas Gazette* as one of the colleges using textbooks that are "suspect." It irks and sorely distresses me to see Americans afraid to call their soul their own. Any fool or fanatic can open his mouth and condemn anyone who does not speak loud and clear about competition, democracy, Christianity, and other conservative notions and ideas. A committee was appointed to study the textbook *Marriage Among the Moderns* and report to the faculty whether they find it subversive or not.

November 26, 1953, Thanksgiving Day

I rode to Fayetteville with the Cooks. It is the first trip to Fayetteville for Thanksgiving without poor, old Mrs. Doolittle, Mrs. Cook's mother, who died last summer. We ate turkey, sweet potatoes, cauliflower, stuffing, and pumpkin pie with coffee. It was a good meal, and I enjoyed it immensely, although Sh. and I were co-hosts.

The commentators are discussing the weighty matter of whether Ike or McCarthy will prevail in getting hold of the Republican Party. What started as an exposé of the Truman administration's infiltration by communists or leftists may split the Republican Party into McCarthyites and Ikists and whatnot. The old man Truman, when he accused the Republican Party of being taken over by McCarthyism, has succeeded in creating something that distracted attention from the main issue and set the Republicans fighting among themselves.

November 27, 1953, Friday

Life has become very quiet in this small town. I wonder how people used to live in small towns before the invention of newspapers, radio, and television. The present life in small towns may be quiet but not uninteresting or even uninspiring. One can almost have everything a big town has except theater and symphony. Even these are available if one can travel to bigger centers like Tulsa, Fayetteville, or Kansas City. But just the same, there is something deadly and deadening in small town life. One grows narrow in a narrow place. One is bored by the monotony of life. I'm glad I spent my first years in America in New York, Boston, Atlanta, and Minneapolis. It would have been too bad to have started in America in a small town. Even now I'm not quite sure life in a small town is good for me.

December 11, 1953, Friday

Last Sunday I went to Fayetteville; I dined with Sh. and returned home by Westville. On Tuesday evening I drove to Fayetteville with the Haleys and saw Thornton Wilder's *The Skin of Our Teeth*. It was an unusual play dealing with man's perennial danger of being wiped out from the face of the Earth either by ice, by war, or by sheer silliness.

December 14, 1953, Monday

It snowed a little in the morning; it cleared in the afternoon. I taught four hours; the faculty was invited to take the English Proficiency Test tonight at 7 o'clock. I toyed with the idea of taking it for fun. But at the last moment, I decided to stay at home. It is a long test, it takes two hours for one to administer it, and it is given in the English Room 108 with its uncomfortable benches. Above all, I hate taking tests. Since it was voluntary, I don't see why I shall undergo the ordeal simply because D. Woodland or D. Wills got it in their heads that the faculty must take the test in order to prove whether we have the right testing instrument. It might look odd that the head of the English Department did not take it, but I cannot help it.

December 19, 1953, Saturday

This is the first day of Christmas vacation. I spent it reading, walking, and mailing the inevitable cards. I mailed about 20 of them, and by Monday I hope to mail the rest of them. I mailed two to Minneapolis and one to New York. Being away from these cities for more than 10 years, I have lost all friends and acquaintances. I received a letter from Sh. She has already left for Ohio to visit with her sister and will return to Fayetteville on December 30.

December 25, 1953, Christmas Day

A train in New Zealand plunged into a river, and about 150 persons perished. They were on their way to greet the queen.

Last night I drove with Mrs. Thornton to Fayetteville. She and her daughter shopped for an hour and a half while I walked the streets and watched the crowds rushing in and out of the stores. We returned home about 5 o'clock. About 7:30 Mrs. Sweet came by with her son Willie and her daughter Martha and picked me up with my landlady and her sister and drove us through Siloam Springs to see the Christmas decorations. It seems that everybody is too busy making money to devote time and energy to decorate his home or Christmas tree. Most people keep cardboard deer, Josephs, shepherds, and camels in the basements or garrets, and when the season comes they dust them and set them up either in the yard or on the roof for display.

I received many cards, but I've not yet a card from either Roxie or the agency of Atlanta. It seems that, with the passing of the years, people forget their old friends or acquaintances. Anyhow, I thank God that I'm well, that I've a job, and that I've leisure to learn, teach, write, and walk.

December 29, 1953, Tuesday

Last night I drove with Mrs. Thornton and her little son Rexy to Chicken Little for supper, and after the meal we returned to Siloam and went to the Grand Theater, where we saw *From Here to Eternity*. The story, or rather, the picture is about the brutality of the Army. The CO and the stockade guard were cruel, beastly, unimaginative men. The hero was a nice-looking youngster who refused to box for the company, and, therefore, he incurred the hatred of the CO and his minions. He underwent all kinds of humiliation, from KP to digging ditches. In the end he kills the stockade guard who was instrumental in the death of his friend, escapes into the apartment of the girl whom he met at the Congress Club whom he wants to marry. Meanwhile, the Japs attack Pearl Harbor, and he tries to join his unit but is shot by the guards. To relieve this beastly Army life, two intrigues, rather than love affairs, were introduced. The first sergeant falls, or rather, he is made to fall in love with his commanding officer's wife, and the hero falls in love with the girl in the Congress Club. The picture was realistic, and to some of us who have been in the Army, it reminded us of many familiar sadistic experiences. I finished *The Power of Positive Thinking*.

The weather is still clear and warm, the Reds are advancing in Indo-China, and Secretary Dulles is threatening to extend the war to China if the Chinese send armies to help the Indo-Chinese Reds.

January 1, 1954, Friday

I listened to the news over the radio. The western powers agreed to meet with the Russians in Berlin on January 25, Michigan beat the University of Southern California 26 to 20, and Oklahoma beat Maryland 7 to 0. Since this is New Year's Day, I thank God for the health, happiness, success, and prosperity I enjoyed during this year. Except for three days in the middle of May when I was violently sick with kidney trouble, I enjoyed almost perfect health. I pray that all the years of my life I enjoy health, happiness, and success in my work. This year I did not travel far and wide. I didn't even visit Kansas City, Missouri. I did not attend the SWMLA meeting at Stillwater, Oklahoma. I visited only Little Rock, Petit Jean Park, Fayetteville, and Tulsa. I like to travel, but I don't like the fatigue and the trouble that trips involve. I prefer to stay at home, read, walk, and occasionally write.

January 4, 1954, Monday

Yesterday I drove to Fayetteville; I dined at Sh.'s, and then we walked to the station. The Blacks were seeing their boy Larry off to Hendrix College, and they gave me a ride to Siloam. On the way, we stopped for a cup of coffee at the Venesian Inn in Tontitown and visited for a few minutes with Rakestraw Jr. The elder Rakestraw was in Fayetteville with Mary.

January 21, 1954, Thursday

I listened to the news on the radio. The first atomically propelled submarine *Nautilus* has been launched. The Big Four are going to meet in Berlin among prophecies for failure: our admirals, statesmen, and generals. It seems that we expect the Russians to make all the concessions, sacrifices, and surrenders while we generously accept them and thus contribute to the peace of the world. Compromise is regarded as appeasement. All the commentators, to prove themselves 100 percent patriots, are clamoring for a set policy backed by the Air Force and atomic weapons. It seems that we Americans have fallen heirs to the Nazis and Fascists. We brag about our bases and the blows we can deliver. While we talk peace, we spend 70 cents of every dollar for armaments and foreign aid. Then we wonder why the others regard us as imperialists. Let us hope that sanity and moderation will prevail over folly and pride. We have had enough of wars, armaments, and hatred.

January 26, 1954, Tuesday

I met my first class. It consisted of four students who enrolled for Contemporary Lit. It is the smallest class in Contemp. Lit. I have ever taught. It was drizzling all day. I walked both ways to school and home. I need exercise, and a little "wetness" will not harm me. Mrs. Wills is in the hospital; she has been operated on, from what I can gather, for a tumor on the breast, which might or might not prove malignant. I received a letter from Sh. She was really mad at me for not visiting Fayetteville last Sunday. She said that she phoned to the bus station and was told that the roads were clear. Of course, no one told her about the road from Westville to Siloam, the small, unheated busses, and the old bus driver. Anyhow, the less said about these occasions, the better.

February 5, 1954, Friday

Last Saturday I attended with D. Wills, D. Ellis, and the Kennedys the graduation exercises at the Field House of U of A. Mr. Weathers received a doctorate of education degree, and Mr. Willie D.

Sweet got a B.S. degree. I returned to Siloam with Mrs. Sweet. On the way we stopped at the Venesian Inn in Tontitown for a late supper. I ate spaghetti with sauce and cheese and Italian salad. Neither agreed with me. Last Sunday I rode on the bus to Fayetteville. I dined with Sh. and returned by the way of Westville and Watts.

All this week it has been clear and cool. I'm glad of it. They have upturned the road to the Hill by putting sewage pipes to Dr. Weathers' new home, and if it were cold and rainy, I would have been forced to call a taxi. I dropped my golden watch last Monday evening. It developed all kinds of trouble. I took it to Mr. Hastings, who agreed to make it behave for $7.50.

March 19, 1954, Friday

Last Sunday I could not go to Fayetteville. The bus service that connects Westville with Siloam Springs has been discontinued. This means that I'll either quit visiting Fayetteville or go Saturday evening and return by Sunday noon. That means spending a night in a hotel. I hope the service will be reestablished. All this week I did not feel very well. There were moments when I felt dizzy. It is due either to my eyeglasses, which need checking, or a touch of the flu, which I must have contracted by my contact with students in the classroom. Anyhow, today I felt better, and my vigor and health have been restored. I'll take it easy and relax over the weekend. It seems that it is not work, but worry, that's getting me down. I really don't have anything to worry about. God has blessed me abundantly. I have accumulated about 6,000 dollars in the School Exchange, 7,000 in my savings bank account, and about 2 to 3,000 thousand in my insurance policies. I even got a raise last month. My salary, which was previously 325 a month, has been raised by 32.50, which makes 357.50 a month.

March 23, 1954, Tuesday

I received a long letter from Sh. She returned safely from Arkadelphia, where she attended a meeting. She flew from Little Rock to Fayetteville in an hour and a half. During the last few days we have heard nothing except atomic weapons, hydrogen bombs, McCarthy, and Secretary Stevens. The war in Indo-China is still going on. Both the French and the so-called communistic rebels want to win a victory so they can bargain in Geneva next month.

April 22, 1954, Thursday

It has been nearly a month since I wrote in my diary. During this month, first, I got rid of the spot that was on my face on the upper part of my nose. D. Blaw burned it up with acid, and it has healed completely. It had given me a great deal of anxiety and worry since 1947. I attended, as usual, the Arkansas Teachers of College English Association on April 9 and 10. I stayed one night at the Mount Inn Hotel in Room 237. It cost me 3.50 plus tax. I was elected vice president of the association with Mrs. K. Brown as president. The honor does not entail any duties, but it was widely advertised by the press. I also, on April 5 and 6, went to Cowskin Lodge on Grand Lake. The lake was very low, but I had a good time sunning myself and looking at the blue waters of the lake.

May 10, 1954, Monday

I spent the weekend in Fayetteville attending the South Central Renaissance Conference at the U of A. I left at noon on Friday and returned on Sunday. I stayed at the Mountain Inn Hotel in Room 230. I attended three, four, or five general assemblies, and I was chairman of the II group on Saturday from 1 to 5 o'clock. I did not do a good job. I was tired—everybody was tired—and I did not feel like making any remarks worth noting. I must have been a sight both physically and mentally. Sh. was ill most of the time and did not attend any meetings. I escorted Mrs. Wills to two or three meetings.

May 16, 1954, Sunday

The news is as usual: the McCarthy-Army feud, Indo-China war, Geneva Conference, Recession or Depression or Readjustment. As for me, the immediate concerns are giving tests, correcting papers, turning in grades, attending committee meetings, and keeping myself healthy, happy, and wise. I'm planning to write a novel based on my Uncle George, whom I have never seen, and he will become the mouthpiece for my educational, political and moral ideas. The first chapter of *I Meet My Uncle* is already in my mind. The educational system, the Blackwood School System, would be a glorified JBU; happiness would be Aristotelian and politics, Platonic. All these Aristotelian and Platonic ideas will be modified by my experiences in the great American Democracy as teacher, worker, soldier, and traveler. In form it will be a philosophical tale in the tradition of Voltaire and Anatole France. It will be a short one.

May 28, 1954, Friday

This is the last day of the short vacation between the closing of the semester on May 24 and the starting of the summer semester on May 29. On Sunday I attended Baccalaureate service. I acted as chief usher; D. Brown spoke on "Of Making Eagles." At 7:30 p.m. I attended another service. D. Brown talked about the need for money and praised the teacher who has left over 6,000 dollars in the Exchange. That teacher is I. On Monday I attended Commencement

Exercises. I again acted as chief usher, having under me about nine juniors. Today D. Wills drove Sh. to Siloam Springs and delivered to me the fan that Sh. does not need anymore. It is a big fan. I'll use it at home for the time being, but if the weather gets really hot, I'll take it to my classroom, C108, where I'm scheduled to teach from 1-3:45 p.m. every day except Saturday.

June 4, 1954, Friday

Last Tuesday the Haleys drove Mrs. Thornton and me to Ginger Blue for supper. The ride was delightful, but the food not worth the price, the waiting, and the drive. I visited Ginger Blue once before with some soldiers while stationed at Camp Crowder, Missouri. I remembered we stayed late, and some of my company got drunk, but they had sense enough to let the wife of one of the soldiers do the driving. Last night I took Mrs. Thornton to Chicken Little. We were accompanied by Richard and his sister and Patsy. After eating we deposited the three youngsters at Collier's Drugstore, where they were going to meet Jack, who was going to take them to a show and then drive them to Siloam. We proceeded to the apartment of Sh., where we visited 'till 9:30, and then we left for Siloam.

Today is the 10th anniversary of the landing of the Allied Forces on Normandy. I remember that; at the time I was mail clerk of Company B-31st and was stationed at Camp Crowder.

June 7, 1954, Monday

Last Sunday I rode with the Kennedys to Fayetteville, where I attended the Commencement of Exercises at U of A stadium. We were rather late; we did not see the procession but heard the address. We left early in order to reach the Chicken House ahead of the crowds and reserve seats for twelve persons who went to see Charles Willis get his B.A. in Architecture. They came in by 7 o'clock; we ate chicken and left by 8:30, returning to Siloam about 9:10.

Yesterday I went to church; Mr. Haley drove me home and told me that he was leaving for Little Rock on Wednesday morning to see his son John marry on Thursday, June 10.

It has been raining and mildly storming since June 1. It is wet but cool; I ate at noon in the school cafeteria with Mrs. Jaderquist, Mrs. Carlson, and Miss Alton. Miss Steyer, who used to eat with us, has resigned to accept a position at Taylor, and the other young lady, Mrs. Hill, has left for further studies. So by a process of elimination, I'm the youngest at the table, although I'm 54 years old.

June 8, 1954, Tuesday

We have an oversupply of politicians both unscrupulous and vocal, but with the exception of Winston Churchill and Nehru, we have no wise statesmen. Our politics has been reduced to name calling and glittering generalities. We call everything treason, aggression, communism. We can't distinguish between appeasement and compromise. We want to preserve Indo-China and unite Korea, but we want these accomplishments on our own terms. Some legislators like McCarthy and others see treason everywhere in the Army, the Navy, in the H-bomb, A-bomb plants, in factories, farms, schools, and whole parties. "He who does not agree with us," they seem to say, "is wrong; he is our enemy, therefore, the enemy of the country because we are the country." How one Catholic Irishman and two young Jews have become the "country" with rights to investigate everyone and serve subpoenas to everyone is one of the mysteries of our time. But the fact is that even the president of the United States is afraid to put down McCarthyism because McCarthyism has become synonymous with the persecution of communists, and who dares declare himself a friend or protector of the communists? To such a pitiful state has been reduced a great and powerful country!

June 10, 1954, Thursday

Today it grew hot. I turned on the fan in the classroom. The fan was given to me by Mr. Whaley last year. I went to school early and spent some time reading under the tree. D. Woodland and D. Oiesen brought to the dining hall a middle-aged lady whom they were interviewing for the position of teacher of music at JBU. She looked sweetly ripe; she is probably a grandmother. I received two notes from Sh. I don't know whether the bus strike is settled and the communication between Siloam and Fayetteville is resumed. I'm planning to spend the weekend in Fayetteville; I've not been anywhere since May.

June 11, 1954, Friday

It is relatively hot; I was intending to go to Fayetteville tomorrow, but the buses between Tulsa and Fayetteville are not running on account of the drivers' strike. I just phoned Sh. to cancel my reservation for tomorrow night at the Mountain Inn. I finished the book called *Literature*. Both the introduction and the selections are excellent and often inspiring. I started a new book called *Modern Minds*. All these books are anthologies of freshman or sophomore English. Someday when I become world famous, I might declare to the universe that I got my education from freshman books. I obtain these books as complimentary copies, and after I read them, sometimes I sell them to a Chicago firm and collect a few dollars.

They don't cost me anything. Even the stamps on the cards, with which I applied for them, are paid by the publishers. These books are the only things that I get free, absolutely free.

June 12, 1954, Saturday

I spent the entire day at home. I took only two trips to town: the first to deposit 40 dollars at the bank, the second to buy soap and blades. It was warm in the morning (92 degrees), but it fell to 79 degrees by 4 o'clock. It grew cloudy and windy. The radio announced that certain parts of Oklahoma were to be visited by tornadoes. The Laniel government resigned, Dulles is talking about interference in Indo-China, Senator McCarthy is accusing everybody, and he is accused by everybody. It seems that the sons of Adam are getting neither wiser nor nobler nor better. They are still ruled by passion rather than reason. They still think of Army, wars, and heroes. This time it is our security and the freedom of the world that are menaced by the communists. Ten years ago we were menaced by the Japanese, the Nazis, and the Fascists. There is no end to threats to our security and our liberty. Now that the weapons of war have become terribly destructive, we might at least begin to think in terms of universal peace, one world, and one government. But we are as far from universal peace as ever.

September 8, 1954, Wednesday

I've not written in this book since June. It has been a very hot and dry summer; as a matter of fact, it is the driest and hottest since 1936 or 1934. Many states have been declared "disaster areas." I tried to keep fit by staying out of the sun, keeping cool, and not overworking. In Summer I, I taught from 1 to 3:50; in Summer II I taught from 9:30 to 10:45 and from 1 to 2:20. Since there was a "bus strike" since June 6, I did not take any trips to Fayetteville except with Mrs. Wills, Mr. Kennedy, or Mr. Haley. Summer school came to an end on August 28. On September 2 I went for vacation to Kansas City, Missouri. I stayed at the Dixon Hotel in room 609; it was a comfortable room, air conditioned and quiet. I took two or three bus rides a day, saw three shows, visited the zoo at the Swope Park, bought a new suit of clothes, and returned home on Sunday afternoon, September 5.

September 17, 1954, Friday

Today I met and dismissed my classes for the first time. I got about 40 students in my two sophomore courses, English Lit. and Essentials of English, and about 30 in my three upper division classes, English Grammar, Am. Lit., and World Classics. For the first time I got a decent program. I'll work only three days, MWF, and am off on Tuesdays, Thursdays, and Saturdays. I ought to devote these three days to productive work, writing a play, story, or novel. It is about time that I do something to conquer time, something to make me immortal, something to enable me to live in the memory of future generations. I received a letter from Sh. She had just returned from a vacation in North Carolina and had had a hectic week registering students. Tomorrow evening is the reception of students by the faculty. I'll put on the new suit I bought in Kansas City and also the new pair of shoes I bought at the Family Shoe Store in Siloam Springs. I hate to put on new clothes, but it is absolutely necessary this time since my old suit does not look good on special occasions.

September 23, 1954, Thursday

The bus service between Siloam Springs and Fayetteville has not yet been resumed. A strike that started on June 6 is still unsettled. The strike has caused me great inconvenience. I can't go to Fayetteville and visit Sh. or see a show or eat a good meal or simply travel for the sake of relaxation. I hope that very soon the service will be reestablished and I'll be able to get out of Siloam once or twice every month.

September 24, 1954, Friday

I taught five hours today. The weather was cool in the morning, but it warmed in the afternoon, so I taught in my shirtsleeves. I took an x-ray chest picture. The mobile unit was parked in front of the Arkansas Building. I'm glad I don't have to go anywhere tonight. It has been a busy week. Tomorrow I might attend the banquet given by the student council in order to welcome the new students. By an indirect way, by pumping the students, I got the information that the enrollment this year is 243 students and that last year it was 223. There is an increase of but 20, it is not sufficient enough to ensure full capacity of faculty and physical plants. We can easily accommodate 600 students. Why we don't get more students has always been a mystery to me. About half of our students are on scholarships or loan funds or some other subsistence. Very few are fully paying students. A situation like this must be remedied before the University advances to greatest heights of service. I got a card from Sh. She wrote that she had secured tickets for the University Theater performances next year. There will be six of them, the first of which, *Death of a Salesman* by Arthur Miller, will run the last week of October.

September 30, 1954, Thursday

Last night a violent thunderstorm hit Siloam; it rained hard for the first time since May, but somehow the storm did not break the heat. I spent the day at home reading *Fathers and Sons* and the October issue of *Reader's Digest*. I'm lucky this year to be able to stay away from the Hill at least one or two days. I must utilize the time in writing. It is about time I write a book. I've the idea or the conception of one, but my laziness prevents me from sitting down and putting it on the paper. One can't amount to anything unless he creates something. I was never ambitious to create children, but I've been always desirous to create books or at least a book. I'm 54 years old, and I've not yet published even an article or a short story or essay. It seems that it is too late, but it is never too late. I'm just now wiser and better and nobler than ever before.

October 4, 1954, Monday

Last Saturday I rode with G. Rogers and Mr. Hutcheson to Fayetteville. We started at 8 a.m., reached Fayetteville at 9 o'clock, and returned home before 1. Both are members of JBU faculty and are taking some courses at the U of A. I visited with Sh. from 9 to 11. She offered a good meat sandwich, a cup of coffee, and rice pudding. It was a cool, rainy day, and I enjoyed the trip.

Today I taught five classes. By 3 o'clock I felt weak, so I taught for half an hour sitting on my class chair. I don't like to teach sitting. A man on his feet is worth two on his seat. But five hours teaching is too strenuous for a man of 55.

October 7, 1954, Thursday

It was cool in the morning, but by noon it was comfortably warm, and I spent the afternoon sitting on the porch. Even the news has grown stale and flat. It seems there is no enthusiasm for the coming elections. The people are listless and apathetic. I don't blame them. Our politicians have done their best to arouse unconcern and disgust among them. They accuse one another of being communists, on the pay of utilities as corrupt, fifth-amendment communists, or whatnot. The result is loss of prestige for the politicians and interest for the people. Although I don't strongly recommend it, it would be better for the politicians to wash their dirty clothes in private. Too much publicity brings contempt for them.

On the political scene the problem is whether to arm or not to arm West Germany. The United States and her allies agreed to rearm West Germany. The Russians offer reunited but unarmed and neutralized Germany. The French have not yet made up their minds which of the two evils to prefer.

October 16, 1954, Saturday

I rode with Glenn Rogers and Hutcheson to Fayetteville at 8 o'clock. I visited with Sh. 'till 11:45 and then rejoined them at the Student Union and returned to Siloam at 12:40. At 2:30 it was the funeral of Mr. McKleskey. I didn't attend it. Funerals upset me badly. I bought 120 One-A-Day multiple vitamins. I'll take one or two a day to banish that tired feeling that sometimes takes hold of me. At Sisco's I met Mr. Clark who works at Hastings, and I asked him to test a stone that Mr. Cline got at Millsaps'. He said it was glass. I asked him how he knew it. He said that one can see through glass but not through a diamond. Everybody is talking about the victories of the U of A in baseball games. Today the U of A team defeated Texas University to the surprise and delight of every Arkansan.

October 24, 1954, Sunday

It has been a glorious week. I worked only Monday and was off the rest of the week. On Wednesday there were no classes, being Intramural Day. On Thursday and Friday I rode with D. Woodland to the Rockfeller's farm and saw his famous Santa Gertrudis cows. We also saw the interior of his home with its glass venetian blinds and glass-walled kitchen. On both ways, we stopped at the Gabler on the top of Mount Gaylor. We returned home on Friday evening. Yesterday I went with the Haleys to Fayetteville, where we saw *Death of a Salesman*. It was well staged and well acted. Mr. Norman DeMario played Willy Loman, the frustrated salesman. Before the theater Sh. and I were guests of the Haleys at Chicken Little.

Today, it rained in the morning. I did not go to church; I stayed at home and read D. D. Runes' *The Soviet Impact on Society*.

November 10, 1954, Wednesday

A week ago about this time (8:22 p.m.) I took the train for New Orleans, Louisiana. It was cold and rainy. I slept on the chair 'till 7 a.m. and then began to look at the scenery. By that time the train approached Baton Rouge. I reached New Orleans at 10:20, and then at 10:40 I took the L &N train for Biloxi, Mississippi, which I reached about 12:30 noon. I registered at the Buena Vista Hotel, got moved into my room (48) and then sallied forth to look at the Gulf of Mexico and eat lunch at a seashore restaurant. The meetings didn't start 'till Friday morning. I attended a few of them and listened to some papers. I saw and talked to all my old friends and colleagues from the Arkansas colleges and universities. Eve Ringler, whom I met at Princeton, was there. I took the train for New Orleans at 2 o'clock and, therefore, missed my connection with the Southern Belle and had to spend four hours in New Orleans. Mr. Garrison and I took the So. Clairborne bus and went through the city to the end of the bus line. Then we got transfers and got on the St. Charles car and rode as far as Tulane and Loyola Universities. At 9 o'clock I boarded the train for Siloam, which I didn't reach 'till 2:45 on Sunday. Mr. Wayne White, the superintendent of the Fayetteville schools, rode with me from Texarkana, and his company helped him make the trip less tedious and monotonous. Thus ended my third trip to the S.C. Modern Language Association meeting.

November 11, 1954, Thursday

Today is Armistice Day or, as they call it today, Veterans Day. I remember the first Armistice Day in 1918; it was the first year I taught; it was 36 years ago. I also remember the first Armistice Day in the United States in 1920. I was teaching then in Lynn, Massachusetts, and Lucille and I attended a short ceremony held on the steps of city hall, not two blocks away from the school in which she and I were teaching. I wonder how many of those who attended that brief ceremony 34 years ago are at present alive. At that time Armistice Day celebrations meant something; today, after another war, Armistice Day is not even observed by school and stores.

November 12, 1954, Friday

Everybody is excited about tomorrow's game at Fayetteville between the U of A and Southern Methodist University. Until now U of A has been unbeaten and untied. It is rated as fourth in the nation, even above the Army, the Navy, and Notre Dame. Mr. Wayne White, who rode with me last Sunday on the train from Texarkana to Siloam, told me that the new coach at the U of A is an unusual man. He inspires confidence and affection in the hearts of the players, who are willing to play well in order to justify his expectations. Anyhow, it is a long time since the U of A team has won a string of such remarkable victories. Let us hope that tomorrow it will emerge victorious.

November 24, 1954, Wednesday

Thanksgiving vacation started yesterday at 5 o'clock, but since I don't have classes on Tuesday, my vacation started Monday at 4. During the last week three events worthy of note happened. On Wednesday JBU entertained at noon the Lions, the Rotarians, The Chamber of Commerce, and whatnot. D. Brown spoke for half an hour about his new plan for starting an Arkansas foundation to handle money destined to help JBU. On Thursday evening Mr. Russell, Mr. Haley, and I took D. Oeisen and Woodland to Chicken Little for dinner as reward or compensation for their driving us in their cars to the Petit Jean Conference. On Saturday evening the Haleys, Sh. and I attended at the University Theater *Two Wives Under One Roof*, a Chinese drama. The presentation of the play and the acting were new to me since I never saw a Chinese play on the stage before. The matter was trivial, but the costumes, the scenery, the music, and the acting were interesting

November 25, 1954, Thursday

It is Thanksgiving Day, cold and clear. I read at home 'till 10:15, and then the Cooks picked me up and drove me to Fayetteville. At Sh. I had Thanksgiving dinner with the Wills, the Cooks, Sh's aunt, and Sh. We ate turkey, peas, salad, and pumpkin pie with coffee. We talked until 4:13 and then drove back to Siloam Springs. I thank God for the health, happiness, and success I enjoyed during the year. I thank God for the opportunity for work and study. I thank God for all the friends I have and all the acquaintances that I know.

November 29, 1954, Monday

I went back to work after a six-day vacation. I walked up the Hill at 7:30 at a fast pace to keep warm. Temperature was down to 20 degrees above zero. I enjoyed a good vacation. On Friday I rode with the Cooks, Sh, and her aunt to White Rock, a mountain peak about 30 or 40 miles south of Fayetteville. We went by a long, torturous road, but we returned by Combs, which is located about 28 miles south of Fayetteville on Highway 16. The mountain road was wild, dusty, rough, and unending. I was glad to be back on paved roads and in the comforts of civilization. Three events occupy the radio and the newspapers at present: the McCarthey censure, the imprisonment of 13 Americans by the Chinese, and the celebration of the 80th birthday of Winston Churchill.

December 3, 1954, Friday

Tomorrow at 10:30 Santa Claus comes to town. Since I'm free and the parade will pass only one block from the place where I stay, I'll go venture out and see it. I saw two or three of them already. There is nothing to brag about. In this small, quiet, sleepy town where all activities except moneymaking and church going are stamped out, a parade, a banquet or a party afford change, and change is always sweet. At last the Senate has condemned McCarthy, and let us hope that this is the end of McCarthy. The commentators who have proved thus far to be invariably wrong, are seeing the Republican Party split with McCarthy forming a third party and Eisenhower heading the remnants of that party.

December 24, 1954, Friday

It is Christmas Eve. Everybody in the house has left from home. My landlady has gone to Little Rock to visit with her niece Evelyn; Jim and Martha Sheets have gone to Enid, Oklahoma; James Webb and his wife have gone somewhere in Oklahoma. So I've the house to myself. I tried my hand at cooking today. I ate sardines at noon. I did not like them; I fried sausage and German fried potatoes. They did not taste good. The big news today is the rejection of rearming of Germany by the French Assembly. The Americans and the British got really excited. There will be a final vote on Monday, and they expect the French Assembly to reverse its vote. I personally don't understand why the Anglo-Americans are in such a hurry to rearm Germany unless they intend to invade Russia. Everybody in Europe is afraid of the Germans. They invaded and destroyed every country from Norway to Greece, from France to the Volga. Besides that, of what use are soldiers nowadays when wars are going to be fought with atomic weapons, guided missiles, and H-bombs? The point of NATO is to bargain with the Russians from a position of strength, but this is ambiguous. Why do they need strength if they really want peace? The Europeans also know that if a third World War comes, they will be exterminated by H-bomb, and there is no point in raising armies, keeping alliances, and building air bases. These thoughts—war, H-bombs, peace, goodwill, rearming Germany, threatening China, sending ships loaded with food to nations—disturb Christmas Eve. Mankind can't make up its mind between goodness and force, peace and war, love and hate. Everybody talks peace, goodwill, and love, but everybody acts war and practices hate.

December 26, 1954, Sunday

Yesterday I was guest at the Wills with Sh. and the Cooks. The Cooks drove me to their place after the meal, and after a short visit they drove me home. Sh. gave me as a Christmas present two wash rags, two face towels and two bath towels.

Today I stayed at home; I didn't go to church for many reasons, one being that I don't like to be in church and sit with Sh. It somehow compromises a man to be seen with a woman in church—at least that was the opinion of my old friend Bitzer, from whom I've not heard these last five years. I promised, however, to see her off at the bus station tonight at 8.

Tomorrow the French Assembly will vote on German rearmament. Of course, it will not make the slightest difference in the world how the French will vote. The United States and Britain have already decided to rearm Germany. But a French vote against rearmament may be a moral rebuke to the United States, which speaks of peace and yet builds air bases over the globe and sends arms to everyone. All these are done in the name of freedom.

December 31, 1954, Friday

It is New Year's Eve. I'll go to bed at the regular time. I was invited by the Russells to attend their "Watch Party" from nine to 12. I declined by telling a white lie. Since they can see the light in my room, the lie was unnecessary. I simply don't enjoy parties anymore. Since this is the last day of the year, I thank God for the health, happiness, and success I enjoyed during this year. I thank God for the books I read, the friends I have, the shows I saw, the trips I took. The most memorable event of the year was the unusually hot summer, during which I taught from 1 to 4 o'clock. I also took a trip to Biloxi, Mississippi, where I attended the SCMLA meeting. After

18 years I looked on the ocean again. I also caught glimpses of New Orleans. Sometime in May the bus communication between Siloam Springs and Fayetteville was discontinued. It was not resumed 'till a few weeks ago. The schedule, however, makes my trip to Fayetteville inconvenient. I have, therefore, to depend on the Haleys for the trip to Fayetteville. My grief is that I've not yet created anything. One does not start living until one creates something. I've notes and notes, and I review them every morning; I acquired a certain amount of knowledge, but the power to create, to write, to think original and bold thoughts has yet to visit me. It may be I'll get that power by creating. One can't learn harping except by playing the harp, and one can't learn writing (imaginative works) except by writing. The only writing I do is writing in this book. It is neither literary nor creative. It is simply recording what I saw, felt, and experienced. I must do better if I ever hope to amount to anything.

January 1, 1955, Saturday

I got up as usual at 6 o'clock. I took a bath, which I do every day of the year, I ate breakfast rather late, about 8, and read and walked the rest of the day. I listened to the radio. Arkansas U was beaten by Georgia Tech at Dallas 14 to 6, Ohio beat SCLU 20 to 6, Army beat Miss. 21 to 0, and Duke beat Nebraska at Miami. This ended the football excitement for the year.

February 1, 1955, Tuesday

I've not written in this book for some time. The first semester is already over. I started the new semester last week. The world situation is very delicate. The United States will defend Formosa; Red China will liberate Formosa; the UN began talks on cease-fire. Formosa Chinese reject it; Red Chinese have not yet accepted; our admirals and generals are eager to unleash war. Unless wisdom, patience and compromise prevail, we are heading for another war. It would be a pity indeed if we get into war for the sake of some island off the Chinese coast that we declared necessary to our defense but that the Chinese claim as their own territory.

February 4, 1955, Friday

It rained nearly all night; I had to call a taxi to drive me to school. I taught two hours in the morning and three in the afternoon. It is really the heaviest work in a day I have had for years. Some of the students have the same heavy schedule on MWF's. D. Brown was on the campus, and he told me that the library is going up nicely. I had a discussion with Mr. Pickle about the Formosa situation. He thinks that we ought to show the Chinese that we mean business and start bombing them with H- and A-bombs. Of course, I think the Americans, as well as the Russians, the British, and the French, do not have any business to be so far away from home either defending liberties or spreading the blessings of our civilization. To defend liberties means to occupy a country, or exploit a country, to use it for your own purposes. Any nation that keeps soldiers, sailors and armies outside its own geographical borders is imperialistic. The Chinese might be wrong, but at least they do not occupy bases outside San Francisco or New York, and their fleets are not 15,000 miles away from their home bases. According to our opinion, it is defense; according to other nations, it is aggression.

[At this point, the journals of Dr. John H. Panage end, and he evidently kept no record from this point on of his daily activities. He lived until the mid-1970s and died from complications from a fall, leaving the bulk of his estate to John Brown University and his surviving relatives in Cyprus.]